DISCARD

All Things Darwin

All Things Darwin

An Encyclopedia of Darwin's World

VOLUME 2
J–Z

Patrick H. Armstrong

GREENWOOD PRESS
Westport, Connecticut • London

Library of Congress Cataloging-in-Publication Data

Armstrong, Patrick, 1941–
    All things Darwin : an encyclopedia of Darwin's world / Patrick H.
Armstrong.
        p. cm.
    Includes bibliographical references and index.
    ISBN 978–0–313–33492–4 (set : alk. paper) — ISBN 978–0–313–33493–1
(v.1 : alk. paper) — ISBN 978–0–313–33494–8 (v.2 : alk. paper)
1. Darwin, Charles, 1809–1882—Encyclopedias. 2. Naturalists—
England—Biography—Encyclopedias. 3. Natural history—Encyclopedias.
4. Evolution (Biology)—Encyclopedias. I. Title.
    QH31.D2A7894 2007
    576.8'2092—dc22
    [B]   2007026482

British Library Cataloguing in Publication Data is available.

Library of Congress Catalog Card Number: 2007026482
ISBN-13: 978–0–313–33492–4 (set)
        978–0–313–33493–1 (vol. 1)
        978–0–313–33494–8 (vol. 2)

First published in 2007

Greenwood Press, 88 Post Road West, Westport, CT 06881
An imprint of Greenwood Publishing Group, Inc.
www.greenwood.com

Printed in the United States of America

The paper used in this book complies with the
Permanent Paper Standard issued by the National
Information Standards Organization (Z39.48–1984).

10 9 8 7 6 5 4 3 2 1

Contents

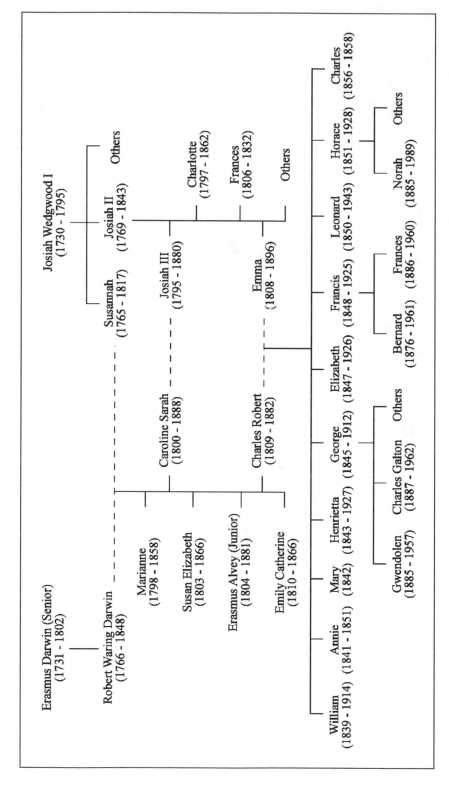

Simplified family tree of the Darwin and Wedgwood families. Note the close connections: three marriages in two generations.

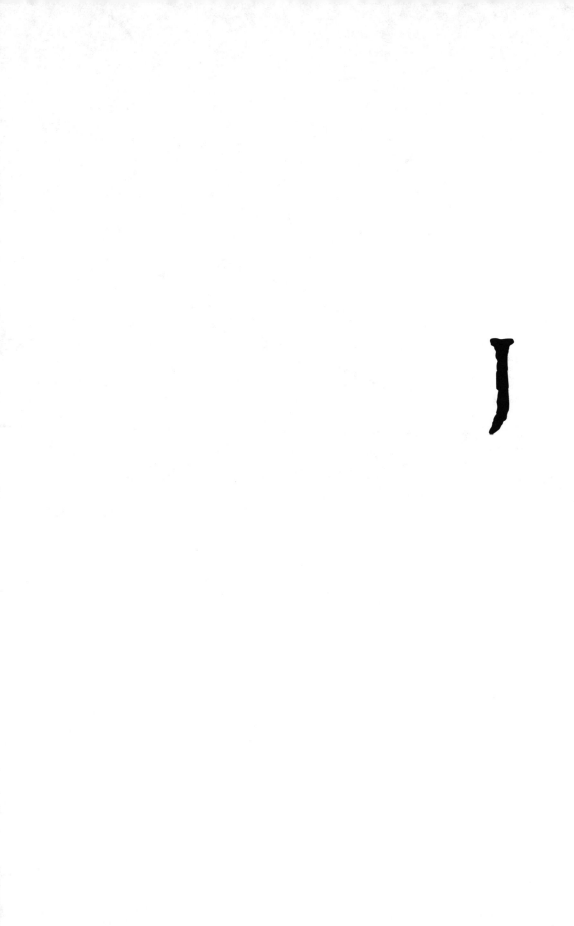

Jenyns, Leonard (later Blomefield) (1800—1893)

Parson-naturalist, polymath, close friend of Charles Darwin.

Leonard Jenyns was a member of that distinctive group, the English parson-naturalists, who formed backbone of English natural history, indeed of British science, for several centuries. He shows many typical characteristics of the genre. His life and work connects Charles Darwin's at a number of critical points.

Leonard was born at 85 Pall Mall, London, the home of his maternal grandfather, an eminent physician. His father was a clergyman, the Reverend George Jenyns, of Bottisham Hall, Cambridgeshire, Vicar of Swaffam Prior and Prebendary (Canon) of Ely Cathedral. His godfather and great uncle was another Church of England clergyman, the Reverend Leonard Chappelow, who encouraged his natural history interests and from whom the young Leonard eventually inherited an extensive library. At Eton College, where he was sent in 1813, he read with great joy Gilbert White's *Natural History of Selborne*, an edition which later edited. The book was also read by the youthful Charles Darwin.

He entered St. John's College, Cambridge, in 1818, where he came under the influence of **John Stevens Henslow,** professor of botany in the University—the person who mentored Darwin and, indeed, generations of Cambridge naturalists. Henslow and Jenyns worked on a number of natural history projects together. In 1832, Henslow married Leonard's sister Harriet, strengthening the link between the two parson-naturalist families.

Meanwhile, Leonard Jenyns graduated BA in 1822, becoming an MA in 1825. He was ordained deacon in the Church of England in May 1823 and became curate of Swaffam Bulbeck, close to his father's parish in Cambridgeshire, preaching his first sermon on June 1, 1823. A year later, he was ordained priest and on January 1, 1828, became Vicar of Swaffam Bulbeck, an office he held until 1849. Jenyns married twice: his first wife, Jane, died, apparently of consumption, at the age of 44; his second wife, Sarah, whom he married in his sixties, survived him and lived into the twentieth century. Both his wives were the daughters of clergy.

Although he traveled throughout Britain (never abroad), much of his work was in the woods, fields, and fens of Cambridgeshire. He dragged local water bodies seeking new species of fish; he collected plants extensively and was a competent entomologist; his notebooks are full of detailed descriptions of butterflies he had found close to his home.

It was, however, **beetles** that brought him in contact with Darwin; Darwin was an enthusiastic collector of beetles—*Coleoptera*—during his school days and as an undergraduate. In early 1830, Charles went to see Leonard at his vicarage, but apparently did not initially warm to him. They exchanged specimens, but Darwin felt he had come off worst (Jenyns seems sometimes to have driven a hard bargain when exchanging, buying, and selling specimens). But the friendship became firmer, perhaps on some of the walks they shared with Henslow or at the soirées the Henslows held in Cambridge for those interested in natural history.

In the summer of 1831, when **Robert FitzRoy** was searching for someone interested in natural history to accompany him on the voyage of HMS *Beagle* around the world, Jenyns was first approached. He seriously considered the offer for some days but, because his health had not been good and he was only a few years into his parish work at Swaffam Bulbeck, he declined. Henslow also briefly considered taking the position. However, Jenyns did have a strong link with the *Beagle* voyage, because on his return Darwin asked Jenyns to describe the large collection of fish that he had collected. Jenyns had only studied the fish of the British Isles, but he rose to the challenge magnificently. His detailed and well-illustrated work was published in 1842 as part 4 of *The Zoology of the Voyage of the Beagle.* He later light-heartedly remarked that the mere mention of Darwin's name conjured up a fishy smell!

Jenyns was a careful observer who made detailed measurements and extremely accurate drawings. He wrote papers on wide range of subjects, including weather, vertebrates (amphibians, bats, shrews, fish), and insects, as well as theological topics. He took an important role in the affairs of Section D (Natural History) of the **British Association for the Advancement of Science.** A special interest was the classification of organisms and the nature of variation: he saw the naturalist's task as the search for order. He gave a paper to the Edinburgh meeting of the Association in 1834 titled "Report of the Recent

Progress and Present State of Zoology," in which he asserted "that the true and legitimate object of zoology is the attainment of the Natural System"— the natural or true system of classifying species and other biological groups.

> My intention, then, is principally to notice those researches which of late years have tended to elucidate the characters and affinities of the larger groups of animals, and thereby advance our knowledge of their natural arrangement.

A year later, he published "Some Remarks on Genera and Subgenera, and on the Principles on Which They Should Be Established."

This search for order in nature was compatible with Paleyan natural theology, whereby each organism was precisely adapted to its way of life and environment and through the creator's ingenuity or providence. There also existed a broader pattern, system, or order of which all organisms were a part. Yet the idea was also very modern in a way. Taxonomists today emphasize that the classification and naming of organisms should reflect their evolutionary relationships. Indeed, just a couple of years before the publication of *On the Origin of Species,* Jenyns published an article titled "On the Variation of Species," of which Darwin requested a copy. Leonard Jenyns corresponded frequently with Darwin, and they frequently provided one another with information for their respective research. Jenyns was an early supporter of many of Darwin's views, although his correspondence with Henslow (and others) shows that he was unable to "go all the way."

When his first wife became ill, he moved south, hoping that the warmer climate would benefit her. He went first to the Isle of Wight and then to Bath. He continued with some parish work and was active in the affairs of local institutions, especially the local Field Club and the Bath Royal Literary and Scientific Institution. He was vice president when the British Association met in Bath in 1864 and again when it met there in 1888. At the time of the latter meeting, he had Charles Darwin's son **Francis Darwin** to stay with him for a week.

In 1871, he changed his name to Leonard Blomefield. Under a term in the will of a distant cousin who had died over fifty years previously, he was required to do this in order to inherit the estate. He obtained a royal license from Queen **Victoria** enabling him to do so.

Leonard Jenyns is important for several reasons. As a parson-naturalist from a family of parson-naturalists, he represents an example of a type of person who, quietly in the study and in the countryside, contributed massively to British science in the Victorian period. He was intimately associated with Darwin for nearly fifty years—they were profound influences on each other. And he was one of an important group of English clergy who did not immediately oppose all evolutionary ideas. While he found parts of Darwin's theory attractive, he remained neutral in regard to certain aspects and opposed others. A letter from Henslow to Jenyns dated January 26, 1860 (a few weeks after the publication of *On the Origin of Species*), encapsulates the views of both these friends and colleagues of Charles Darwin:

> My views correspond with yours. The Book is a marvellous assemblage of facts and observations—and no doubt contains much legitimate inference, but it pushes hypothesis . . . too far . . . I believe . . . that Darwin attempts more than is granted to Man.

FURTHER READING

Wallace, I., ed. 2005. *Leonard Jenyns: Darwin's Lifelong Friend*. Bath, England: Bath Royal Literary and Scientific Society.

K

Kelp and Kelp Beds

Over large areas of the cool, temperate, subantarctic, and subarctic regions, rocky sea floors below the low tide line are covered in growth of large brown algae, which grow into extensive, almost forestlike, kelp beds. The term kelp is particularly used for algae of the genera *Macrocystis, Nereocystis,* and *Laminaria.* Typically they are found along the shorelines washed by cold currents in the Atlantic and Pacific Oceans to a depth of 60 to 100 feet (20 to 30 meters).

Kelp beds are largely restricted to cold-water environments because warmer waters tend to lack the rich supply of nutrients that kelp needs to thrive and proliferate. Several different species of kelp are found in a typical kelp bed, along with other smaller species of seaweed. Amid the stalks and blades of the kelp live many marine animals, including sponges, sea anemones, sea squirts, barnacles, sea stars (starfish), and many types of gastropod (sea snails). A number of species of fish also live in this complex habitat.

Darwin spent many hours studying the organisms that inhabited the kelp bed communities that existed along Berkeley Sound in the **Falkland Islands** and along the coasts in **Tierra del Fuego.** He wrote the following account in April 1834, combining material from his two sojourns at East Falkland and material from similar researches he had undertaken in Tierra del Fuego. (It is an almost exact transcription; the scientific names of many of the organisms mentioned have changed.)

The Zoology of the Sea is I believe the same here as in Tierra del Fuego: Its main striking feature is the immense quantity & number of aquatic beings which are intimately connected with the Kelp. The plant (the Fucus giganteus of Solander) is universally attached to rocks, from those which are awash at low water & those being in fathom water: it is frequently attached to round stones lying in mud. From the degree to which these southern lands are intersected by water & the depth in which Kelp grows the quantity may be imagined, but not to a greater degree than it exists. I can only compare these giant forests to terrestrial ones in the most teeming part of the Tropics; yet if the latter in any country were to be destroyed, I do not believe nearly the same number of animals (a) would perish, as would happen in the case of the Kelp: All the fishing quadrupeds & birds (& man) haunt the beds attracted by the infinite number of small fish which live amongst the leaves: (the kinds are not so very numerous, my specimens I believe show nearly all.) Amongst the invertebrates I will mention them in order of their importance. Crustacea of every order swarm, my collection gives no idea of them, especially the minute sorts. Encrusting Corallines & Aztias are excessively numerous. Every leaf (excepting those on the surface,) is white with such Corallines . . . & compound Ascidia. Examining these with a strong microscope minute crustacea will be seen. . . . On shaking the great entangled roots it is curious to see the heap of fish, shells, crabs, sea-eggs, cuttlefish, star fish, Planaria, Nercilae which fall out. This latter tribe I have much neglected. Amongst the Gasteropoda [*sic*], Herobranchus is common: but Trochus & patelliform shells abound on all the leaves. One single plant forms an immense and most interesting menagerie. If this Fucus was to cease living, with it would go many of the Seals, the Cormorants & certainly the small fish & sooner or later the Fuegan Man must follow. The greater number of invertebrates would likewise perish, but how many it is hard to conjecture. (*Zoological Notes*, Cambridge University Library, Darwin Archive)

A note on the back of the page refers to the "(a)" added in small handwriting to the text, perhaps when Darwin reviewed his work sometime later. It reads, "I refer to numbers of individuals as well as kinds."

This description forms one of the most significant passages in Darwin's notes from the *Beagle* voyage. It reveals how insightful Darwin had become in evaluating environments by April 1834 (about halfway through the voyage). He has clearly compared the beds of East Falkland with those of Tierra del Fuego (which the ship visited between the two Falklands visits), and there are a number of ecological concepts embedded (in some cases, implied) in the account. Darwin is comparing the productivity of the kelp beds on the shores of the Southern Ocean with that of the tropical rain forests he had recently seen in Brazil. He distinguishes carefully between number of individuals (population) from number of species (diversity). He comes close to using the concepts of food chain, food web, ecological niche, and dominant or perhaps keystone species—although these ecological terms were not coined until a century or more later. He understands that the complex assemblage of plants and animals that comprises the kelp bed is an

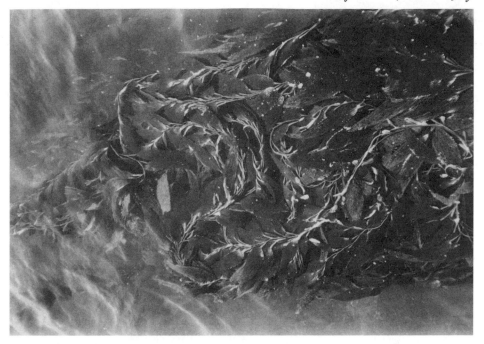

Kelp Berkeley Sound, East Falkland. Photo: Patrick Armstrong.

integrated whole. He also accepts that humans ("Fuegan man") are part of the system; they interact with, and form part of, the environment in a manner comparable with that of other creatures. The young naturalist is describing an environment—a modern scientist would say ecosystem—in a remarkably integrated, holistic way. This is of great significance, because the notion of the relationship between organisms and their environment—a dialogue—is fundamental to the concept of natural selection that he was to develop a few years later.

See also: Ecology.

King, Philip Gidley (junior) (1817—1904)

Shipmate and close friend of Charles Darwin aboard the *Beagle*. He was son of Captain (later Admiral) Phillip Parker King, grandson of Philip Gidley King (senior), also a naval officer and the third governor of New South Wales.

Philip King was born at Parramatta, New South Wales, Australia. When he was five years old, he traveled to England with his parents. At the age of nine, he sailed with his father on the first surveying voyage to South America with the *Beagle* and *Adventure*. After a period of shore leave, he joined the second voyage as midshipman. Soon after sailing, King developed a close friendship with Darwin that they remembered throughout their lives. Several times, after they had gone their separate ways, they reminded each other in their letters of the evenings when they sat on the booms of the *Beagle* as the ship sailed through tropical seas under the influence of the trade winds, yarning over present and past voyages. It may be that the friendship of the young midshipman, several years Darwin's junior, was a support as he bore sickness and loneliness on the long voyage.

King, having spent more than half his life aboard ships, left the *Beagle* and the Royal Navy in Sydney in January 1836. He proceeded to his father's property at Dunheved, inland from Sydney. After Darwin's visit there, he assisted his father with the compilation of the first part of the *Narrative of the Voyage*. Later he followed his father into a number of business ventures in agriculture and mining. He became involved in local politics and became director of an Australian bank.

In later life, King corresponded with Darwin and provided information on Aborigines, the behavior of dogs, sheep-breeding in Australia, barnacles, and other matters. Some of this material was used in Darwin's publications. Late in life, King prepared, from memory, a sketch of the *Beagle* as it was during the voyage (he was a proficient amateur artist) and cooperated with Charles Darwin's son, Francis, by providing information for a volume of his letters.

King was the last of the *Beagle* shipmates to die, surviving into the early years of the twentieth century.

King, Phillip Parker (1791—1856)

A member of a distinguished naval family, most members of whom had strong links with Australia. Although they only met on a few occasions, his life and work intersected those of Charles Darwin at critical times.

King was the eldest (legitimate) child of Philip Gidley King, senior (1758–1808), the founder of the settlement of Norfolk Island and later governor of New South Wales. He was born on Norfolk Island in 1791. Phillip Parker King was educated in England and joined the Royal Navy as a teenager and was eventually the first Australian to become an admiral. A distinguished hydrographer, in 1817, he was given command of an expedition to complete the exploration of the northwestern coast of Australia. Sailing in the cutter *Mermaid* through the Bass Strait to North West Cape, he commenced a survey along the coast toward Arnhem Land. During four voyages off the northern and northwestern coasts, King named Port Essington and Buccaneer Archipelago and established that Melville Island was indeed an island and charted the coastline. He also surveyed the west coast of Australia from Rottnest Island to Cygnet Bay (in King Sound) and charted the entrance to Macquarie Harbour on the west coast of Tasmania. He was elected fellow of the Royal Society for this hydrographic and exploration work in 1824. He was sent in 1826 to command of HMS *Adventure* and HMS *Beagle* during the first surveying voyage of the *Beagle* to South

America. During the period February to April 1827, he made a base at Port Famine and dispatched HMS *Beagle,* then under the command of Captain Pringle Stokes, westward to survey the complex, uncharted Pacific end of the Magellan Strait with its complex network of inlets, islands, and peninsulas— or at least to accurately fix certain key points for navigators. *Adventure* went to the east and south. In the second season, after wintering and picking up stores in Rio de Janeiro and Montevideo, Stokes again proceeded to the western part of the Strait. But possibly through the effects of the privations and the bad weather, Pringle Stokes deteriorated psychologically, spending weeks at a time in his cabin. His notes became fragmentary and disorganized. He attempted to kill himself several times, ultimately shooting himself in the head on August 2, 1828, and died, in great pain, 10 days later. Captain King had to sort out the mess. He arranged a for a postmortem to be carried out by the ship's surgeon, went through Stokes's papers and journals attempting to put them in order, compiled a detailed report for Sir Robert Otway, commander-in-chief of the Royal Navy's South American station, and nursed the two ships north to Rio. After re-equipment and repairs, *Adventure* and *Beagle* went south a third time, because much of the Admiralty's surveying work was incomplete. This was the segment of the voyage during which the *Beagle,* now under the command of Captain **Robert FitzRoy,** collected a small group of Fuegians and took them to England. The need to repatriate this group provided one of the bases for the ship's return to southern waters two years later with the young Charles Darwin aboard.

King remained in the active service of the navy while he completed work from the voyage (including work on the charts) and was on the wharf at Plymouth on December 27, 1831, when the *Beagle* departed on the voyage that Darwin accompanied.

However, not long after, King retired from his active naval career and, having spent much of his earlier life in the Australian colonies, established himself at the King family property at Dunheved, an estate near Penrith, New South Wales, 100 miles (160 kilometers) from Sydney. Here he was working on his part of the massive *Narrative of the Surveying Voyage of His Majesty's Ships* Adventure *and* Beagle *between the Years 1826 and 1836 Describing Their Examination of the Southern Shores of South America and the* Beagle*'s Circumnavigation of the Globe* when Darwin visited on January 26–27, 1836. (Large sections of this work were written by Fitzroy, and volume 3, Darwin's account, was eventually retitled *The Voyage of the Beagle* and published separately.) Because southern South America and particularly Tierra del Fuego had been a focus for both voyages of the *Beagle,* they had a great deal to discuss. Darwin noted that he "spent a very pleasant afternoon walking about the farm and talking over the Natural History of T del Fuego." King had been a keen collector of natural history specimens during his voyages and had published some of his observations. He gave Darwin a signed reprint of a paper he had written on barnacles and mollusks.

The monographs that Darwin later compiled on barnacles helped to establish his scientific reputation. Darwin had already made observations on barnacles in South America, but perhaps the discussions at Dunheved encouraged him to think that there was much more of interest in this biological group.

In retirement, King took an active interest in the affairs of the colony. He was for many years a commissioner of the Australian Agricultural Company and briefly a member of the New South Wales Legislative Council. He took an active interest in local church affairs and supported science in the colony in every possible way. Both local enthusiasts and visiting naturalists had great encouragement from him. He took part in explorations in inland Australia and New Zealand and was one of the first to make systematic meteorological observations in Australia. He made one last trip to England in 1849. He heard that he had been promoted to rear admiral in early 1856, but he collapsed and died a few weeks later.

Kingsley, Charles (1819—1875)

Church of England clergyman, writer, and enthusiastic supporter of Charles Darwin's ideas.

Charles Kingsley published relatively little in the field of serious science, although he produced a number of articles on popular natural history and a somewhat wordy, rather sentimental book on the sea coast (*Glaucus or Wonders of the Shore,* 1855). He was a professor of history at Cambridge University, a poet, social activist and commentator, and prolific novelist and essayist, in addition to holding senior appointments in the Church (chaplain to Queen Victoria, canon of Chester Cathedral and of Westminster Abbey). He did, however, have scientific training, and one of his greatest contributions was his enthusiasm for Darwinian ideas and his vehement assertion that religion and science were not only compatible, but complemented each other. Born in the same year as Queen **Victoria** (and also **Karl Marx**), he was friends and corresponded with **Charles Lyell, Thomas Huxley,** and **Alfred Russel Wallace.** After reading *On the Origin of Species,* Kingsley wrote to Charles Darwin that it was:

> just as noble a conception of Deity, to believe that He created primal forms capable of self-development . . . as to believe He required a fresh act of intervention to supply the lacunas which he himself has made. . . . I question whether the former be not the loftier thought. (Charles Kingsley to Charles Darwin, November 18, 1859, *Correspondence,* Vol. 7, 379–380)

Darwin was so delighted with this idea that, with permission, he inserted it into the final chapter of the book in later editions (including the U.S. edition of the work), attributing the remarks to "a celebrated author and divine."

It was Kingsley's positive attitude to the theory of evolution, together with his natural enthusiasm and powers of persuasion that was responsible for the favorable reception of Darwin's views within a certain section of the English Church, and indeed among the educated British population as a whole.

Despite the wide range of his activities and achievements, Kingsley's love of and enthusiasm for science is a theme that runs through his life. The dean of Chester Cathedral took as a text for Charles Kingsley's obituary sermon a couple of verses from the Old Testament:

> And he spake three thousand proverbs: and his songs were a thousand and five. And he spake of trees, from the cedar tree that is in Lebanon, even to the hyssop that springs from the wall: he spake also of beasts, and of fowl, and of creeping things and of fishes. (*I Kings* 4, 32–33)

His mother (Mary Lucas, 1788–1874) was of the opinion that if, before his birth, she took delight in the beauties of the countryside as she wandered over the moorland of Dartmoor, they would become part of him for the whole of his life. Whatever was the basis of this supposition, Charles was born in Devonshire, in the west of England, had a lifelong interest in landscape, and a concern for it.

Kingsley's father (also named Charles, 1781–1860), although educated at Harrow School and Oxford and Cambridge Universities, was for many years an impecunious country curate; there was a long tradition in English clergy families of son following father into the Church, the daughters in such families often also marrying into the Church. One of Kingsley's sisters (Charlotte, 1828–1882) married a clergyman.

A devotion to natural history was another family tradition. Kingsley's maternal grandfather, Nathan Lucas, had been a judge in the West Indies, and was a significant amateur scientist, as well as a great traveler. His sister Charlotte wrote a book on ferns.

After several years of moving from curacy to curacy in the Fen country of eastern England, Kingsley's father resettled in Devonshire, where he became rector of the picturesque fishing village of Clovelly, a single street of white cottages clinging to a steep valley on the north Devon coast.

Kingsley thrived in the Devon village environment, enjoying its "green amphitheatre" of oak and ash trees and the way in which the sunshine fell on "the wings of gorgeous butterflies . . . which

Charles Kingsley, Darwin's Church of England publicist. National Portrait Gallery, London.

fluttered from woodland down to the gardens." Another interest shared by the whole family was conchology—the collection and study of shells—under the guidance of a local Dr. Turton, then one of the world's authorities on shelled creatures.

Perhaps because of the ill health that dogged him throughout much of his life, the young Charles Kingsley was not sent to school until he was 12. After a short period at a small school in Bristol, he went to a little-known grammar school at Helston in the adjoining county of Cornwall (1832–1836), where he came under the influence of the Reverend C. A. Johns, author of *Flowers of the Field*. Throughout his teens, natural history was a consuming interest: he collected birds' eggs and geological specimens, and he pressed (dried) flowers. His interest was metaphysical as well as scientific, and he developed for himself a sort of pantheism, having a holistic view of nature, shunning orthodox Christian religion.

In 1836, his father became vicar of St. Luke's, Chelsea, in London, and the family had to leave Devon. Two years of study at Kings College followed, to prepare him for admission to Cambridge University. He walked the four miles each way daily, but he did not like London, nor did he enjoy the company of the parishioners that attended his father's church.

He was admitted to Magdalene College, Cambridge, in the autumn of 1836. He was supposed to be studying classics and mathematics, but beer-drinking, playing cards, rowing (in the college's second boat), boxing, fishing, and smoking (he always used long "churchwarden" pipes) meant that his books were somewhat neglected; he and one or two friends dabbled in mesmerism or "animal magnetism." However, he attended the lectures given by geology professor **Adam Sedgwick,** who was an inspiring teacher. An undated fragment from Sedgwick's public lecture notes reads: "I cannot promise to teach you all geology, I can only fire your imagination." Sedgwick's lectures were sometimes given in the field, on horseback. Charles Kingsley was a superb horseman and an enthusiastic foxhunter in addition to being, from his schooldays onward, a keen geologist. He greatly admired Sedgwick.

Adam Sedgwick was an important influence on the reform of Cambridge University. He argued that three branches of study were necessary in a university: the laws of nature, the laws of ancient literature, and the laws of humans, considered as social beings. He argued that geology, "like every other science, well interpreted, lends its aid to natural religion." It showed that there existed a driving force, Sedgwick argued, contriving a means adapted to an end, and thus afforded a proof that "the first great cause" continues as a "provident and active intelligence."

This search for laws or governing principles that might give an insight to the mind of the creator, caught from Sedgwick, aided perhaps by his study of mathematics, became an important theme in Charles Kingsley's later work. For example, in his inaugural lecture on the occasion of his installation as professor of modern history at Cambridge (a position, incidentally, for which he was not really qualified), he declaimed:

> Without doubt History obeys, and always has obeyed, in the long run, certain laws. But those laws assert themselves and are to be discovered not in things but in persons; in the actions of human beings; and just as in proportion as we understand human beings, shall we understand the laws they have obeyed. . . . [T]he rapid progress of science is tempting us to look at human beings rather as things than as persons. . . . Discovering, to our delight, order and law all around us, in a thousand events which seemed to our fathers fortuitous and arbitrary, we are dazzled by the magnificent prospect opening before us. (*The Limits of Exact Science as Applied to History,* 1860, London: Macmillan, 8)

It was not quite as simple as that, however (as the title of the lecture implies), but clearly this search for order and law was an important preoccupation throughout Kingsley's life.

The last few weeks before his final examinations were spent trying to make up for the previous neglect of his studies, but he eventually passed with first-class honors. He had thought, while at Cambridge, of becoming a barrister, and in April 1839 his name was entered at Lincoln's Inn, one of London's Inns of Court (it was removed in 1841, when he changed his mind). As happened several times in his life, overstrain—in this case, brought on by excessive study—brought him to the verge of a nervous breakdown, and he retreated to his beloved Devon for several weeks to recover.

In the summer of 1839, during one of the vacations from Cambridge, he met Frances (Fanny) Eliza Grenfell, one of a group of sisters from a wealthy, High Church Anglican family. Although Fanny was several years older than Charles, they fell in love at once. It was the extremely devout Fanny who was largely responsible for his decision to abandon his somewhat hedonistic life-style and his resolving to become a priest of the Church of England. Her family, however, were resolutely opposed to her marriage to a penniless nobody, and it was five years before they were married. Their voluminous correspondence during this period reveals a mixture of sexual passion and extreme religious devotion.

Kingsley was ordained deacon in July 1842 and obtained a curacy (a position as assistant to the rector or priest) at the parish of Eversley, in Hampshire in southern England. Although he still enjoyed following the foxhunt, he immersed himself in life among the rural peasant folk with enthusiasm, campaigning for schools and better sanitary conditions.

Less than 18 months after Kingsley had moved to Eversley, his boss, the rector, was involved in an incident "of a most revolting nature" with a woman in the congregation and fled. Charles became rector in his stead. This was a time of widespread poverty, and its relief provided a major focus to his ministry. In 1848, the Chartists—campaigners for voting rights for all—took their campaign to the Westminster Parliament, and the Christian Socialist movement was born. Kingsley assisted with the editing of its journal *Politics for the People,* with its message of the need for education and the improvement of conditions for working people. As well as his parish work and his political and social activism, he was active as a journalist and novelist and also taught part-time at Queens' College, London. His wife Fanny had expensive tastes, and he had to work hard to support her in the manner that she regarded as appropriate. Another breakdown was imminent, and he retreated to Devon for some months. This pattern of alternating periods of overwork and depression and poor health, during which he retreated to the countryside of the West of England, continued for some years. Natural history, particularly an enthusiasm for sea creatures, was an enthusiasm during these visits. Yet at Eversley, too, there was much of interest: toads inhabited a grassy bank; sand wasps returned each year to a crack in Kingsley's dressing-room window; and there was a favorite slow worm (a species of legless lizard) in the churchyard.

Partly to expose social inequalities and partly to earn money to indulge Fanny and to educate his family, Kingsley wrote a series of novels. *Alton Locke* and *Yeast* were very popular and are said to have been appreciated by the royal family. He also had a growing reputation as a preacher, and thus in 1859 he was invited to become a chaplain to Queen Victoria. Further honors followed. Despite having little academic background in the subject, he was appointed Regius Professor of Modern History at Cambridge in 1860, where, incidentally, he is said to have had a beneficial effect on the Prince of Wales—the future King Edward VII. Although he was regarded as a popular lecturer, there were stresses during these Cambridge years. A protracted and somewhat ill-tempered theological dispute with John Henry Newman—the Anglican theologian who later became a Roman Catholic and eventually a cardinal—eventually affected his heath badly. Despite this loss of dignity, in 1870, he became a canon of Chester Cathedral, where he endeared himself to the local community, giving classes in geology and botany to the townspeople, and founding, as did many parson-naturalists of his generation, a local natural history society. In May 1873, he was translated to a canonry at Westminster Abbey, an appointment he held until his death in January 1875. Several months of this period were spent on a lecture tour of the United States, where he enjoyed the excitement of Boston, New York, Philadelphia, and San Francisco; found a visit to Niagara Falls an almost religious experience; and marveled at the landscapes of the West, especially Yosemite. He met poet Henry Wadsworth Longfellow. Yet he found the weeks of travel a strain, particularly because of some severe, very cold weather he experienced. He was reluctant to go on this tour, but he needed the money. His wife Fanny was becoming more and more extravagant and insisted that both the Eversley and London houses needed major improvements and redecoration. And some of his relations were literally begging him for money. Much of the rest of his life was spent in a poor state of health, often drugged with opiates. Fanny was also then dangerously ill (or considered herself to be), and Charles often had to nurse her. Fanny survived, living on until 1891, and it was Charles who perished. Although burial in Westminster Abbey was suggested, he was interred at Eversley.

The preaching of the Christian faith, a love of nature, and an enthusiasm for science were intertwined throughout much of Kingsley's life: to worship nature was to worship God. He was also a great propagandist, performer, and publicist. Although he was an early campaigner against pollution and has been described as an early "ecotheologian," he was not a strikingly original thinker. Nevertheless, he did much to win over many of Britain's more educated classes, particularly churchmen, to the view that there was no conflict between science and religion and that the acceptance of evolutionary ideas was entirely compatible with being a Christian.

We have seen that Kingsley had training in field geology under Sedgwick (as did Darwin) and felt an imperative to search for guiding principles in nature. He wrote in *Glaucus* (1855): "All laws that made the world are . . . busy in the commonest mountain burn" (chapter 1). Indeed, several times in the 1840s and 1850s, he came close to uttering vaguely evolutionary thoughts.

His mind was, therefore, prepared for Darwin's ideas. In *Glaucus* he wrote:

> Let us, therefore, say boldly, that there has been a "progress of species," and that there may be again, in the true sense of that term. (257)

He tended to believe at this stage, perhaps influenced by Jean-Baptiste Lamarck, that the changes occurred more during the lives of individuals, rather than in species as a whole or populations. Two pages later, he quotes the following passage from *Harvey's Sea-side Book*, describing it as "excellent":

> Thus it is that Nature advances step by step, gradually bringing out, though successive stages of being, new organs and new facilities; and leaving, as she moves along, at every step, some animals which rise no higher, as if to serve as landmarks of her progress through all succeeding time. (160)

Although the notion that the more complex animal forms were developments of their more simple ancestors is rejected by Harvey a line or two later, it seems that four years before the publication of *On the Origin of Species*, Charles Kingsley had thought about the matter.

Also interesting is *Alton Locke*, published in 1850—five years earlier—portraying the terrible living conditions in East London at the time and containing a remarkable dream sequence. The hero dreams that he is a madrepore (a type of coral, a very simple form of life); as he crawls out of a primeval sea, he is transformed into a crab, and then into a mylodont (an extinct giant sloth) among the tree ferns of South America, and then into an ape. Ultimately, the hero declaims: "I feel stirring within me the germs of higher consciousness." Again, the transformation seems to take place from within.

This is perhaps an allegory for evolution or transformation within society. Kingsley's Christian Socialism, although it espoused the cause of both the rural farm laborer and the urban artisan, was a lot less radical than some maintained. He believed that workmen should attempt to improve their lot by education, including self-education, and by cooperation rather than revolution. He also remained a staunch monarchist and greatly respected the aristocracy, making him a complicated man!

His love of nature and of landscape revealed a remarkable understanding of the integrated nature of the environment; his thinking was occasionally quite close to that of modern ecologists. Here is a quotation from an address he gave in 1871:

> As the marvellous interdependence of all natural objects and forces unfolds itself yet more and more, so the once separate sciences, which treated of different classes of natural objects, are forced to interpenetrate (as it were) and supplement themselves by knowledge borrowed from each other. Thus . . . no man can now be a first-rate botanist unless he is also a meteorologist, no mean geologist, and as Mr Darwin had shown in his extraordinary discoveries about the fertilization of plants—no mean entomologist. (F. Kingsley, *Charles Kingsley: His Letters and Memories of His Life, Edited by His Wife*, Vol. 2, 1877, London: Henry S. King, 371)

Kingsley saw Charles Darwin's *The Fertilisation of Orchids*, published in 1862, as a most valuable addition to natural theology—the doctrine that the exquisitely complex, integrated nature of the universe (and particularly the living world) provides evidence for the existence of a divine creator. In another address, he stated:

> I sometimes dream of the day when it will be considered necessary that every candidate for ordination [entry into the priesthood] should have passed creditably in at least one branch of physical science, if it be only to teach him the method of sound scientific thought. And if it be said that the doctrine of evolution, by doing away with the theory of creation, does away with that of final causes—let us answer boldly—Not in the least. We might accept what Mr Darwin and Professor Huxley have written on physical science, and yet preserve our natural theology on exactly the same basis as that on which Butler and Paley left it. That we should develop it, I do not deny. That we should relinquish it, I do. (F. Kingsley, *Letters and Memories*, 347)

Kingsley saw Darwin's ideas as liberating: no longer were enlightened Christians expected to believe what they found impossible to believe. He was understanding of those who, while accepting Christian standards of conduct, rejected much of Christian dogma. His good friend **Thomas Huxley** ("Darwin's bulldog") was in that category. Although Huxley described himself as an agnostic, Kinglsey carried on a friendly correspondence with him following the death of Huxley's son. He also corresponded with Charles Darwin: following a shooting party on Lord Ashburton's estate, during which a rock dove had been shot, he argued that the various species of pigeons and doves—rock dove, stock dove, wood pigeon—had a common ancestor.

> My view is—and I coolly stated it, fearless of the consequence—that the specimen before us was only to be explained by your theory, and that cushat [wood pigeon], stock dove and blue rock, had all once been one species; and I found—to show how your views are steadily spreading—that of five or six men only one regarded the notion as absurd. (Charles Kingsley to Charles Darwin, January 31, 1862, *Letters and Memories*, Vol. 2, 135)

Charles Kingsley was a man of intellectual integrity; he believed that all truth was God's truth. The universe, the natural world, and humanity were all subject to God's laws. It was this integrity and his formidable powers of persuasion that played an important part in increasing the level of acceptance of the notion of evolution through natural selection among Britain's intellectual classes.

FURTHER READING

Chitty, Susan. 1974. *The Beast and the Monk: A Life of Charles Kingsley.* London: Hodder and Stoughton.

Chitty, Susan. 1976. *Charles Kingsley's Landscape.* Newton Abbot, England: David and Charles.

Colloms, Brenda. 1975. *Charles Kingsley: The Lion of Eversley.* London, Constable.

Thorp, Margaret Farrand. 1937. *Charles Kingsley 1819–1875.* Princeton, NJ: Princeton University Press. Reprinted by Octagon Books, New York, 1969.

Kirby, William (1759–1850)

Parson-naturalist, botanist, and entomologist.

William Kirby, who came from a long line of naturalists, was associated with the parish of Barham, in Suffolk,

William Kirby, entomologist and source of some of Darwin's ideas on instinct. From: *Introduction to Entomology,* 1815.

eastern England, for 68 years, first as curate, then as rector. He corresponded with a Yorkshire businessman, and together they wrote *Introduction to Entomology,* the first volume of which was published in 1815 (two others followed). This was a standard work for several decades: one of its important emphases was on insect behavior. The treatment of animal behavior in this work, although extremely detailed, tends to be somewhat anthropomorphic: bees are referred to as "citizens of the hive"; flies poisoned by nectar from a poisonous plant are "imprudent." Nevertheless, the work was very influential: Darwin had a copy with him on the *Beagle* and used it extensively.

See also: Instinct.

L

Lamarck, Jean-Baptiste (1744–1829)

French naturalist and pre-Darwinian evolutionary theorist.

Jean-Baptiste Pierre Antoine de Monet, Chevalier de Lamarck, was born in the village of Bazentin-le-Petit in northern France into a family with a long tradition of military service. Lamarck entered a Jesuit seminary in Amiens in about 1756, but in the summer of 1761 he joined the French army and campaigned in Germany. In his first battle, he distinguished himself by acting bravely under fire and was promoted to officer. Some years later, an accidental injury compelled him to leave the army. He worked in a bank in Paris for a period, while he began to study medicine and botany, subjects in which he soon became expert. In 1778, his book on the plants of France, *Flore Française,* was published and was well received. On the strength of this work, he was appointed to the staff of the Jardin de Roi. The position paid poorly, but in 1793—the year of the execution of Louis XVI and Marie Antoinette—the old garden was reorganized as the Musée National d'Histoire Naturelle (National Museum of Natural History). This was to be run by a group of 12 professors: Lamarck was appointed to the less-than-prestigious professorship of the natural history of insects and worms—a field about which he knew little. However, he effectively established the field of invertebrate zoology (he coined the term invertebrate).

He published *Philosophie Zoologique* in 1809 and the two-volume *Histoire Naturelle des Aninmaux Vertèbre,* 1815–1822. He revolutionized the classification of the invertebrates, separating the Crustacea (crabs, prawns, lobsters), Arachnida (spiders), and Annelida (worms) from the Insecta. He appreciated that barnacles were not mollusks.

The concept of a chain of being—the idea that it was possible to arrange all organisms (plants, animals, fossils) into a single graded series from the simplest to the most complex—is an ancient one. In *Flore Française,* he suggested that there were two entirely separate chains or series: plants and animals. To order plants in the series, he, like his Swedish colleague **Carolus (Carl) Linnaeus,** used functional criteria, especially the organs associated with reproduction. Later he used similar principles in regard to his reorganization of invertebrate animals (making use of the enormous collections of specimens in the Musée).

In *Philosophie Zoologique,* he developed the idea of a static chain or series into a theory of transformation. He claimed that the system was a dynamic one and that life had developed over long periods of time from the simplest to the more complex. "Time has no limit," he remarked at one point, and, therefore, throughout time, great changes might be possible. The simplest forms had been spontaneously produced, and subsequent life forms had been transformed by two mechanisms: *pouvoir de la vie* (power of life), a force that was responsible for the general trend toward increasing complexity; and the inheritance of acquired characteristics. Animals, he argued, changed according to their environment, first in their habits or behavior and then in their structure. These changes, Lamarck maintained, could be passed on to the animals' offspring. The example often quoted is that of the giraffe, which had to stretch up its neck to reach the leaves of the trees in the African savanna, thereby, over time, extending it. Perhaps his most important contribution was to emphasize that the diversity of life now present in the world was the product of natural processes that operated according to ascertainable laws, and not as the result of divine whim.

[B]y the action of the laws of organisation . . . nature has . . . multiplied her first germs of animality, given place to developments in their organisations, . . . and increased and diversified their organs. Then . . . aided by much time and by a slow but constant diversity of circumstances she has gradually brought about . . . the state of things which we

Jean-Baptiste Lamarck, eighteenth-century evolutionary thinker. From a nineteenth-century book.

now observe. (Text of a lecture by J-B Lamarck, Musée National d'Histoire Naturelle, Paris, May 1803)

Lamarck's ideas were not well received at the time nor subsequently. Paleontologist **Georges Cuvier** opposed him. It has to be admitted that Lamarck could cite very little evidence for his theories; in this he differed from Darwin, who supported his theory with massive amounts of evidence. Another important difference was that Lamarck's system was essentially linear, teleological: it was as though evolution (although Lamarck did not use the word) was directed toward an end point, almost a goal. Darwin's model allowed more room for random processes and a branching system. Nevertheless, Darwin acknowledged Lamarck as one whose ideas were forerunners of his own. He admired Lamarck as a great zoologist who had performed a valuable service by "arousing attention to the probability of all changes in the organic, as well as the inorganic world, being the result of law and not of miraculous interposition." Some of Lamarck's notions were, in fact, similar to those of Darwin's grandfather, **Erasmus Darwin** (senior). However, as far as is known, neither was aware of the other's work.

Lamarck, when he worked at the Jardin des Plants and while he held the professorship at the Musée, was not well paid and was constantly at the mercy of official cost-cutters. In his last years, he went blind, and he died in poverty. He was given a pauper's funeral, although his colleague Geoffroy St. Hillaire gave a eulogy.

Linnaeus, Carolus (Carl von Linné) (1707–1778)

Swedish physician and botanist; he developed a "natural system" for the classification of organisms. His binomial system of nomenclature, by which an organism is known by a generally latinized generic name and a species name, is still (with modifications) in use today.

Linnaeus was born in Småland, in southern Sweden, the son of a Lutheran pastor who was a keen gardener. He studied medicine at Lund, at Uppsala, and then at Harderwijk and Leiden in the Netherlands. However, plants were his main interest, and he traveled to many parts of Sweden to study and collect them. He practiced medicine in Stockholm (he specialized in the treatment of syphilis) before accepting a professorship at Uppsala in 1741. There, he restored the university's botanical garden (arranging the plants according to his natural system of classification). (In those days, botany was seen as a logical extension of medicine, because most drugs were prepared from plants.) He also arranged for his students to be attached to voyages of exploration to all parts of the world. Perhaps the best known of these was Daniel Solander, the naturalist on Captain James Cook's first round-the-world voyage, who brought back to Europe the first plant collections from Australia and the South Pacific. He eventually became physician to the Swedish royal family, being granted a title 1757.

In strongly advocating a natural system of classification, Linnaeus sought to distinguish and group organisms on the bases of criteria of fundamental scientific importance. His system contrasts with arbitrary or artificial systems, which tended to reflect human convenience, or those that used superficial characteristics (e.g., the colors of flowers) of little fundamental significance. Linnaeus often used the reproductive system for plants, and the reproductive and (later) the circulatory systems for animals. His emphasis on the reproductive systems of organisms was not always popular with his scientific colleagues; some of his imagery was sexually explicit and was vigorously attacked. Botanist Johann Siegesbeck referred to "loathsome harlotry." (Linnaeus rather cunningly, named a small, useless weed *Siegesbeckia*.)

Linnaeus published the first edition of his classification of organisms, the *Systema Naturae,* while still studying medicine. He revised it many times, so that it grew from a slim pamphlet to a multivolume work, as concepts were modified and as more and more plant and animal material was sent to him from all over the world. There were also scientific difficulties, and subsequent systems of classification largely follow the practice of using morphological evidence from all parts of the organism and in all stages of its development. This notion was pioneered by **John Ray.** What has survived of the Linnaean system is its method of hierarchical classification and custom of binomial nomenclature.

For Linnaeus, species of organisms were real entities, which could be grouped into categories called genera (singular, genus). These were then grouped into orders according to shared similarities and then into classes, classes being linked together as kingdoms. For example, the kingdom Animalia contained the class Vertebrata, which contained the order Primates, which contained the genus *Homo* with the species *sapiens*—humans. Later taxonomists added additional levels in the hierarchy between these to express other levels of similarity.

Previously, practices for naming species varied. Many naturalists gave species long, unwieldy Latin names, which tended not to be fixed and standardized: John Ray's scientific names are often six or eight words long. A naturalist comparing two descriptions of a species might not be able to tell which organisms were being referred to. The need for a workable naming system was made all the greater by the huge number of plants and animals that were being brought back to Europe from Asia, Africa, and the Americas, and Linnaeus's system simplified naming immensely. His two names (genus and species) make up the binomial name. For instance, in his two-volume work *Species Plantarum* (The Species of Plants), Linnaeus renamed the briar rose *Rosa canina*. The name remains.

The extent to which Linnaeus was an evolutionist has been much discussed. He certainly abandoned an early belief in the fixity of species, yet he remained a creationist of sorts. The process of generating new species, in his view, was not unlimited. Whatever new species might have subsequently developed from the original kinds of organisms present in the Garden of Eden were nevertheless part of God's creation, for they had always potentially been there. Linnaeus also commented on the struggle for survival for example in his *Critica Botanica*, 1736—he called nature a "butcher's block" and described competition in the living world a "war of all against all." Nevertheless, he considered struggle and competition necessary to maintain the balance of nature, and a part of the divine order.

Linnaeus's hierarchical classification and binomial nomenclature, much modified, have remained the standard for over 200 years. His writings have been studied by every generation of naturalists, including both Erasmus and Charles Darwin. The search for a natural system of classification continues; however, what systematists now try to achieve and use as the basis of classification are the evolutionary relationships of taxa. Without Linnaeus's nomenclature, Darwin's task, and that of his contemporaries and successors, would have been much more difficult.

Linnaeus died in 1778. His son, also named Carl, succeeded to his professorship, but achieved little as a botanist. When the younger Carl died five years later without any heirs, his family sold the elder Linnaeus's library, manuscripts, and collections to Sir James Edward Smith, who founded the **Linnean Society of London** to conserve them. This society remains one the premier biological societies in Britain. It was at its June 1858 meeting that the cobbled-together Darwin-Wallace paper first setting out the essential points of natural selection was presented.

FURTHER READING

Hagberg, K. 1952. *Carl Linnaeus*. London: Jonathan Cape.

Koerner, L. 1999. *Linnaeus: Nature and Nation*. Cambridge: Harvard University Press.

Lindroth, S. 1983. "The Two Faces of Linnaeus." In T. Frängsmyr (ed.), *Linnaeus: The Man and His Work*. Berkeley: University of California Press.

Linnean Society of London

A scientific society founded in 1788 for the "cultivation of the Science of Natural History in all its branches." Charles Darwin presented papers to the Society and published in its journals several times.

The Linnean Society and its publications remain leading vehicles for contemporary discussions on natural history, particularly systematics, genetics, and the history of plant and animal taxonomy (classification). It is the world's oldest still-active biological society. The Society takes its name from the Swedish naturalist **Carolus (Carl) Linnaeus** (1707–1778), whose natural history collections and library have been in the Society's care since 1829, having been purchased from the executor of the will of the Linnean Society's first president, Sir James Edward Smith (1759–1828).

When Linnaeus died in 1778, Sir Joseph Banks, the secretary of the Royal Society, had tried to buy the collections, which had been inherited by the Swedish naturalist's son. When the younger Linnaeus died in 1783, the collections passed back to Linnaeus's widow, who decided to sell them. They were offered to Banks, but he decided not to purchase them. A young medical student, James Edward Smith, was attending a reception at Banks's home when the offer arrived, and Banks persuaded Smith to acquire the collections. There is a tale that when the King of Sweden heard of the sale of the collections, he immediately dispatched a warship to intercept the ship carrying Smith's new acquisitions back to England. However, the English ship had a good head start, and the collections arrived in Britain, without mishap, in 1784. James Smith founded the Linnean Society to enable scientists to study the collections, and, in due course, the Society bought them from Smith's widow. The collections remain expertly cared for in London, along with a number of other historically important collections, and are available for consultation by scientists of any nation.

Charles Darwin was a fellow of the Linnean Society and through the Society and its journals, he published some of his most important findings, although he was not among its most active members. The joint presentation with Alfred Russell Wallace that set out the notion of evolution through natural selection was made before the Linnean Society in July 1858, was published as "On the Tendency of Species To Form Varieties; and on the Perpetuation of Varieties and Species by Natural Selection"; and was published in the Society's *Journal and Proceedings (Zoology)*, a few months later. Darwin's experiments on seeds' survival in salt water and the implications of this for **long-distance dispersal** were published in the Society's botanical journal a couple of years previously.

Long-Distance Dispersal

The distribution of organisms across substantial distances, especially across oceans; the concept has been described as "the handmaiden of evolution."

If it is accepted that all life on Earth has evolved throughout geological time from a single source or from a very limited number of simple forms, then it follows that all forms of life on remote oceanic **islands** (coral or volcanic islands that have never had any direct connection with a continent), or the ancestors of such life forms must have made the journey in some way. Mechanisms of dispersal include wind (for birds, tiny insects, spores, some seeds); flotation on the ocean surface, movement perhaps facilitated by ocean currents (coconuts); carriage by birds, either inside their bodies to be excreted later or as seeds or fruits adhering to their feathers. Small mammals and reptiles, and perhaps creatures such as snails, may have made the journey by rafting in or on a floating tree trunk or on a mat of decaying vegetation. Ice floes have been suggested as mechanisms for the transport of large animals in polar regions.

These dispersal mechanisms may be involved in the movement of plants and animals between continents (or large subcontinental masses such as

Madagascar). Two widespread species of *Barringtonia* are among a long list of mangrove swamp and coastal species (sometimes referred to as the Indo-Pacific strand flora) to have reached Madagascar by transoceanic dispersal. Both are present along the coast of parts of northern Australia and the southern shores of the Asian mainland. Nevertheless, the distributions of *B. asiatica* and *B. racemosa* in the Indian Ocean basin contain a significant stochastic or random component: *B. asiatica* is present on Mauritius but not on the nearby island of Reunion, and it has not reached the African coast; *B. racemosa* has reached the East African shore, but is not present in the Mascarenes (Reunion and **Mauritius**); both are present in the Seychelles island group. One is naturally present on the **Cocos (Keeling) Islands,** the other on Christmas Island, some 900 kilometers away.

Because the carriage of a seed, fruit, or a pregnant female animal to an island is a rare event, it follows that the biota (the floras and faunas) of remote islands will be few; to use the modern expression, the biodiversity will be low. Moreover, the species that are found in such habitats will only include those that can readily disperse. Tiny insects that could be blown by the wind and mosses and ferns that have very small easily dispersed spores occur frequently on islands; so do trees with floating fruit or seeds, such as coconuts (*Cocos nucifera*) or fruit of the tree *Neisosperma oppositifolium*, both of which Darwin noted on Cocos. The latter he described: "the fruit is bright green, like that of a walnut." He seems to have noted the remains of seeds, possibly including coconuts and *Neisosperma*, washed up on the outer shores of the islands, and, in modifying his account for *The Voyage of the Beagle,* he wrote:

> As the islands consist entirely of coral, and must at one time have existed as mere water-washed reefs, all their productions must have been transported here by the waters of the sea. (*Voyage of the Beagle,* chapter 20)

Of a solitary tree growing near a beach he wrote: "without doubt the one seed was thrown up by the waves."

Although he did not adopt his evolutionary outlook until after his return to England, Darwin noted again and again the poverty of island biota. Notwithstanding the thick, tangled, junglelike vegetation of the island of **Tahiti** and parts of the Cocos (Keeling) atoll, he noted that the number of plant species was very low. He commented that there were few insects on some of the islands he visited (the **Falkland Islands, St. Paul's Rocks,** Cocos). Certain groups of species—such as earthworms, freshwater fish, and amphibians (frogs, toads, newts)—that cannot survive salt water were absent from islands; where they did occur, they had probably been introduced (as in Mauritius). Mammals, too, were rare on islands. Of **New Zealand,** Darwin commented:

> [I]t is a very remarkable fact that so large an island, extending over nearly a thousand miles of latitude, and in many parts one hundred and fifty broad,

with varied stations, a fine climate and land of all heights from 14,000 feet downwards, should not possess one indigenous animal [i.e., mammal] with the exception of a small rat. (*Diary*, December 24, 1835)

In the Chonos archipelago, a group of tiny islets near the southern tip of South America, he recorded:

I caught in a trap a singular little mouse (*Mus brachiotis*); it appeared common on several of the islets, but the Chilotans at Low's Harbour said it was not found in all. What a succession of chances, or what changes of level must have been brought into play, thus to spread these small animals throughout this broken archipelago! (*Voyage of the Beagle*, chapter 13)

However, he added a footnote, possibly written some years later:

It is said that some rapacious birds bring their prey alive to their nests. If so, in the course of centuries, every now and then, one might escape from the young birds. Some such agency is necessary, to account for the distribution of the small gnawing animals on islands not very near each other. (*Voyage of the Beagle*, chapter 13)

During his voyage, therefore, Darwin noted the poverty of island biotas; he noted that some types of organisms were absent from islands or were rare; he speculated about possible mechanisms of dispersal (the waves, wind, birds). But the full evolutionary implications of these observations and speculations did not fully form in his mind until after his return.

As ideas on the transmutability of species began to form in his mind, he increasingly came to appreciate the importance of long-distance dispersal. In a letter to his mentor, **John Henslow**, on March 28, 1837—a matter of days after his probable conversion to his theory of the transmutability of species—he wrote:

At some future time I shall want to know [the] number of species of plants at Galapagos and Keeling, and at the latter whether seeds could possibly endure floating on salt water. (*Correspondence*, Vol. 2, 14. Original letter at Royal Botanic Gardens, Kew)

Clearly, as Darwin became more convinced of the correctness of the notion of transmutability, the idea became more closely associated with those of long-distance dispersal and the poverty of island floras.

Later, as his evolutionary thinking progressed, the capacity of seeds to survive in sea water became an important focus for experimentation, and he conducted experiments on how long the seeds of several dozen species of seed would float, publishing the results in the *Gardeners' Chronicle* and in a paper presented to the **Linnean Society of London.** He found that some species would survive in salt water for 120 days and still germinate. A problem, nevertheless, was that many seeds, after a while, sank.

> Some few seeds, however, do float. . . . From knowing that timber is often cast on the shores of oceanic islands far from the mainland, and from having met with accounts of vegetable off estuaries, I assumed that plants with ripe seeds, washed into the sea by rivers, landslips, &c might be drifted by sea currents for some weeks. The closing of the capsules, pods and heads . . . when wetted, and their reopening when cast on the shore and dried . . . seemed to favour such means of transport. ("On the Action of Sea-water," *Journal of the Proceedings of the Linnean Society (Botany)* 1 (1857): 130–140)

The mechanisms of dispersal of animals also fascinated him. In chapter 12 of *On the Origin of Species*—the second of two chapters titled "Geographical Distributions"—he wrote:

> Some species of fresh-water shells have a very wide range, and allied species, which on my theory, are descended from a common parent and must have proceeded from a single source, prevail throughout the world.

He explained this by giving instances of snails and other organisms being transported in weeds adhering to the bodies of water birds or directly attached to their feet. He also mentioned finding a water beetle on the *Beagle*, blown by the wind, 45 miles (72 kilometers) from land: "How much farther it might have flown with a favouring gale no one can tell."

Other scientists adopted other explanations—building hypothetical land bridges to connect mainland to island and continent to continent—to explain striking plant and animal distributions. Australia was connected to New Zealand, and remote Madeira was connected to the mainland by some naturalists. Another land mass bridged the North Atlantic and another stretched around the world connecting Africa, via the Islands of Kerguelen, to Australia. Darwin would have none of it; in a letter to his friend Charles Lyell written in June 1856, he claimed that his "blood gets hot with passion & runs cold alternately at the[se] geological strides."

Although Charles Darwin placed considerable emphasis on earth movement and the rise and fall of sea levels over geological time, he preferred to be a gradualist rather than a catastrophist. The slow accumulation of species on islands by long-distance dispersal and movement of organisms within and between continents by simple processes involving ocean currents, wind, and migrating organisms appealed to him more than throwing massive land bridges across the oceans. His emphasis on long-distance dispersal, possibly occurring over long periods of time, was more compatible with his developing evolutionary views.

See also: Hooker, Joseph Dalton.

Lyell, Charles (1797—1875)

Geologist; author of *The Principles of Geology,* which profoundly influenced the young Charles Darwin.

One of the ironies of the history of science is that a copy of volume 1 of *The Principles of Geology* was given to Darwin by **Robert FitzRoy,** the captain of HMS *Beagle* on the eve of their great voyage. Ideas in this book greatly influenced the young naturalist while he was developing his evolutionary views, and he is quoted as saying: "The greatest merit of the *Principles* was that it altered the whole tone of one's mind, and therefore that, when seeing a thing never seen by Lyell, one yet saw it through his eyes." But FitzRoy, an evangelical, fundamentalist Christian, became a firm opponent of Darwin's ideas, the disagreement causing a breach between them.

Charles Lyell the geologist was the eldest son of Charles Lyell, senior, of Kinnordy, Forfarshire, in Scotland. He was born on the family estate. His father (1767–1849) was a botanist; the plant genus *Lyellia* was named after him. He also translated Dante's *Vita Nuova* and *Convito.* From his boyhood, the young Lyell had a strong inclination toward natural history, especially entomology, an interest that he cultivated at Bartley Lodge in the New Forest, in southern England, to which his family had moved soon after his birth. In 1816, he entered Exeter College, Oxford, where he studied mathematics, but where also the lectures of **William Buckland** first stimulated his interest in geology. After taking his degree of BA in 1819 (MA followed in 1821), he entered Lincoln's Inn to train for a legal career. In 1825, after a delay caused by chronic weakness of the eyes, he was called to the bar, and practiced as a lawyer (with no striking success) for two years.

He had been elected a fellow of the **Linnean Society of London** and the **Geological Society of London** around the time he completed his undergraduate course, and he presented his first paper, "On a Recent Formation of Freshwater Limestone in Forfarshire," to the Geological Society in 1822; he acted as honorary secretary in 1823. In that year, he went to the continent of Europe with introductions to **Georges Cuvier, Alexander von Humboldt,** and other men of science. In 1824, he made a geological tour in Scotland with Buckland, and these were the first of many travels throughout Europe and North America. In 1826, at a young age, he was elected a fellow of the **Royal Society.**

The first volume of Charles Lyell's *Principles of Geology* was published in 1830, the second in 1832, and the third in 1833. The work went through 11 editions in his life time; a 12th, the revision of which was completed by his nephew, Leonard Lyell, appeared shortly after his death. The subtitle was *An Attempt To Explain the Former Changes of the Earth's Surface by Reference to Causes Now in Operation,* which emphasizes his approach.

Until the nineteenth century, most geologists were adherents to **catastrophism:** they believed that the surface of the world—the formation of mountains, gorges, sea coasts, and erratic boulders—was to be explained with reference to occasional, sudden, dramatic changes caused by processes quite different from those now operating. Lyell and his Scots predecessor, James Hutton, adopted the view of **uniformitarianism** or **gradualism.** All the features of the Earth's surface could be understood with reference to the normal processes that one can see in operation today, over very long periods of time. One of the implications of this theory was that the earth was in a steady state and "the present is the key to the past." Thus, the ripple marks visible along sandy beaches today are very similar to those in sandstones millions, or hundreds of millions, of years old and were formed by similar processes.

There is evidence that Darwin was reading the first volume of Lyell's *Principles* very early during the *Beagle*'s voyage. Volumes 2 and 3 reached him while he was in South America, part way through the circumnavigation. The book profoundly influenced how Darwin perceived the world. There are a number references to Lyell's work in his *Beagle* notes. Yet there is evidence that, from time to time, catastrophist and uniformitarian ideas were battling in his mind. For example, in the Falkland Islands, Darwin noticed the way in which deposition was gradually accumulating in some of the long inlets of the sea, but he also speculated that the stone runs (now thought to have been formed by periglacial action [frost action in and on semifrozen ground] at the end of the Ice Age) might have been formed by the shaking down of rocks from the valley sides by spectacular earthquakes.

Sometimes during the voyage, although he accepted Lyell's general hypothesis, Darwin differed from him in detail. For example, Lyell suggested that that coral atolls (circular or horseshoe-shaped islands formed entirely of coral) formed on the lips of submerged circular volcanic craters. Darwin explained them in terms of coral growth around a gradually sinking volcanic island (or through a rise in sea level eventually overtopping such an islet). Lyell was later convinced of the correctness of this idea.

Lyell and Darwin eventually became firm friends and corresponded over many scientific matters. When, in 1844, he drafted instructions to his wife Emma for the publication of an essay (the **Essay of 1844**) setting out the framework of his evolutionary idea in the event of his early death, Charles Lyell was suggested as someone who might assist with this. And when it appeared that **Alfred Russel Wallace** was developing similar ideas in 1858, Lyell was among those who assisted Darwin to prepare a combined presentation to be put before the Linnean Society.

His important work *The Geological Evidence of Antiquity of Man* appeared in 1863; it went through three editions in one year. The book gave a general overview of the arguments for man's early appearance on the Earth derived from the discoveries of flint implements in post-Pliocene deposits both in Britain and on the European continent. He also discussed in some detail the deposits of the Ice Age (the Quaternary **glaciation**). In the first few pages of this volume, Lyell gave general support to Darwin's evolutionary ideas. Nevertheless, there is evidence that he was not in entire agreement with every aspect.

Lyell was knighted in 1848 and was made a baronet (i.e., awarded a hereditary knighthood) in 1864, the same year he was president of the **British Association for the Advancement of Science** for its meeting at Bath. He was elected corresponding member of several European academies of science. He was a leading member of the **Royal Society,** from which he received both the Copley and the Royal medals.

During the last years of his life, his sight, which had always been weak, failed him completely. He died on February 22, 1875, and was buried in Westminster Abbey. The Lyell Medal, established in 1875 according to Charles Lyell's will is awarded by the Council of the Geological Society of London for distinguished work in the field.

Lyell's uniformitarianism in geology and Darwin's evolution of life through natural selection can be seen as different sides of the same coin. Both sets of ideas depend on the notion of gradual change though normal processes, and both depend on those processes continuing over immense periods of time. The two were enormous influences on each other, and they typify the scientific revolution in the middle decades of the nineteenth century.

See also: Hooker, Joseph Dalton.

M

Malthus, Thomas Robert (1766–1834)

Clergyman, political economist, demographic theorist, and author of *Essay on Population,* the work that is credited with providing Darwin with the mechanism for his theory of evolution through natural selection.

Despite having a profound influence on much of modern thought, Malthus attracted ridicule and opprobrium in his own time and afterward. One nineteenth-century biographer wrote:

> He was the "best-abused man of his age." [Napoleon] Bonaparte himself was not a greater enemy of his species. Here was a man who defended small-pox, slavery and child-murder; who denounced soup-kitchens, early marriage, and parish allowances; who "had the impudence to marry after preaching against the evils of a family"; who thought the world so badly governed that the best actions do the most harm; who in short, took all the romance out of life and preached a dull sermon on the threadbare text—"Vanity of vanities, all is vanity." Such was the character of Malthus as described by his opponents. (J. Bonar, *Malthus and His Work,* 1885. London: George Allen & Unwin, 1926)

As unfair as much of the criticism was, there is a certain dreariness about parts of Malthus's message.

Thomas Robert Malthus—he preferred the name Robert—was born into a scholarly family that lived in a house perhaps aptly named the Rookery (rooks are among the most social of birds) near Guildford, Surrey, not far from London. His father Daniel was influenced by the French educational philosopher Rousseau and may have employed some of Rousseau's ideas in the education of the young Robert, for he was educated partly at home. He entered Jesus College, Cambridge, in 1784 to study mathematics, graduating with honors in mathematics. He also studied classical and modern languages and history. He was self-conscious in his early life about a speech defect—perhaps a cleft palate—but he nevertheless read regularly in the college chapel and received prizes for speeches in Greek and Latin. But later in life his speech was described as imperfect. It is not clear when he was ordained a priest in the Church of England, possibly in about 1788; he was appointed to a minor clerical appointment close to his home in Surrey in 1793. Around the turn of the century, he made several tours to Scandinavia, Russia, France, and Switzerland. He married a young cousin—Harriet Eckersall—in 1804 (she was 11 years younger). Despite advocating restraint and discouraging early marriage among the laboring classes, he seems to have enjoyed the company of attractive young women.

At the end of 1805, he became professor of political economy and history at the East India College at Haileybury—an institution founded to provide administrators for British India. He held this post for almost 30 years, writing a series of articles and pamphlets on economic and political topics. He advised the government and gave evidence to a House of Commons committee.

He died, probably of a heart attack, on December 29, 1834, while spending Christmas at his wife's family home near Bath. He is buried in Bath Abbey, where a commemorative plaque describes him as:

> Long known to the lettered world by his admirable writings on the social branches of political economy, particularly the "Essay on Population."
>
> One of the best men and truest philosophers of any age or country . . . His writings will be a lasting monument of the extent and correctness of his understanding.

By far the most influential of his works was the *Essay on Population,* first published before the Haileybury appointment. Early in the essay (in fact, a work of almost 400 pages), he succinctly sets out the ideas for which he will be remembered, arguing from first principles:

> I think I may make two postulata. First, that food is necessary to the existence of man. Secondly, that passion between the sexes is necessary, and will remain nearly in its present state. . . . Assuming then, my postulata as granted, I say, that the power of population is indefinitely greater than the power in the earth to produce subsistence for man. Population, when unchecked, increases in a geometrical ratio. Subsistence increases only in arithmetic ratio. A slight acquaintance with numbers will show the immensity of the first power in

comparison with the second. By the law . . . which makes food necessary, . . . the effects of these two unequal powers must be kept equal. This implies a strong and constantly operating check on population from the difficulty of subsistence.

Famine and pestilence, he goes on to argue, are the mechanisms that provide the check to the otherwise inexorable growth in human numbers; he sometimes added war to this list. This pessimistic outlook was somewhat moderated in the second (1803) edition. Here the checks were portrayed not as insuperable obstacles, but as defining limits or problems that had to be overcome if social progress was to be maintained. He did not advocate the spread of smallpox to control the rising population of the poor, but he pointed out that hunger, poverty, and disease went together and with very large families. He advocated what he called moral restraint, discouraging marriage (and reproduction) among those who could not support themselves. He discouraged the distribution of money and food to the poor, arguing that it caused the price of food to rise and encouraged the poor to breed. To those who sided with the poor, Malthus was the devil incarnate; to the middle classes, who saw themselves as highly taxed, he was a savior.

To some extent, Malthus has been vindicated, and, to some extent, his prophesies have been found wanting. The world's population has increased by at least three times since Malthus's day. In Ireland, between 1846 and 1850, the combined effects of famine and the typhus outbreak that followed the potato blight caused the deaths of 1.5 million people. A figure of 3 million is sometimes suggested. Hundreds of thousands emigrated. The population of the island fell from 8.175 million in 1841 to 6.624 million in 1851. And more recently (in the 1930s and 1940s), famine in China and India has been linked to high population densities.

On the other hand, the famine in the Soviet Union in 1920 to 1921 in which 5 million people died, and subsequent periods of food shortage have been seen by some as the product of the incompetence and maladministration by the Communist government. Although populations are still rising in some parts of Africa and Latin America, they have leveled off in most parts of North America, Europe, and Australia. (HIV and AIDS have contributed to the leveling out and a local decline in parts of Africa.) Malthus did not foresee such factors as the enormous improvements in agriculture, industrialization, the widespread availability of contraception, and greater affluence and social change, all of which contributed to the decline in average family size in the developed world.

Malthusian ideas were in wide circulation in fashionable (especially Whig) circles in London in the 1830s, the period when Charles Darwin returned from his voyage. Indeed Harriet Martineau, the early feminist and a propagandist for Malthusian doctrines, was a girlfriend of Erasmus Darwin, Charles's elder brother, for a while. Charles never met Malthus, but the families had a number of mutual acquaintances. Darwin read the *Essay* (the sixth edition) in about September 1838, a little over a year after his unpublicized conversion to an evolutionary view. It provided him with a key—a mechanism for the evolutionary process. Malthusian competition eliminated less favored individuals from the population, preventing them from passing on their characteristics to later generations, and thus encouraging a progressive adaptation to environment. Darwin referred to this process as natural selection, and it was a critical component in the suite of his evolutionary ideas.

Mantell, Gideon Algernon (1790—1852)

English geologist and paleontologist, born at Lewes, Sussex, on the south coast of England.

Like many of his scientific contemporaries (e.g., **Thomas Huxley,** Charles Darwin, **Joseph Hooker,** and **Richard Owen**), Mantell trained for the medical profession. He first practiced in his home town, later in Brighton (a seaside resort a few miles away), and finally in Clapham, near London. He made a special study of the rocks and fossils of southern England, publishing *The Fossils of the South Downs* in 1822. This remarkably includes the fossil reptiles known as *Iguanodon, Hylaeosaurus, Pelorosaurus,* and *Regnosaurus.* For this research he was made a fellow of the **Royal Society** and was awarded the Wollaston medal by the **Geological Society** and the Royal medal by the Royal Society. He was influenced by **Charles Lyell** and popularized science. His best-known work, *The Wonders of Geology or A Familiar Exposition of Geological Phenomena* (2 volumes, 1838), was extremely popular and went through six editions in 10 years. The seventh edition appeared in 1857. **Thomas Hardy** owned a copy of the sixth edition and probably obtained a good deal of his knowledge of geology, and indeed his enthusiasm for science, from it.

Maori

The native or indigenous people of **New Zealand** and the name of language they speak. Darwin spent just over a week—December 21–30, 1835—at the **Bay of Islands,** North Island, New Zealand, and had a good deal to say of Maori customs and way of life.

New Zealand was one of the last areas of the planet, apart from Antarctica and small remote islands, to be colonized by humans. Archaeological and linguistic evidence suggests there were probably several periods of migration from Polynesia to New Zealand between about A.D. 800 and 1300. Moreover, because European settlement of New Zealand also occurred relatively late, it has been asserted that they represented the last major human community to remain untouched and unaffected by Western civilization.

Early European explorers, such as Captain James Cook, had encounters with Maori. These reports described the Maori as a fierce, proud warrior race. Intertribal warfare was a way of life, with the conquered being enslaved or sometimes eaten. From as early as the 1780s, Maori had encounters with European and American whalers and sealers. Also in New Zealand at the time were a few escaped convicts from Australia and a number of deserters from visiting ships.

By 1830, it was estimated that living among the Maori were as many as 2,000 persons of European origin whose status varied from slaves to high ranking advisors, from prisoners to those who abandoned European culture and identified themselves with the local people. The Europeans were valued for their ability to introduce certain skills and the facility with which they could obtain European items in trade, particularly weapons.

During this period, the acquisition of muskets by tribes in close contact with Europeans upset the existing balance of power between the various Maori tribes, and there was a period of bloody intertribal warfare, during which several tribes were effectively exterminated and others were driven from their traditional lands. Diseases introduced by the Europeans also killed a large, but unknown, number; estimates vary between 10 and 50 percent of the Maori population.

With increasing European missionary activity and settlement in the 1830s as well as European lawlessness (both of which existed at the time of Darwin and Captain **Robert FitzRoy**'s visit in late 1835 and on which Darwin comments in some detail), the British government was under pressure to step in, and Queen **Victoria** annexed New Zealand (it had already been claimed by Cook in 1769), originally as part of the colony of New South Wales and then, with the appointment of William Hobson as governor, as a separate colony. FitzRoy returned to New Zealand as governor as Hobson's successor 1843 to 1845. His governorship was not a success, because he did not get along well with the Maori chiefs nor the white settlers.

Numbers of Maori declined as the result of wars with the colonizers and disease throughout much of the nineteenth century, and traditional Maori society became fractured. In the later twentieth century, there was a substantial rise in their numbers and in their cultural awareness and improvement in the status of their language.

Darwin's notes on the Maori are of interest because they described the customs of the people before the social decline accelerated. He describes the way of life and customs in some detail. Here are his notes about tattooing by the Maoris; they show, perhaps, the influence of his less-than-successful time at Edinburgh Medical School:

The complicated but symmetrical figures, covering the whole face, puzzle & mislead the unaccustomed eye; it is moreover probable that the deep incisions, by destroying the play of the superficial muscles, would give an air of rigid inflexibility. (*Diary*, December 22, 1835)

Darwin also described in some detail the Maori custom of rubbing noses:

> The women on our first approach began uttering something in a most dolorous and plaintive voice, they then squatted down & held up their faces; my companions standing over them placed the bridges of their own noses at right angles to theirs, & commenced pressing; this lasted rather longer than a cordial shake of the hand would with us; as we vary the force of the grasp of the hand in shaking, so do they in pressing. During the process they utter comfortable little grunts, very much in the same manner as two pigs do when rubbing against each other. (*Diary,* December 22, 1835)

Darwin compares, quite objectively, the Maori custom with the Western handshake and, in a somewhat uncomplimentary way, the vocalizations with those of pigs. Beyond that, there is little attempt at analysis and interpretation, although in his later work—particularly in *The Descent of Man* and *The Expression of Emotions in Animals and Man*—he emphasizes comparisons between the behavior of humans and animals more strongly.

Early in his visit, in his diary entry for December 22, 1835, he noted that the Maoris and Tahitians belonged to the "same family of mankind." A little later, he attempted to place the various societies that he had encountered in relationship to one another on a ladder or scale:

> If the state in which the Fuegians live should be fixed on as zero in the scale of government, I am afraid New Zealand would rank but a few degrees higher, while Tahiti, even as first discovered would occupy a respectable position.

The idea of a family relationship between races and of a ladder of civilization recur in his writings. Later he was to write about the Australian Aborigines and the Cocos Islands Malays in a similar way. These same concepts were later developed, for example, in the *Descent of Man.*

The idea that there exists a close relationship between organisms and their environment is an idea that is fundamental to Darwin's work. Humans were no exception. The Maori people manipulated their environment and were influenced by it. Darwin had heard it asserted that the extensive open country was once covered by forest but had been cleared by the Maoris with the help of fire; he stated that the local people "had an evident motive for thus clearing the country," because tracts of fern flourished where the fire

Maori, North Island, New Zealand. From: *Narrative of the Surveying Voyages,* 1839.

had been and this was a "staple . . . article of food." Moreover, in many of the cleared areas, digging revealed large lumps of resin, such as flowed from the kauri trees. He also noted that pas (fortified settlements or hill forts) were an important element in the landscape:

> The summits were cut into steps or successive terraces & they had frequently been protected by trenches. . . . That the Pas had formerly been used was evident from the piles of shells & the pits in which I was informed, sweet potatoes were buried as reserved provisions. (*Diary*, December 2, 1835)

Darwin did not particularly like New Zealand, and he saw Maori society as being in decline. Yet he very strongly approved of what the missionaries were doing, writing of the "excellence of the Christian religion" and asserting that the missionaries were "improving the moral character" of the Maoris. The natives he met at a mission station, Waimate, he described as "respectable," "honest," "clean, tidy and healthy," and "very merry and good humoured." Darwin, although he tried to be objective and fair in describing the people with whom he came into contact, saw the world through the lens of his background and education. Nevertheless, Darwin's experiences among the Maoris were important and gave him material that he developed in his later work.

Marsupials

A group of mammals frequently described as pouched. Although they give live birth, they do not have long gestation periods as do placental mammals. They give birth to incompletely developed young—little more than embryos—which climb from the mother's birth canal to the nipples (which, in most forms, are in the pouch), where development continues.

Marsupials probably evolved in North America in the Cretaceous period (about 100 million years ago), finding their way to South America, and then through Antarctica into **Australia** when the southern continents were joined together as the Gondwana supercontinent. There are about 140 species of marsupials in Australia, most of which are found nowhere else in the world (although some of them appear in New Guinea, which was connected to Australia in geologically recent times). The only naturally occurring marsupial in North America today is the opossum, *Didelphis marsupialis*. Marsupials were more abundant in the Americas in the past and mostly died out in North America during the Tertiary period. The opossum represents a relatively recent reinvasion from South America, where some forms persisted.

The Australian marsupials belong to about eight groups: the koala; the kangaroos and wallabies; the wombats; the possums, and gliders; carnivorous marsupials such as the Tasmanian devil and the extinct thyracine; the numbat; the bandicoots and billbies; and the marsupial mole.

Darwin had some, but not much, personal experience of marsupials while he was in Australia in early 1836. On January 19, he went kangaroo hunting with a local farm manager. There was poor sport, and Darwin bemoaned the fact the greyhounds (and, of course, firearms) had led to the destruction of wildlife: "now the Emu is banished to a long distance, & the Kangaroo is become scarce," he noted in his diary. However:

> The Grey hounds pursued a Kangaroo Rat [*Potarous tridactylus,* a potaroo] into a hollow tree out of which we dragged it; it is an animal as big as a rabbit, but with the figure of a Kangaroo.

Darwin very early in his visit noticed the distinctiveness of the Australian environment, at one stage wondering whether there had been two creations: one for Australia and one for the rest of the world. But he soon rejected this notion. But he did notice how places in "the economy of nature" in the Australian environment were occupied by different, but analogous, creatures to those that elsewhere occupied the same ecological niche (as modern terminology would put it). Marsupial forms replaced the placental forms of other continents (the kangaroo rat represented a rodent—rat or rabbit—elsewhere).

He developed these ideas in *On the Origin of Species,* over twenty years later:

> A set of animals, with their organisation but little diversified, could hardly compete with a set more perfectly diversified in structure. It may be doubted, for instance whether the Australian marsupials, which are divided into groups differing but little from each other, and feebly representing . . . our carnivorous, ruminant, and rodent mammals, could successfully compete with these well-pronounced orders. In the Australian mammals, we see the process of diversification in an early and incomplete stage of development. (*On the Origin of Species,* chapter 4)

Darwin slightly overemphasized the point, but he was in a number of respects very perceptive. In his remarks can be seen the concept of adaptive radiation (the development of many different forms from a single ancestral stock, as organisms adapt to different environments or ecological niches). Here too is the idea of **convergent evolution.** Marsupials and placental forms have converged—or have come to resemble one another despite their belonging to different groups. Marsupial moles in Australia occupy a similar environment to the burrowing moles of northern climes; the thyracine and the Tasmanian devil represent the Carnivora of other lands.

Darwin was also perceptive in the manner in which he foresaw the way in which the combined effects of human slaughter and the introduction of placental mammals from elsewhere would devastate the Australian native mammal fauna. (Apart from bats, seals, and a few small mouselike forms, there were no placental mammals in Australia other than the dingo, which arrived several thousands of years ago.) The effects of foxes, rabbits, feral cats, mice, and rats through direct predation and competition have been substantial.

See also: Ecology.

Marx, Karl Heinrich (1818–1883)

Founder of international communism; strongly approved of Darwin's evolutionary ideas, but the respect was not reciprocated.

Karl Marx was born in Trier, Germany, to upper-middle-class parents. He studied law at Bonn and Berlin but later took up history and philosophy. He edited a radical periodical that was soon suppressed. He moved to Paris in 1843 and to Brussels in 1845. There, with Friedrich Engels (1820–1895) as his collaborator, he reorganized the Communist League and, in 1848, completed the *Communist Manifesto,* which painted the state as an instrument of oppression of the common people and religion and culture as ideologies of capitalism. On expulsion from Brussels, he settled in London (1849), notoriously working long hours in the British Museum Library. *Das Capital* was completed in 1867, and further volumes were added in 1884 and 1894.

Marx was initially ambivalent to *On the Origin of Species,* calling it a "bitter satire" on humanity and nature, seeing a parallel between the struggles of plants and animals in nature and English society. Marx and Engels, not surprisingly, detested the ideas of **Thomas Malthus.** But the parallelism between what Darwin saw as evolution of increasingly complex living things and the notions of the progression of society from feudalism through capitalism to socialism appealed to Marx, and in 1873 he sent a copy of a new edition of *Das Capital* to Darwin, with an inscription that it was from a "sincere admirer." Darwin appreciated the importance of the work and tried to read the first few pages. But he found the German heavy going, and felt that the character of the book was very different from that of his own work. He wrote a brief appreciative note to Marx, noting the "important subject of political economy" and expressing the wish that he was more worthy to receive it and understood more of the subject with which it dealt. He hoped that the respective efforts toward the "extension of knowledge" would be of benefit to mankind. The note is brief, short, polite, but noncommittal.

The circles in which Karl Marx and Charles Darwin moved overlapped slightly. Jenny, Marx's daughter, attended a lecture given by **Thomas Huxley** in 1866 and was impressed. Edward Aveling, who eventually became Marx's son-in-law, publicized Darwin's work and called on him, urging him to adopt a more stridently atheist posture. But this was not Darwin's way. Besides, although a Gladstonian liberal in much of his outlook, as a well-to-do land-owning squire, he and his family had much to lose from a breakdown of a stable society and the spread of revolutionary ideas.

Although an analogy can be drawn between Darwin's and Marx's ideas, they deal with different phenomena, and the parallelism must not be pushed too far. Marx withdrew from debate in the last few years of his life as his health deteriorated. He is buried in Highgate Cemetery in London, and his grave, despite the partial eclipse of Marxist ideologies with the collapse of the Soviet Union in the 1990s, remains an object of pilgrimage.

Mauritius

Small tropical island in the Indian Ocean, of volcanic origin and surrounded by coral reefs.

Mauritius is an island about 550 miles (880 kilometers) east of Madagascar in the tropical Indian Ocean (20° S, approximately 58° E); it has an area of 720 square miles (1,865 square kilometers). It consists of a mountainous core of volcanic rocks (the highest point is 827 meters) but is surrounded by coral reefs. The island has a population of about 1.3 million. Today, Mauritius is an independent Commonwealth country. It was a British colony until 1968 and was under French administration from 1715 to 1810. The French influence at the time of Darwin's visit (April 29 to May 9, 1836) was still strong, although the island was heavily garrisoned by British troops. The capital then, as now, was Port Louis, which in Darwin's day had a population of 20,000 and which he admired for its well-laid-out design. The production of sugar cane dominates the economy of the island today. Darwin noted that the production of sugar was increasing: he claimed it had increased 75-fold over the preceding 25 years—a fact that he attributed to the emphasis that the British colonial administration placed on building good roads, as well as the importation of Indian workers for the sugar plantations. During his time in Mauritius, Darwin stayed for a few days with a Captain Lloyd, the surveyor general at his residence in the cooler hill country about six miles from Port Louis. He went for leisurely walks and collected a few insect and geological specimens. For the first time in his life, he rode on an elephant. Before the ship sailed, he did a little shopping in Port Louis. He thought the landscape was "exceedingly picturesque."

Despite the leisurely nature of Darwin's time in Mauritius, his few days there were not without significance. Walking along the coast north of the town, he made significant observations on the ecology of coral reefs. He noticed that there was some coralline rock above sea level. He commented on the complex volcanic structure of the islands. He later fitted his geological observation into his comparison of the various volcanic **islands** that he visited and his theory of coral reefs. He argued that there were places where the sea bed was rising, and that these were compensated for by areas of subsidence. He noted the evidence for erosion and down-cutting by some of the rivers and streams in the volcanic uplands of the island.

Darwin collected only one vertebrate specimen—a frog. This he later discovered was introduced, being the same species as is found on a number of other islands in the Indian Ocean. Indeed, the number of natural history observations he made on Mauritius was small. However, his interest in the island remained, for in *On the Origin of Species* he uses the absence of amphibians from Mauritius and other remote islands as evidence for evolution.

Mauritius provided Darwin with an opportunity for rest and recreation rather than constituting a locale for detailed scientific work. Nevertheless, the observations he made there fit with other work elsewhere, particularly on coral reefs and volcanic isles. The limited natural history work that he did triggered his imagination, for he wrote about island biotas, including that of Mauritius, in some of his later books.

See also: Corals and Coral Reefs; Long-Distance Dispersal.

Megatherium

A large, bulky, extinct, slow-moving mammal that lived during the Pleistocene period in South America.

Megatherium probably lived between about 1.8 million and 8,000 years ago. This Ice Age mammal was the largest of the ground sloths; Megatherium's name means great beast. The first Megatherium fossil was found in Brazil in 1789. It was related to the modern South American sloths.

The animal had peg-like teeth, powerful jaws, and a thick, short tail. It had three hooklike claws on each foot. It sometimes walked on all four limbs, but fossil footprints show that it frequently walked on its hind legs. When it stood on its hind legs, it was about twice the height of an elephant, about six meters or twenty feet tall. It weighed several tons. Megatherium, like its living relatives, was probably an herbivore (a plant-eater). It may have eaten leaves from the upper parts of trees while standing upright, using its tail to balance. Its large deep jaw is believed to have housed a long tongue, which it could have used to pull leaves into its mouth. It may have occasionally eaten carrion.

Charles Darwin found several Megatherium fossils in South America.

After breakfast I walked to Punta Alta, the same place where I have before found fossils. I found a jaw bone, which contained a tooth: by this I found out that it belongs to the great ante-diluvian animal the Megatherium. This is particularly interesting as the only specimens in Europe are in the King's collection in Madrid, where for all purposes of science they are nearly as much hidden as if in their primaeval rock. (*Diary,* October 8, 1832)

Note the use of the word "ante-diluvian"—before the flood. Even if Darwin did not intend a literal interpretation, he does not entirely divorce himself from earlier biblical thought forms. He surmised, from the other fossils associated with these bones, that they were of relatively recent date (he was right). The spot where he collected important fossils in 1832 has been built over by an Argentinean naval base, but places where he geologized a few miles away are still available for inspection, and near here spectacular fossil footprints of Megatherium have recently been found.

The fossils Darwin collected were taken back to England and studied in detail by **Richard Owen,** and the results of his studies were published in the first volume of *The Zoology of the Voyage of the Beagle: Fossil Mammalia.*

Darwin made good use of Megatherium in his subsequent publications. Here is an extract from chapter 5 of *The Voyage of the Beagle.*

> The great size of the bones of the Megatheroid animals . . . is truly wonderful. The habits of life of these animals were a complete puzzle to naturalists, until Professor Owen solved the problem with remarkable ingenuity. The teeth indicate, by their simple structure, that these Megatheroid animals lived on vegetable food, and probably on the leaves and small twigs of trees; their ponderous forms and great strong curved claws seem so little adapted for locomotion, that some eminent naturalists have actually believed, that, like the sloths, to which they are intimately related, they subsisted by climbing back downwards on trees, and feeding on the leaves. It was a bold, not to say preposterous, idea to conceive even antediluvian trees, with branches strong enough to bear animals as large as elephants. Professor Owen, with far more probability, believes that, instead of climbing on the trees, they pulled the branches down to them, and tore up the smaller ones by the roots, and so fed on the leaves. The colossal breadth and weight of their hinder quarters, which can hardly be imagined without having been seen, become, on this view, of obvious service, instead of being an incumbrance: their apparent clumsiness disappears. With their great tails and their huge heels firmly fixed like a tripod on the ground, they could freely exert the full force of their most powerful arms and great claws. Strongly rooted, indeed, must that tree have been, which could have resisted such force!

Ideas on the nature and life-style of Megatherium have changed slightly, but what is interesting is that Darwin attempts to place the creature in the context of its environment and way of life. The form, ecology, and behavior of creatures were tightly interconnected. This was as true for creatures that had been extinct for thousands of years as it was for existing animals.

Megatherium also makes its appearance in *On the Origin of Species.* After explaining his possible mechanism for evolution in the earlier chapters on variation (chapter 3) and natural selection (chapter 4) and discussing difficulties of the theory in chapter 6, he turns to the geological evidence in chapters 9 and 10, the latter titled "On the Geological Succession of Organic Beings." If organisms have changed throughout time, one would expect to find evidence of this in their fossil remains in the rocks. Darwin described the way in which creatures come into the geological succession and go extinct, citing Megatherium. He also stresses that fossil creatures are often of the same type in the same region:

[I]n several parts of La Plata . . . Professor Owen has shown in the most striking manner that most of the fossil mammals, buried there in such numbers, are related to South American types.

And a little later:

On the theory of descent with modification, the great law of the long enduring, but not immutable, succession of the same types in the same areas, is at once explained; for the inhabitants of the same quarter of the world will obviously tend to leave in that quarter . . . closely allied though to some extent modified descendants. (*On the Origin of Species,* chapter 10)

FURTHER READING

Bargo, M. S. 2001. "The Ground Sloth Megatherium Americanum: Skull Shape, Bite Forces, and Diet." *Acta Palaeontologica Polonica* 46: 173–192.

Fariña, R. A. and R. E. Blanco. 1996. "Megatherium, the Stabber." *Proceedings of the Royal Society of London* 263: 1725–1729.

Mendel, Gregor (1822–1884)

Austrian Augustinian monk, botanist, and pioneer in genetics.

Johann (he took the name Gregor after entering the cloister) was born to a peasant farmer in a village that was then called Heizendorf, in Austria (it is now Hynice and in the Czech Republic). He did well at school and entered the monastery of the Augustinian Order at Brün (Brno). He was ordained priest in 1847, and a short while later his aptitude for teaching became apparent. In 1851, with the support of his order, he entered the University of Vienna for further training as a teacher of mathematics and biology; although he did not complete the course (he suffered from anxiety and possibly epilepsy), he acquired research skills that became important later. He returned to Brün, teaching part-time.

Gregor Mendel loved plants and was curious about their variations. He was also interested in the views of **Jean-Baptiste Lamarck,** who had suggested that differences in environment might modify organisms and that these acquired characteristics might be passed on to the next generation. With the support of his abbot, Mendel resolved to undertake a series of experiments to test Lamarck's theories and to study the nature of inheritance. These studies commenced in about 1856. At one stage, he grew two varieties of the same species of plant close together (i.e., in more or less the same environment) and then grew their progeny from seed to see whether they became more similar. He found that the offspring retained the characteristics of the parent plants and were thus not influenced by the environment. He became curious about the nature of this heredity and embarked on seven years of experiments in the monastery garden and greenhouse, crossing peas and beans with different characteristics and carefully examining the progeny. Mendel arrived at certain conclusions, which may be simply restated as follows:

Law of segregation: Inheritable factors (now known as genes) are present in pairs in an organism's cells. When an organism forms gametes (reproductive cells), the pairs separate so that each gamete contains only one factor.
Law of independence: When more than one pair of factors is considered, each pair of factors segregates independently of every other pair.

Modern research has confirmed that genes are arranged along chromosomes in most cells of an organism and that chromosomes form homologous pairs that separate when the reproductive cells are formed. Mendel also understood the concept of dominance: some characteristics tend to dominate over other (recessive) factors or genes. A logical consequence of these laws is that the characteristics of organisms are inherited in ascertainable, predictable, numerical ratios.

Although modern research—on DNA, for example—has shown that many aspects of inheritance are much more complicated than Mendel allowed, by and large, his findings have held up. However, at the time, the reception of Mendel's theories was muted. Mendel reported on his research to a local scientific association in Brno in February and March 1865; the monk's remarks were received politely, but few understood the importance of what he was saying. The association published a written account of the experiments under the title of *Versuche über Pflanzen-Hybride* (Treatise on plant hybrids) in 1866, and 40 reprints were sent to distinguished scientists, but again there was little response. Mendel was bitterly disappointed by the failure of the scientific community to appreciate the significance of his findings, and this may have been part of the reason that he abandoned his experiments. It was perhaps a small compensation that in 1868 he was elected abbot of the monastery.

It is sometimes stated that part of Mendel's motivation was to refute Darwin's theories, showing that change could occur as the result of cross-breeding. However, heredity alone, as defined by Mendel's concepts, far from promoting evolutionary change, results in predictable segregation ratios.

It was not until nearly twenty years after Mendel's death, and 34 years after their first publication, that his work was rediscovered. Around 1900, Carl Correns in Germany and Hugo de Vries in the Netherlands began to understand the general significance of the work. Some still saw Mendel's theories as an alternative to those of Darwin, rather than complementing them. Darwin's notion of natural selection, working in a population of organisms, required a mechanism of inheritance (about the nature of which Darwin could only speculate). Mendel's work went some way to providing this mechanism, although he did not realize it at the time.

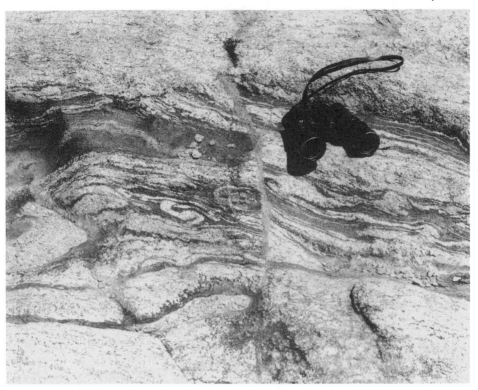

Contorted gneiss, southwestern Australia. Photo: Patrick Armstrong.

Metamorphic Rocks

Rocks originally igneous or sedimentary that have been transformed, deep within the Earth's crust, by high pressure, heat, or chemical action. Examples of metamorphic rocks are schist, gneiss, and slate.

A distinction is sometimes made between regional metamorphism, where large areas have been affected by the intrusions of granites and the contortion of rocks deep within mountain ranges, and contact metamorphism, which is usually more local and caused by the heating of rocks through proximity to hot magma (such as a dyke—a vertical or near vertical intrusion of igneous material).

Darwin encountered regional metamorphism in South America (the Andes and Tierra del Fuego) and in the "gneiss-granites," as he called them, around King George's Sound in southwestern Australia. In Tasmania, he found evidence of contact metamorphism. On a hill behind Hobart Town he found:

> strata of a very impure Coal, carbonaceous Shale, & white Sandstone banded with the finest lines, stained black by a similar substance. Here such layers are penetrated by a great mass or dyke (a hundred yards wide) of a decomposing

Greenstone: on one side the strata dip away at an angle of 60° or 70°, & fragments of Porcelain rock & indurated sandstone, lying on the lines of junction, point out the effect of the igneous mass—on the other side, the confusion is even greater; layers of impure Coal, being now nearly vertical. (*Geological Notes,* Cambridge University Library, Darwin Archive)

Darwin is deducing the geological history of the area from the appearance of the rocks and their orientation. A sequence of sedimentary rocks—coal, shale, and sandstone—has been intruded by a dyke. The hot magma heated the shaly, clay-rich rocks into a porcelainlike substance, modified the sandstone, and contorted the originally more or less horizontally bedded rocks so that they dip at a high, near vertical angle.

Morris, Francis Orpen (1810—1893)

English clergyman and naturalist who campaigned stridently against Darwin's evolutionary ideas.

Francis Morris was born in Ireland and educated at Worcester College, Oxford. He was ordained in 1834 and was rector of the parish of Nunburnholme in Yorkshire, in northern England for nearly 50 years. He was something of an ornithologist and published popular books on birds better known for their amusing anecdotes and large colored pictures than for their scientific accuracy. Nevertheless, he was an early activist in the area of bird conservation. He was one of several Church of England clergy who campaigned against Darwinism.

Francis Orpen Morris. Outspoken opponent of Darwin's views. From a nineteenth-century print.

A paper given before the **British Association for the Advancement of Science** in Norwich in 1868 was followed by a stream of anti-evolution pamphlets with titles such as *Difficulties with Darwinism* (1869) and *The Demands of Darwinism on Credulity* (1890). Although evangelical in outlook, Morris's objections were based on logic rather the Scripture. It was, he argued, absurd to state that organisms varied, and yet were descended from one another. In one of his publications, he expressed his "ineffable contempt and indignation" at the "astounding puerilities" of Darwin's ideas and their "childish absurdities." There were insufficient words in the English language to express his contempt for evolutionary concepts, he asserted. His self-confessed aim was to eradicate Darwinism from English intellectual life. He failed.

Mutations

Changes to the sequence of genetic material (DNA or RNA) in the cells of living organisms.

Mutations can be caused naturally by copying errors in the genetic material during normal cell division and also by exposure to radiation, ultraviolet light, certain chemicals (*mutagens*), or viruses. In multicellular organisms, mutations can be classified into germline mutations, which can be inherited or passed on to descendants, and somatic mutations, which in animals cannot be transmitted to descendants. Plants, however, occasionally can transmit somatic mutations to their progeny asexually (i.e., through vegetative reproduction such as the sending out of suckers or the formation of a new individual by the breaking away of part of a stem) or, rarely, sexually (as when flowers develop in a part of a plant that has somatically mutated).

Mutations cause variation in a population's gene pool and are, therefore, one of the drivers of evolutionary change. The less favorable mutations are usually eliminated from the gene pool through natural selection. Because they cause the development of unfavorable characteristics, the organism with such a mutation is less likely to survive to produce progeny. Some hereditary diseases may be the result of such unfavorable mutations.

On the other hand, favorable, beneficial mutations tend to accumulate, because they give the organism a competitive advantage. But only a small percentage of all mutations have a positive effect and help organisms adapt to their environment. One example may be a specific change in a human gene that seems to confer resistance to HIV, delaying the onset of AIDS. This mutation is more common in people of European descent than in other human groups. It has been suggested that the relatively high frequency of this gene in European populations is because it conferred resistance to bubonic plague, which swept Europe in the fourteenth century, killing 25 million people between 1347 and 1352.

Neutral mutations confer no particular advantages or disadvantages on individuals, populations, or species. These can, however, accumulate over time through genetic drift. Thus, isolated populations of organisms on high mountain peaks or on remote islands may develop characteristics that, although conferring no particular advantage, differentiate them from their parent population.

Mutation rates vary widely from species to species. Some evolutionary biologists have suggested that higher mutation rates can be beneficial, because they allow organisms to evolve and therefore to adapt more rapidly to changing environments. For example, repeated exposure of bacteria to antibiotics and the survival and natural selection of resistant mutated forms can result in the emergence of bacteria that have a much higher mutation rate than the original population.

N

Native Peoples

Groups, races, or communities indigenous to a particular locality or country. Here taken to refer to human groups of non-European origin.

Charles Darwin showed a particular interest in the indigenous peoples of the lands he visited during his sojourn aboard HMS *Beagle*. However, he had no training in anthropology—indeed it was still a very young science—and so he had few concepts around which to arrange his observations. He had, however, undergone two years of medical training in Edinburgh in his late teens, and occasionally signs of this training emerge in his descriptions of people. For example, when commenting on the facial tattoos of the Maori people in New Zealand, he speculated "that the deep incisions, by destroying the play of the superficial muscles, would give an air of rigid inflexibility." His medical experience may have helped him appraise an Indian man he encountered in Mauritius with "an emaciated body and strange drowsy expression" as possibly being an opium addict.

Darwin was an excellent observer, and his descriptions of the Fuegians (the native people of Tierra del Fuego) are detailed. He describes their food (they ate fungi, berries, shellfish, and a little animal food), their clothing (or lack or it), the construction of their crude shelters and canoes, their weapons, and face-painting. But his approach is mainly to compare their primitiveness with Western, civilized humanity—unfavorably. Words with negative connotations such as "savage," "primitive," "hostile," "miserable," "filthy," "hideous," and "wretched" are used throughout his account.

> I never saw more miserable creatures; stunted in their growth, their hideous faces bedaubed with white paint & quite naked. One full aged woman absolutely so . . . Their red skins filthy & greasy, their hair entangled, their voices discordant, their gesticulation violent & without any dignity. . . . They cannot know the feeling of having a home & still less that of domestic affection. . . . How little can the higher powers of the mind come into play: what is there for imagination to paint, for reason to compare, for judgement to decide upon? To knock a limpet from a rock does not even require cunning the lowest power of the mind. Their skill like the instinct of animals, is not improved by experience; the canoe, their most ingenious work, poor as it may be, we know has remained the same for 300 years. Although essentially the same creature, how little must the mind of one of these beings resemble that of an educated man. What a scale of improvement is comprehended between the faculties of a Fuegian savage & a Sir Isaac Newton! (*Diary*, February 25, 1834)

A modern person might see here a case of severe racial, social, and gender prejudice. But the account must be seen in context. Darwin had never before seen tribal people; elsewhere in South America, he had been within a European sphere of influence. Like everyone, he saw the world through the lens of his upbringing and background. He wrote that they had a sense of equality and no social hierarchy. No one, therefore took charge and directed operations; he felt that little social progress would be made until a social structure or hierarchy emerged. These views are not altogether unsurprising in one imbued with the early-nineteenth-century English class system stepping off a Royal Naval ship-of-war with its rigid stratification of captain, officers, petty officers, midshipmen, and common seamen.

Some of Darwin's comments were astute. He noted that different tribes of Fuegians had different dialects. But he was sometimes in error; he thought they had little notion of spirituality when, in fact, they had a complex shamanistic religion and a wealth of tales and myths concerning the origins of things.

Darwin was always intensely interested in the customs of non-European peoples. (For a detailed account of an Aboriginal corroboree that he witnessed at King George's Sound in the southwest of Western Australia, see article on **Australia.**)

In his account of Aboriginal dancing, Darwin made a comparison with the Fuegians, using such words as "rude and barbarous," "lowest barbarians," "hideous," and "savage" (Darwin frequently used his habit of comparison to bring out relationships or themes.)

He went a little further. Throughout the voyage, and indeed to some extent after it, he attempted to arrange the "primitive" societies he encountered as steps on "ladder of civilisation." The Fuegians occupied the lowest rung of this ladder—at one stage he used the expression "fixed on as zero in the scale of government"—with the Australian Aborigines at the same level or a little higher. The Maoris, he felt, "would rank but a few degrees higher, while Tahiti, even as first discovered, would occupy a respectable position." (Nevertheless, he acknowledged correctly that these two groups belonged to the "same family of mankind.") The Malay people of the Cocos Islands he compared to the Tahitians. Some of the Indians he saw in Mauritius he thought were of a "noble" appearance. It was taken for granted that European civilization was at the top of the ladder. Although he had not yet adopted an evolutionary viewpoint when he made these observations, his arranging of groups in ascending order reveals the first features of ideas that were important to him later.

On Chiloé, on the western coast of southern South America, he encountered the suggestion that the different races of humans had different parasites and that lice adapted to one race would not live well on another. He thus seems to have acknowledged that the different groups or "varieties" of humans had sprung "from one stock" (this was the phrase he used) but had "different species of parasites." The implication was that all humans had a common origin (elsewhere he referred to them of being of the same family) but had important biological differences between them.

Some of these accounts might seem initially to be somewhat prejudiced against some non-European groups. In fact, Darwin was remarkably open and friendly to people of many different races and seems to have got along reasonably well with people of many different racial groups and nationalities. Probably because of the liberal tradition of the Darwin family he was more open in this respect than others aboard *Beagle*. He described a group of Aborigines he encountered in New South Wales as being "good humoured and pleasant" and "far from being the degraded beings . . . usually represented." The Tahitians he described as being "charming" and "merry" and displaying a high degree of "intelligence." Although on the whole he approved of the work of missionaries among the non-European people that he encountered, he was far from uncritical. He thought the rigid Sabbatarian outlook of missionaries in Tahiti and their discouragement of traditional dancing and flute-playing were foolish. He admitted that European contact had not always been beneficial. The noted that the Tasmanian Aborigines had been driven virtually to extinction, and he thought that those of the Australian mainland were also in decline, partly as the result of the elimination of game (e.g., kangaroo and emu) and the introduction of disease. The notion of competition between groups would, of course, recur in Darwin's writing.

Some of the anthropological observations that Charles Darwin made on the *Beagle* voyage appear somewhat dissociated. Yet his observations of humanity, especially in relation to its environment, were sometimes excellent, as he adopted a somewhat ecological approach. He medical background (as the son of a physician and from what he had learned at Edinburgh) sometimes helped him. He constantly compared one group with another. Some of the ideas that he employed in his descriptions (the "ladder of civilisation," the "family of man"), although simple, were precursors of later evolutionary ideas. ***Descent of Man*** (1871) applied his evolutionary ideas to humanity, emphasizing the relationships that existed between the different groups of humans.

See also: Expression of Emotions.

New South Wales

Originally a British colony on the southwest coast of mainland Australia. Now a separate state within the Commonwealth of Australia. Visited by Darwin early in 1836.

The British Admiralty, in 1768, instructed Captain James Cook to observe the transit of Venus in Tahiti and then to search for the unknown Great South Land. After his mission to the South Seas was complete, Cook returned to England via **New Zealand** (which he circumnavigated) and the east coast of "New Holland." Cook landed at Botany Bay (named on account of the enthusiasm for botany of HMS *Endeavour*'s enthusiastic naturalist, Joseph Banks) in April 1770 and three other places on Australia's coast, taking possession in the name of King George III under the name New South Wales.

Following the Revolutionary War and the independence of the United States, convicts from Britain who had been transported to the southern American colonies because of overcrowded English prisons had to be sent elsewhere. On January 26, 1788, Governor Arthur Phillip landed at Botany Bay with a group of 750 convicts, a detachment of marines, and a small administration. The Europeans had arrived in Australia, and January 26—now named Australia Day—has been celebrated ever since. The date was celebrated by the decoration of the ships in Sydney Harbour with flags in 1836, while the *Beagle* was anchored there.

At the time of Darwin's visit, the colony of New South Wales included the entire eastern portion of Australia, and it was still a convict settlement (it remained such until 1839). Victoria was made a separate colony in 1855, Queensland in 1859, and what is now the Northern Territory in 1863 (when it was attached to South Australia). In 1901, the separate Australian colonies federated to become the Commonwealth of Australia, and they became states. The state of New South Wales now has an area of 309,433 square miles (801,430 square kilometers) and a population of 6.7 million. The capital, Sydney, on its magnificent harbor, is now one of the world's most spectacular cities. Farming and sheep-grazing country are nearby with substantial heavy industry around Newcastle to the north.

The *Beagle*'s passage from the Bay of Islands to Port Jackson (Sydney) in early January 1836 had taken 12 days because of contrary winds and storms (the trip was often made in 5 days by traders). Darwin was ambivalent about New South Wales. He did not like how the economy and society were dominated by the "convict system." Much of the heavy manual work was done by those who had been transported for crimes committed in England, Ireland, or other parts of the British Empire. As a result, convicted criminals were everywhere—one might be waited on at an inn by a petty thief, and "children learn the vilest expressions," Darwin wrote. He thought the people were excessively mercenary. On the other hand, he commented favorably on the good network of roads and the rapidly expanding economy, especially "on the sheep's back."

The Australian environment fascinated him. He noted and described well, the essential uniform nature of Australian eucalyptus woodland. He noted that the trees stood "tolerably straight" and "well apart." He described the way in which the bark was annually shed and often hung in long shreds, swinging in the wind, giving the landscape an "untidy" and "desolate" appearance. The forest was in many places burnt—fire has been a component of Australia forest communities for millennia. The essential character of the forest was quite different from any other forests he had seen in South America, the Pacific Islands, or in New Zealand. He saw some brightly colored parrots, kangaroos, kangaroo rats (potaroos), and emus, and, while resting by a creek, he glimpsed some duck-billed platypuses swimming. He came across a group of 20 Aborigines "carrying in their accustomed manner a bundle of spears and other weapons." He persuaded them to demonstrate their skills, and "a cap being fixed at 30 yards distance, they transfixed it with a spear, delivered with a throwing stick."

The whole environment—including the **marsupials** (pouched) and the monotreme (egg-laying) mammals, the gum trees, the distinctive birds, the hot sunny climate, fire, and the Aborigines—was unique. Could there, wondered Darwin briefly, have been two creations and creators: one for Australia and one for the rest of the world? After a moment's thought, seeing insects that were similar to those of Europe, he reconsidered: "one hand has worked throughout the universe." Darwin, even at this late stage of his voyage, was not an evolutionist, although the fact that he saw the whole Australian ecosystem as something distinctive was of great importance to his later thinking.

Inland are the mountains of the Great Dividing Range, up to 4,475 feet (1,364 meters); here a massive sandstone plateau is dissected by deep valleys. Darwin, on his journey inland to Bathurst in January 1836 thought (wrongly) that the valleys of the Blue Mountains had been cut the sea, when it was at a higher level than at present. Although he was mistaken, his preoccupation with sea-level change at that time had led him (correctly) to his theory on the origin of coral reefs and atolls and to an understanding of the importance of continuing gradual change in the environment.

See also: Australia; Ecology; Instinct.

New Zealand

Mountainous group of islands in the South Pacific; claimed for the British Crown by Captain James Cook in 1769 and established as a British colony in 1841. New Zealand is now an independent dominion within the British Commonwealth and has a reputation for high standards of democracy and social welfare. The population is 4,150,000, most of whom are of British descent, but there are some 600,000 **Maori** and smaller numbers of Asians and Pacific Islanders.

New Zealand extends from 34° 25" to 47° 17" S and 166° 26" to 178° 33" E and covers about 70,000 square miles (270,500 square kilometers). There are two main islands (North and South Islands), a much smaller Stewart Island to the south and many offshore islets. The South Island is mountainous, and there are permanent snowfields and glaciers. The North Island is volcanic, with three active volcanoes (usually quiet), an area of hot springs near Rotaroa, and many smaller, apparently extinct volcanic cones. The island is affected by earthquakes. The plants and animals are highly distinctive, for, although once part of Gondwana, the former great southern land mass, New Zealand has been isolated for tens of millions of years.

New Zealand was uninhabited until over 1,000 years ago, when several waves of Maoris arrived from Polynesia; they had an appreciable effect on the environment, clearing areas of forest with fire and exterminating the large flightless moas.

Volcanic cone, North Island, New Zealand. Photo: Patrick Armstrong.

HMS *Beagle* visited the **Bay of Islands,** at the northern tip of North Island for just over a week (December 21–30, 1835). Captain **Robert FitzRoy** made astronomical and magnetic observations to fix the locality's position, and, in the short length of time he was there, Charles Darwin completed a surprisingly thorough program of collecting and natural history observations. He traveled inland to a missionary settlement at Waimate, explored an area of limestone hills and caves, collected rock and insect specimens (and a few vertebrates), and commented in detail on the Maori customs, noting the way in which the kauri trees and native flax were utilized. He also noted the distinctiveness of the New Zealand biota (flora and fauna), the absence of mammals, and the extent to which exotic species of plants such as gorse (*Ulex europea*) were establishing themselves.

Early in his visit, Darwin explored Paihia, a small settlement that he thought "hardly deserves the title of a village." He was struck by the English atmosphere: sweet briar, honeysuckle, and stocks grew around the white-washed missionaries' cottages. He and FitzRoy also visited James Busby, the British resident who lived in the small but elegant "Residency" nearby.

The next day (December 22), he and FitzRoy, together with one of the missionaries, explored Koroareka (now called Russell) on the other side of the bay: their impression was very different. Darwin formed a poor view of the place, inhabited as it was by the crews of whaling ships and others who were described with phrases such as "worthless character," and "whole population addicted to drunkenness." Darwin was invited by one of the missionaries to visit Waimate, a missionary settlement about 15 miles (24 kilometers) inland. Two days before Christmas, he set off with a Maori guide. James Busby gave them a lift by boat to Haruru Falls, from where they continued on foot.

At Waimate, Darwin took tea with a missionary family and noted an atmosphere of "cordiality and happiness" among everyone at the mission, both the missionary families and the Maoris. He stayed overnight at the mission and wandered about the farm and garden, noting that some of the Maori children were playing cricket and that the landscape had been modified. He approved of the way in which fields of grain had been planted, and he noted that the gardens were full of familiar English plants and that barns and a watermill had been constructed. He returned the following day, spending Christmas in Paihia and attending a Christmas service there.

Darwin was particularly interested in recent (i.e., geologically very young) volcanic rocks: along much of the road to Waimate, he recorded in his geological notes that there were rocks that:

> were certainly volcanic. There was much grey Basalt, but seldom containing many crystals, sometimes slightly vesicular and amygdaloidal [containing air bubbles], its structure frequently columnar. The other most abundant kind is a kind of greenstone (?) with crystals of glassy Feldspar. At a small village . . . the whole surface was covered with shaggy & highly vesicular Lavas. In a

Kauri trees, North Island, New Zealand. Photo: Patrick Armstrong.

neighbouring broken down hill, the form of a crater could be traced. I heard of another whose figure is perfect. Near Waimate, two or three truncated conical hills are said to be surrounded by deep circular cavities, & clearly have at one time existed as active Volcanoes . . . [but] there is no sign of any recent action. . . . Crystalline or Volcanic rocks in the neighbourhood of the Bay of Islands would appear to be the most prevalent kinds. In the Southern & main part of the island the land becomes very mountainous. . . . In the interior it is confidently asserted there is an active volcano. It is certain that in this part Earthquakes are commonly experienced. Mr Williams [one of the missionaries] described to me a large Volcano which he had seen in full activity, as comprising a small Island in the Bay of Plenty on the East coast. Also another Island covered with rugged & nearly naked streams of lava. On the mainland there are many springs of hot waters. Volcanic districts in the Northern Island of New Zealand, may from its position & direction of its coast, be with propriety described as the SE termination of the great band of Volcanic action which contains the parallel lines of New Caledonia, New Hebrides, New Ireland & New Guinea. (*Darwin's Geological Diary,* Cambridge University Library, Darwin Archive)

There is plenty of sound observation and shrewd deduction here. But Darwin carefully separates his own observations from those of others and separates observation from deduction. Not only is Darwin combining information from a variety of sources, but he is also carefully integrating material on rock types, land forms, hot springs, active volcanoes, and gross structure. In his book on *Volcanic Islands* and to some extent in *Coral*

Reefs, he developed his ideas on what later came to be known as island arcs in more detail. Darwin's early writings of New Zealand provide an early example of the manner in which he was able to integrate information from different sources to reach important conclusions.

North Wales

Mountainous region, now mostly part of Snowdonia National Park; the scene of a field trip in the summer of 1831 where **Adam Sedgwick** taught the young Charles Darwin enough geology and other fieldwork skills to be useful on the voyage of HMS *Beagle.*

The Snowdonia National Park, designated in 1951, covers 823 square miles (2132 square kilometers) of beautiful and unspoiled countryside in northwest Wales. Unlike some national parks elsewhere in the world, Snowdonia is home to just over 26,000 people, who live and work in its towns (such as Dolgellau and Bala) and villages and on its hill farms. Just over 60 percent of the population currently speaks Welsh. An estimated 6 to 10 million visitor days are spent every year enjoying a wide range of leisure activities in Snowdonia. The region includes parts of the old counties of Caenarvonshire, Merioneth, and Denbighshire (names that would have been familiar to Darwin) and is now mostly in the Gwynedd local government area and the borough of Conwy (Conway).

Snowdonia has some of the most spectacular mountain scenery in England and Wales. More than 90 summits are over 2,000 feet and 15 are over 3,000 feet. The highest is Snowdon (*Yr Wyddfa* in Welsh, at 3,560 feet or 1,085 meters). The mountainous character is the result of the underlying resistant, ancient rocks, mostly of Silurian, Ordovician, and Cambrian age, and much folded and affected by volcanic activity. It was partly to study these that Sedgwick went to North Wales in 1831.

Darwin returned to **Shrewsbury** from Cambridge in mid-June 1831 and spent much of the summer learning geology. He made geological maps of Shropshire and visited quarries in nearby Llanymynech. In his *Autobiography,* he recalled:

> Professor Sedgwick in the beginning of August intended to visit N. Wales to pursue his famous geological investigations amongst the older rocks, and Henslow asked him to allow me to accompany him. Accordingly he came and slept at my Father's house.

The next morning, they left on their field trip through North Wales (see main article on Charles Darwin. The *Autobiography* and other sources disagree to some extent on the exact route Darwin took, particularly after separating from Sedgwick. Darwin's own notes show he zigzagged somewhat, looking at rock exposures and quarries.) They studied the geology to the west of Shrewsbury before traveling northward through Llangollen,

353

Ruthin, Denbigh, and the tiny cathedral city of St. Asaph. Then, they headed westward, parallel to the coast, through Abergele, Conwy to Bangor, possibly reaching Anglesey over the period August 5–20, 1831. Darwin probably left Sedgwick at Menai and walked due south, through the core of Snowdonia via the Capel Curig Lakes to Barmouth, making a special visit of Cwm Idwal, where he particularly noticed the junction between the slate and the volcanic rocks. He stayed a few days with friends in the seaside town of Barmouth, which he reached on August 23, and returned to Shrewsbury on August 29 to open the letter inviting him to join the *Beagle* expedition.

One of the tasks of the Darwin-Sedgwick North Wales expedition was to ascertain the extent to which the Old Red Sandstone (desert sandstones of Devonian age) outcropped in North Wales; the tentative result of their inquiries was that it did not. Nevertheless they saw a wide variety of rock types of many geological ages: New Red Sandstone, Mountain (Carboniferous) limestone, conglomerate, greywacke, greenstone, and volcanic rocks. They found fossils (rhinoceros teeth in caverns and corals and brachiopods in the limestone) and examined several slate quarries. They talked to local people and obtained information on the local names for different types of slate. In his notes in several places Darwin discusses the relationship between geological structure and soils, vegetation, and topography. He comments on springs, noticing their relations to the geology (at Abergele). Darwin shows himself (as he did later) to be an excellent integrator. His notes contain many details of the angles of dip of rocks and of the minerals present in them.

But Darwin and Sedgwick did not confine themselves entirely to geology; they noted aspects of the land forms, soils, and hydrology. They also seem to have visited a few ecclesiastical sites (e.g., Valle Crucis Abbey and the ancient chapel at Caerhun) and castles (Darwin also noted that Denbigh Castle was built of limestone).

During that summer, under Sedgwick's tutelage, Darwin gained skills in many aspects of geology, including chemical analysis, use of compass, map, and clinometer (an instrument for measuring the angle of dip of strata), the direct transect across country, the collection of specimens and careful note-taking, all of which were to prove vital in his work on the *Beagle*.

The extent of Darwin's gratitude to Sedgwick can be seen in several letters written to John Henslow from the *Beagle*—for example, on April 11, 1833, just after his visit to the Falkland Islands: "[T]ell him [Professor Sedgwick] I have never ceased to be thankful for that short tour in Wales."

But there was much more to Darwin's time in North Wales than just a supervised geological field excursion. While some of Darwin's notes reflect those of his teacher, for much of the time, Darwin was working on his own. At least once they seem to have separated, meeting up again a few days later. Darwin's geology notes from the excursion contain the occasional anecdote, speculations and ideas detailed observations, comments on relationships, and bald facts—as do his notes and diaries from the *Beagle*. He had, on several occasions, to deal with innkeepers on his own (in his diary entries for the Blue Mountains in New South Wales, years later, he comments about on the similarity of Australian inns to those of North Wales). He had to walk long distances over difficult country. On one day in Snowdonia, he covered 20 miles (32 kilometers), probably with a heavy pack, for on arrival at Barmouth one his friends later recalled, he "carried with him, as well as his other burdens, a hammer of 14 lbs weight" (about 5 kilograms). He coped with a variety of weather conditions, and on at least one occasion, he and Sedgwick were caught in a thunderstorm. He had to converse with the local country people and navigate with map and compass. In every possible way, the "short excursion" to North Wales was an invaluable training run for the adventures of the *Beagle* years that lay just a few weeks ahead.

FURTHER READING

Barrett, Paul H. 1974. "The Sedgwick-Darwin Geologic Tour of North Wales." *Proceedings of the American Philosophical Society* 118: 146–164.
Roberts, Michael. 2000. "Just before the Beagle: Charles Darwin's Geological Fieldwork in Wales, Summer 1831." *Endeavour* 25: 33–37.

Notes and Notebooks

The many thousands of pages of Charles Darwin's notes provide a remarkable insight to the way in which he worked. Many are held, often in the order in which he left them, in the Darwin Archive of the Cambridge University Library. Some are at Down House.

One of the joys of studying the life and work of Charles Darwin is that so much material is available that illustrates the manner in which he worked. Because of his family's foresight in preserving his notes, notebooks, diaries, letters, and ephemera, it is possible to reconstruct his thought processes in some detail.

"The habit of comparison leads to generalization," wrote Darwin during his final days aboard the *Beagle*. On the voyage, Darwin was constantly comparing the plants, animals, people, rocks, and landscapes of one locality with those of another. When he visited a place more than once, as he sometimes did, he compared the observations that he made on the several occasions. Also, aboard the *Beagle* were copies of the books of many earlier travelers and navigators, and Darwin was able to compare his observations and ideas with those of his predecessors. In later life—when, for example he was working on his species theory—he used broadly the same technique, collecting vast amounts of information from correspondence and from his reading, and, in correlating it, he attempted to find generalizations.

Darwin constantly reworked the same material as new information came to hand or as his ideas changed, and he often kept early drafts with their deletions and annotations. For example, on the reverse of pages of notes

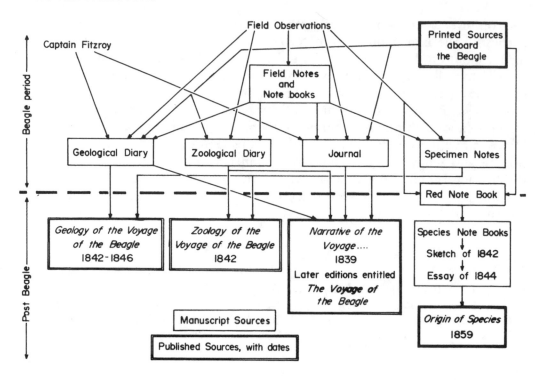

Diagram showing flows of information among Darwin's sources. Drawn at Geography Department, University of Western Australia.

from the *Beagle* period, there are often further notes of where he had seen an organism or phenomenon, perhaps months or years after it was first encountered. Sometimes he drew vertical or diagonal lines through notes with which he was finished, perhaps after the publication of the material or its transcription into other memoranda.

Frequently information from several sources was combined. On the *Beagle*, Darwin kept his diary or journal, but he also kept several other types of notes. There was a series of about 18 leather-covered notebooks in which he wrote short pencil jottings while he was in the field. These notebooks sometimes contain memoranda of a practical nature—such as shopping lists of items to be purchased at ports of call—as well as scientific observations.

Darwin's usual procedure was to write up these informal jottings into more complete, formal accounts when he had a little leisure. These were on much larger sheets of paper and were written with pen and ink. The pages are usually carefully dated and numbered and often include the name of the locality at the head of each page. He usually wrote only on one side of the paper, although, as explained above, further memoranda, comparisons, and afterthoughts were sometimes written on the reverse. These notes were presumably written up as the vessel was sailing from port to port at the great table in the cabin of the *Beagle,* with specimens, instruments, notebooks, and reference works scattered around him. Separate zoological and

An anticline (a set of upfolded rock strata), East Falkland. Photo: Patrick Armstrong.

geological notebooks were kept. The detail is almost always excellent, and ecological information is often included. (See articles on **anemones, sea** and **corals and coral reefs** for examples of the level of detail in his notes.)

Briefer notes were kept on some of the specimens he collected. He knew that the alcohol in which he kept some of his specimens would destroy the original color, so, for example, for a fish "caught by net in Princess Royal Harbour" at King George's Sound, Western Australia, he recorded in his *List of Fish in Spirits of Wine:*

> Fish, sides dark green, and pale silvery green, fins tipped with red. It is fine green, handsome fish.

There were separate lists of the rock specimens, insects, and shells he collected during the voyage.

Charles Darwin also kept his diary or journal in a narrative form; this included more personal material, anecdotes, and accounts of activities. Although the entries are dated, it was sometimes written up retrospectively, days or weeks later (occasional mistakes were made). This diary formed the basis for what eventually became his book *The Voyage of the Beagle.* The style was improved for the book, but large sections of material from the zoological and geological notebooks (and occasionally other notes) were included. When he prepared the manuscript for the printer, he must have had several sets of notes around him.

The **Red Notebook** forms an important link between the patterns of note-making from the *Beagle* voyage and that of the periods of review, thought, and concept development in years that followed. The Red Notebook was opened toward the end of the voyage, possibly during, or just after, the visit to Australia and continued in the months that followed his return to England in October 1836. It contains his first known writings on evolutionary change and material on changes of sea level—a theme that had preoccupied him during the voyage. Entries were continued until about April 1837, just after his adoption of a transmutationist or evolutionary view.

When filled, it was replaced, in about July 1837, by two notebooks: A, which highlights geological themes, particularly changes in sea level, uplift, and subsidence; and B, which continued the species theme. For example, in B we read the rhetorical question: "Has the creator since Cambrian formations gone on creating animals with same general structure? [What a] miserable limited view." And "My theory will make me deny the creation of any new quadruped [mammal] since the days of Didelphus [a primitive mammal from the Jurassic period described by **William Buckland** in 1826]." These thoughts were uttered probably in the privacy of his notebooks very late in 1837 or early in 1838.

Notebook B was superseded by C, D, and E in 1838 and 1839. By mid-1838, Darwin was beginning to think that important clues to the mechanism of evolution could be adduced from studies on the behavior of organisms, and notebook M was opened, followed by N a few months later.

The development of his evolutionary theories can be traced onward through these his early notebooks, compiled in the 1830s, through his *Sketch of 1842*, his *Essay of 1844*, the manuscript of his *Big Species Book* (not published until the 1970s), and the compilation **Linnean Society of London** presentation (jointly with Wallace's paper) to *On the Origin of*

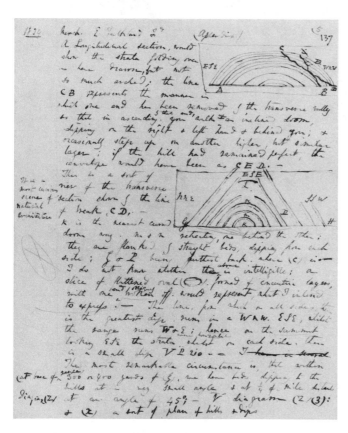

A page from Darwin's geological notes on the site shown in the photo on page 357. Photo: Cambridge University Library.

Species published in 1859, and then on through the various editions of that work.

See also: *Beagle* Diary.

FURTHER READING

Barrett, P. H., P. J. Gautry, S. Herbert, D. Kohn, and S. Smith. 1987. *Charles Darwin's Notebooks, 1836–1844.* Cambridge, England: Cambridge University Press.
Herbert, Sandra. 1980. *The Red Notebook of Charles Darwin.* London: British Museum (Natural History).

On the Origin of Species

Book published in 1859 that sets out Charles Darwin's theory of **evolution through natural selection.**

First published on November 24, 1859, *On the Origin of Species* (the full title was *On the Origin of Species by Means of Natural Selection, or the Preservation of Favoured Races in the Struggle for Life*) is one of the most important and fundamental books in the history of science; some assert that it is the most important work in biology ever published. In it, Darwin develops an argument, with numerous empirical examples as support, for his theory that groups of animals and plants—rather than individual organisms—gradually evolve or change over time through a process of natural selection. The work presents detailed scientific evidence he had accumulated during the voyage of HMS *Beagle* (1831–1836) and afterward, setting out his ideas and thereby attempting to refute the doctrine of independent creation of organisms, which was then widely (but far from universally) accepted.

The book is remarkably readable, written in a very clear rhetorical style, even if some of the sentences are rather long and the style somewhat quaint to the modern ear. The book attracted widespread interest on its publication (which the first presentation of the ideas of evolution to the scientific world—a hastily cobbled-together piece put before the **Linnean Society of London,** jointly authored by Darwin and **Alfred Russel Wallace** in July 1858—did not). Although the concepts presented in the book are supported by overwhelming scientific evidence and are widely accepted by scientists today, they are still, in some parts of the world, regarded as controversial by people who see them as contradicting religious doctrines.

During his voyage, Darwin read **Charles Lyell**'s *Principles of Geology* and became convinced of the doctrine of **uniformitarianism**—the idea that the Earth's features are the result of very gradual change and that the processes of change are those that can be observed in operation today. Moreover, during the voyage, Darwin collected many thousands of specimens—birds, fish, reptiles, mammals, insects, and fossils—which he discussed with "the leading men of science" in the months following his return to England in 1836. For example, **Richard Owen** examined some of the mammal fossils that Darwin collected in South America and found that they were of extinct species related to species still living in the same region. **John Gould** startlingly revealed that, in the Galapagos Islands, there were species of finches that differed from island to island.

By early 1837, Darwin was speculating on the transmutation of species. His first clear written reference to the possibility of the change of one species into another was in the **Red Notebook;** there followed a series of private notebooks in which he gradually developed his ideas. He investigated the breeding of domestic animals—artificial selection—and read a pamphlet by John Sebright, which commented that "a severe winter, or a scarcity of food, by destroying the weak and the unhealthy, has all the good effects of the most skilful selection." At the London Zoo in 1838, Darwin had his first sight of apes, and their antics impressed him as being "just like a naughty child"; recalling his experience of the Fuegians, Darwin began to think that there was perhaps only a narrow gap between humans and animals.

In late September 1838, he began reading **Thomas Malthus**'s *Essay on Population* and was struck by the statistical demonstration that, while human populations increase geometrically, the production of food increases at a lower rate—arithmetically. Humans, therefore, reproduce at a rate beyond which available resources can expand; thus, they must compete in order to survive. Social thinking at the time, partly influenced by **Adam Smith,** emphasized economic competition, without handouts for the weak, the inefficient, and the lazy. By late 1838, Darwin saw a congruence between animal breeders selecting traits they sought and a Malthusian nature selecting from random variants so that on organism's structure became "fully practised and perfected."

Darwin pressed on with his work on the species question through the 1840s, producing a short outline, the **Sketch of 1842,** and then a much fuller account, the **Essay of 1844.** Meanwhile, he continued with much other work, including his important publications on **barnacles.** Sharing his ideas with only a few close colleagues such as **Joseph Hooker** and **Charles Lyell** and his American correspondent, botanist **Asa Gray,** in the period 1856 to 1858, he commenced work on a massive technical monograph simply titled *Natural Selection,* but sometimes referred to as the *Big Species Book,* that was not published until 1975. In this work, he used the phrases "the struggle for existence" and "natural selection" as chapter headings. However, he received in June 1858 a "bolt from the blue" in the shape of a letter from Alfred Russel Wallace enclosing the draft of a paper containing ideas almost identical to his own, asking him (Darwin) to consider submitting it to a scientific journal. With the support of Hooker and Lyell, the compilation mentioned above, containing Wallace's paper, part of a letter Darwin had written to Asa Gray, and other material, was put before London scientific community at the **Linnean Society of London** on July 1, 1858. Neither Darwin nor Wallace was present.

Thereafter Darwin worked hard for many months to produce a digest of his *Natural Selection* manuscript. It was this that was published as *On the Origin of Species* in November 1859. The price was a comparatively expensive 15 shillings, and yet all 1,250 copies were sold at once. The second edition appeared six weeks later, in January 1860. Perhaps to assuage religious susceptibilities (his wife Emma was very religious), the words "by the Creator" were inserted into the famous closing sentence of the book so that it read:

> There is grandeur in this view of life, with its several powers, having been originally breathed by the Creator into a few forms or into one; and that, whilst this planet has gone circling on according to the fixed law of gravity, from so simple a beginning endless forms most beautiful and most wonderful have been, and are being evolved.

During Charles Darwin's life time, the book went through six editions, each with changes and revisions attempting to answer criticisms leveled at the work and to deal with the various counter-arguments raised. The third edition was published in 1861, and the fourth in 1866. The fifth edition appeared in February 1869 and incorporated more changes; for the first time, the book included Herbert Spencer's phrase "the survival of the fittest."

The seventh edition appeared in early 1872; in response to a perceived demand, the price was reduced to seven shillings and sixpence, but the size of the print used was also reduced. Sales increased considerably. Hundreds of reprints of the various editions have subsequently appeared, and the book has been translated into at least thirty languages.

Darwin's approach has been described as rhetorical, as he attempts to present an argument supported by evidence, then suggests possible objections and in due course answers them. Almost every chapter ends with a concise summary, so that readers can assess the argument as it develops and prepare for the next step.

The structure is extremely logical and conceived so as to persuade. Darwin starts with the familiar: Chapter 1 is titled "Variation under Domestication," because everyone can be expected to be familiar with the various breeds of domestic animals and farm and garden plants. The varieties of pigeon are taken as a particular case study. In chapter 2, Darwin extends the discussion to "Variation under Nature." In chapter 3, the concept of competition—or, as he puts it in the first edition—"the struggle for life" is introduced, and the Malthusian doctrines of geometrical increase and the checks on increases are discussed. Chapter 4 leads into "Natural Selection," comparing it to selection by humans and shows how it may work "on characters of trifling importance" over time. Chapter 5 is headed "Laws of Variation" and links the idea of inheritance to natural selection; working before Mendel's experiments were widely known and the science of genetics was developed, Darwin's treatment was necessarily incomplete.

Having set up his "theory of descent with modification," chapter 6 addresses the "Difficulties of the Theory"—in particular, the absence or rarity of transitional varieties. Chapter 7 is directed toward instinct; here, Darwin claims that similar generalization in terms of variation, competition, and inheritance apply to animals' instincts, and the habits of animals apply to their physical form. A wide range of examples are provided: parasitism in the cuckoo and in other organisms, the taking of slaves by some ants, the cell-making instinct in hive bees.

The next group of chapters seeks to bolster his arguments with evidence from particular sources. Chapter 8 discusses hybridism and the sterility of some hybrids.

Chapter 9 again raises the possibility of difficulties, headed as it is "On the Imperfection of the Geological Record." The rarity of intermediate forms in the fossil record, as well as among living organisms, is acknowledged, and attempts are made to explain it in terms of the intermittence of geological formations and the poorness of fossil collections that existed at the time. Nevertheless, essays in chapter 10—"On the Geological Succession of Organic Beings"— show how, to some extent, paleontology supports his theories. Two chapters on geographical distribution follow; these show how the distribution of organisms—particularly the occurrence and nonoccurrence of certain biological groups on islands—supports the theory of evolution. Chapter 13 marshals the evidence in support of the notion of affinities between biological groups, embryology, and the presence of rudimentary organs. Classification of plants and animals, Darwin argues, should be based on their evolutionary relationship. The final chapter (14) is headed "Recapitulation and Conclusion"; after again discussing "the difficulties on the theory of natural selection," he summarizes the evidence in favor and briefly mentions some of its implications. The book is indeed "one long argument"—logically structured and carefully crafted.

In the 1860s, Darwin's book and the ideas it contained were widely discussed and debated by scientists, clergy, and in the fashionable salons of Britain. **Thomas Huxley** acted as an efficient publicist and attracted the interest of the general population: he has been described as "Darwin's bulldog" for his support and advocacy of Darwin and his theories. It was he who defended the concept of evolution in the Great Debate at the **British Association for the Advancement of Science** meeting in 1860.

Many of the established scientists, especially those of the older universities, were clergy of the Church of England. Even if they did not accept the literal truth of every detail of the creation stories in the book of Genesis, they certainly believed in the idea of divine design and were attracted to the doctrine of natural theology outlined in a book of that title by **William Paley.** There was also the feeling among some that the rejection the notion of divine creation might lead to the rejection of the moral basis of Christianity, of the belief in man being created in the image of God, and the notion of the human soul might follow.

It may have been for this reason that much of the debate centered on whether evolution had occurred at all, rather than on Darwin's proposed

> ON
>
> ## THE ORIGIN OF SPECIES
>
> BY MEANS OF NATURAL SELECTION,
>
> OR THE
>
> PRESERVATION OF FAVOURED RACES IN THE STRUGGLE FOR LIFE.
>
> BY CHARLES DARWIN, M.A.,
> FELLOW OF THE ROYAL, GEOLOGICAL, LINNEAN, ETC., SOCIETIES;
> AUTHOR OF 'JOURNAL OF RESEARCHES DURING H. M. S. BEAGLE'S VOYAGE
> ROUND THE WORLD.'
>
> LONDON:
> JOHN MURRAY, ALBEMARLE STREET.
> 1859.
>
> *The right of Translation is reserved.*

Title page of first edition of *On the Origin of Species*, 1859.

mechanism of natural selection. Darwin did not take a very active part in the defense of his ideas in public. The person who, as a young man, had thrashed through tropical forests, ascended mountain ranges, and explored volcanoes and coral reefs was, at this time (or at least thought himself to be), too much of an invalid to do this. His old friends Joseph Hooker and Charles Lyell were among Darwin's prominent supporters (although Lyell seems to have been ambivalent on the evolution of humans).

In the United States, Asa Gray worked in close correspondence with Darwin to assure the theory's acceptance (despite opposition of one of America's most prominent scientists of the time, Louis Agassiz) and helped to arrange the publication of the book in the United States.

In the twenty-first century, almost all professionals in the fields of earth and life sciences consider correct the ideas put forward in Darwin's *On the Origin of Species.* Nevertheless, a significant proportion of the general population—particularly in the United States but also in the Islamic world and in some traditional Catholic communities—continue to disagree on religious grounds.

Origin of Life

One of the ultimate mysteries. When the Earth formed about 4.6 billion years ago, it was lifeless; a billion years later, the oceans were full of algae-like forms. Where had life come from?

Some medieval and early modern (i.e., up to the seventeenth century) thinkers believed that life could be generated spontaneously from nonliving sources: for example, some held that insects, amphibians, and other creatures could form spontaneously from decaying matter. Louis Pasteur (1822–1895) demonstrated that bacteria and other microorganisms were derived from parents similar to themselves. Life begets life.

Darwin provided a mechanism for evolution and hinted that all life on Earth must have been derived from a single original simple form or from a few simple forms and that living things have become more complex throughout geological time: "From so simple a beginning, endless forms most beautiful and most wonderful have been and are being evolved." But Darwin had little to say publicly on the ultimate origin, although in private correspondence he hinted that it might have arisen "in some warm little pond with ammonia, phosphoric salts, heat, light and electricity present."

In the twentieth century, some scientists proposed that all life on Earth was descended from disseminules (mobile living particles such as spores) from elsewhere in the universe—that the first living things on Earth were derived from outer space. This merely pushes the question of the origin of life to another place. Nevertheless, searches have been made for organic chemicals and other evidence of past life on the moon, on Mars, in meteorites, and elsewhere in the solar system in the hope that the discovery of such signs might shed light on the matter—so far with little success.

It seems likely that the early atmosphere of the Earth was very different from that of today—providing a reducing rather than an oxidizing environment. The atmosphere and oceans of this early Earth may have been rich in methane, ammonia, and hydrogen, as well as water, in contrast to the oxygen-rich environments of today. Experiments aiming to replicate this environment have subjected flasks containing these substances to electrical discharges to simulate lightning and have led to the production of molecules such as those of amino acids. With the passage of long periods of time, it is hypothesized that these might eventually combine into a substance that could self-replicate. Possibly RNA (now present in viruses) appeared first, and **DNA** (now present in most other forms of life) developed later. Natural selection may have operated at this early stage, which has been compared to a soup of organic chemicals, some molecules having more efficient powers of self-replication than others. The enclosure of such materials in some bubblelike structure would produce something resembling a living cell.

See also: Evolution through Natural Selection.

Origin of the Beagle Voyage

Darwin was a supernumerary aboard HMS *Beagle*. On an earlier voyage of the *Beagle*, Captain FitzRoy thought it would be appropriate to carry someone with some scientific knowledge "to examine the land; while the officers and myself would attend to hydrography." Darwin had thus no official position and had little say in determining the route or the ports visited— although, while the ship was in port or at anchor offshore, he was often able to make use of the ship's boats, arranging to be set down at particular sites to make observations or collect specimens and to be picked up later. Sometimes while the ship was in port for several days for repairs or to resupply provisions, while business was being conducted ashore, or the ship's company were undertaking an extensive offshore hydrographic survey, Darwin was able to explore ashore for more extended periods.

On the earlier voyage, FitzRoy captured a group of four natives of the island of **Tierra del Fuego.** They had originally been taken as hostages against the return of a ship's boat that had been stolen, but FitzRoy had resolved to take them to England to educate and Christianize them. Thus it was that the group had been taken to Plymouth and to London. They had been schooled by a Church of England schoolmaster and presented to the King and Queen. At one stage, it seemed that the British Admiralty might not continue the hydrographic survey of South America, and Captain FitzRoy resolved to charter a vessel at his own expense to return the Fuegian hostages. But the Admiralty authorized an expedition, and the *Beagle* set sail again for southern latitudes two days after Christmas 1831 with the party of Fuegians and Richard Matthews, a young man whose intention it was to establish a missionary colony. The Admiralty's instructions to FitzRoy included the completion of the survey of the coasts of South America, but he was also to establish a chain of meridians around the world. The fixing of longitude was still a relatively young science, and the exact position of many points, particularly remote islands, was still uncertain. There were a number of chronometers (very accurate clocks, resistant to disturbance, needed to establish the exact time of astronomical observations at sea) aboard, and at many places throughout the voyage navigational and other instruments were set up at temporary observatories, and magnetic and astronomical observations were taken.

It was therefore FitzRoy's zeal to return the Fuegians to their home and to establish the mission station, the Admiralty's need for hydrographic charts of certain locations, and their instructions to establish a chain of meridians that determined the route, the landfalls, and the locations of Darwin's explorations.

Owen, Fanny Mostyn (later Biddulph) (1807—1886)

Second daughter of William Mostyn Owen of Woodhouse. Her family lived close to the Darwin family home in Shrewsbury, and she was a youthful friend of Charles Darwin.

Fanny was a close friend of Charles Darwin before the *Beagle* voyage, and there is every reason to believe they had a considerable fondness for each other. She was a competent artist. They went riding together and exchanged gifts. He also taught her to shoot pheasants. Darwin wrote of his "dearest Fanny" and in a letter to his cousin **William Darwin Fox** described her as the "prettiest, plumpest, [most] charming personage that Shropshire possesses." The passion seems to have declined somewhat by mid-1831, as Darwin became devoted to his new love, geology, and there was a romance between Fanny and the Reverend John Hill, which was stopped by his mother, apparently for "political reasons." Nevertheless, Darwin was much affected when, a few months into the voyage of the *Beagle,* in 1832, he heard that Fanny had married a local rakish member of Parliament, Robert Myddleton Biddulph, and had gone to live in Chirk Castle. Despite her husband's social position (member of Parliament 1832–1835 and 1852–1868, colonel of the local militia, lord lieutenant of the county of Denbighshire), the marriage does not seem to have been a very happy one. She might well have been happier with her first love. Charles, on the other hand, found a loving, devoted and entirely suitable partner in his cousin **Emma Wedgwood.**

Owen, Richard (1804–1892)

Close contemporary of Charles Darwin, paleontologist, and comparative anatomist. Idiosyncratic and brilliant, Owen changed the way science was practiced and understood by the public. He remained, nevertheless, a believer in special creation and was strongly opposed to Darwin's theories of evolution through natural selection.

Although there are a number of points of similarity in the lives and work of Darwin and Owen, their backgrounds were very different. In contrast to the gentry upbringing and education of Charles Darwin, Owen came from a poorer family, being born in Lancaster in the north of England on July 20, 1804. His mother Catherine was widowed twice, and on the death of her second husband, Richard's father, she had to open a boarding school for girls to support the family. Richard entered Lancaster Grammar School at age five and remained there for 10 years, strongly encouraged by the headmaster (who was also Richard's godfather), the Reverend J. Rowley. On leaving school, he was apprenticed to surgeon and apothecary Leonard Dickson; his indenture (deed of apprenticeship) was dated August 11, 1820 (shortly after Richard's 16th birthday). However, Dickson died two years later, and the apprenticeship was transferred to Joseph Seed. A year later, Owen was transferred again, this time to James Stockdale Harrison, because Seed had accepted a post as surgeon in the Royal Navy. Attached to the indenture to Seed is a certificate dated January 10, 1827, in Seed's handwriting, to the effect that "Mr. Owen's general conduct during the time he was with me has my highest commendation, and at all times I shall be happy to bear testimony to his most deserving merit, as well as to his respectability."

His master was surgeon to the inmates of Lancaster Gaol, an ancient building of stone towers and corridors through which the wind used to howl on cold winter nights, when the young Owen used to sometimes attend postmortems. Owen later told tales of how his thoughts ran away with him in these circumstances, lapsing into weird ghostly imaginings. Some of his experiences there were, indeed, macabre. On just such a stormy night, the trainee surgeon wished to secure the head of an African for study and dissection, and, probably without proper authorization, removed the head from a body being prepared for burial. With the specimen in his bag, he hurried down to the gate, giving the gaoler on guard the signal that the corpse was now ready for interment. This was received with a nod of understanding, which assured the rapidly retreating Owen that no awkward questioning was likely from within the castle walls.

As he hurried homeward, however, the pavement being coated with ice, he slipped and fell forward with a shock that jerked the severed head out of the bag and sent it hurtling down the street. He could not retrieve it before it bounced against the door of a cottage, with him slipping and sliding in pursuit. The door flew open, and as he was unable to stop his rapid descent, he crashed into the front room of the dwelling. A woman screamed and fled into an inner part of the house. Owen followed his treasure and grabbed it, and did not pause until he reached his master's surgery.

In 1824, Owen attended **Edinburgh** University Medical School (as did Darwin a year or two later) and attended private classes in anatomy given by John Barclay (whom Darwin may have met while at Edinburgh but with whom he did not study). In 1825, with Barclay's support, Owen transferred to St. Bartholomew's Hospital in London, where he worked with John Abernethy. In 1826, Owen obtained his membership of the Royal College of Surgeons and set up as a medical practitioner in Lincoln's Inn Fields (in London's legal quarter), gradually establishing a small practice among the lawyers. However, Owen's ability as a dissector and his interest in comparative anatomy had not escaped the attention of Abernethy, then president of the College of Surgeons. Abernethy was concerned about the neglect of the collections formed by pioneer surgeon John Hunter (1728–1793), which had recently been purchased by the government and handed over to the College; he determined that his old pupil should undertake their arrangement, and he appointed Owen as assistant to the conservator of the Hunterian Museum.

Owen's task was to identify and label a collection of 13,000 specimens. By 1830, he had largely accomplished this and was publishing a catalog. This work provided an excellent training in comparative anatomy that he could not possibly have obtained if he had remained in medicine.

In 1830, the distinguished French anatomist and paleontologist **Georges Cuvier** (1769–1832) visited Richard Owen, and the following year he returned the visit, calling on Cuvier in Paris, where Cuvier held a senior academic position as well as exerted considerable political influence. Owen witnessed the evolutionary debates between Cuvier and Isodore Geoffroy Saint-Hillaire (1805–1861), an omen perhaps of the role he would play in the great evolutionary debates in England three decades later.

Richard Owen published an anatomical work *Memoir of the Pearly Nautilus* in 1832 and was appointed Hunterian Lecturer in Comparative Anatomy in 1837. His election to a fellowship of the **Royal Society** had already occurred in 1834. Always one for the dissemination of scientific knowledge, he established a name for himself in presenting series of Hunterian Lectures to the public; these were widely attended by fashionable London, including members of the royal family and a young Charles Darwin. Another venture into the popularization of science was Owen's attempt to create large models of dinosaurs, with the encouragement of Prince Albert (Queen **Victoria**'s husband) for exhibition at the rebuilt Crystal Palace in 1854; these were constructed on the basis of the best information then available and were an immense popular success. Always one for a gimmick and publicity, he entertained 21 eminent scientists to a dinner in the hollow interior one of the dinosaur models. However, as new fossil evidence emerged, it was clear that the models contained significant errors, and Owen faced acerbic criticism for this.

Owen's desire to bring the beauty and interest of the natural world to the public as well as his desire to document Britain's imperial destiny led to his campaigning for many years for a building where natural history specimens could be displayed and studied on an appropriate scale. It took years of debate and utilization of his considerable influence in high places for this dream to become a reality. The building was to be "a monument to God's creation," and it is no coincidence that the British Museum of Natural History (now the Natural History Museum) was built in a cathedral-like, ecclesiastical style of architecture. The London *Times,* reporting on the opening of the museum in April 1881, referred to it as "a true Temple of Nature, showing, as it should, the Beauty of Holiness."

Owen was, in fact, the originator of the term dinosaur, following his first research on extinct reptiles in the late 1830s: his first published use of the term was in 1842. He described and named several dinosaurs in the years that followed and identified many species of plesiosaur and ichthyosaur (aquatic Mesozoic reptiles) in addition to several species of flying reptile (e.g., *Pteradactylus manselli*). Fossil and extinct birds also came within his purview; he wrote a *Memoir on the Dodo* in 1866 and papers on the fossil moas of New Zealand in the 1840s. Numerous papers on fossil and living mammals and invertebrates also appeared under his name. Interestingly, his work on extinct mammals began with his description in 1837 of *Toxodon,* a hoofed creature the bones of which had been brought back from South America by Charles Darwin. In much of this work, Owen was assisted by the custom of taking specimens from the expanding British Empire to

London. In the early and middle years of Victoria's reign, the colonies such as Mauritius, New Zealand, and Australia had few scientific institutions of their own.

Owen believed, like Darwin, that plants and animals had changed throughout time. He accepted (as did his French mentor Cuvier) that the animals of the geological past were very different assemblages from those that existed today. Many creatures had become extinct. But Owen believed in the notion of special creation—that God had created each organism in a way that uniquely adapted to its environment and way of life. In this thinking, he was an intellectual descendant of **William Paley** (1743–1805). Owen maintained that all vertebrates were based on the same basic design, blueprint, or archetype. The wings of birds and bats, the flippers of seals and whales, the arms and legs of humans all had certain structures and the arrangement of their bones and muscles in common. He used the term *homology* for this basic similarity of structure. Each archetype was an idea in the mind of the creator; the changes were not linked to one another through ancestry. The term homology is still used in evolutionary biology and comparative anatomy.

Owen knew Charles Darwin quite well; they attended a meeting of the **Geological Society of London** in 1838, where Owen ridiculed the transmutationist ideas of Jean-Baptiste Lamarck. When Darwin was ill in 1841, Owen visited him. Indeed, it was Owen who was asked to describe some of the fossil mammals that Darwin had collected on the *Beagle* voyage in South America, and his work was published as part 1 of *The Zoology of the Voyage of the Beagle*. However, the two men later came to detest each other: Owen's attempts to ensure the elimination of official support for **Joseph Hooker**'s Botanic Gardens at Kew were particularly hurtful to Darwin.

Owen's friend and mentor, George Cuvier, was a catastrophist, and he developed the concept of extinction. He argued that each layer of rock contained a distinctive assemblage of fossil organisms, and the era it represented had been brought to an end by an enormous catastrophe or upheaval. Cuvier recognized that even the youngest of sediments were extremely old, that life in the sea had preceded that on land, and that reptiles had preceded mammals. Cuvier has been described as an egomaniac who used his reputation and influence to bully and intimidate others (as, in time, did his protégé, Richard Owen). Cuvier's opponent Isodore Geoffroy Saint-Hillaire was a progressionist who thought that ichthyosaurs had eventually changed (progressed) into crocodiles. These exchanges provided the pattern for debates in which Owen would engage later. Owen's studies of the differences between humans and apes led to his assertion that the human brain had an organ, the hippocampus minor (known today as the calcar avis), which was unique to humans—thus confirming humanity's uniqueness: "There is a gradation of cerebral development from the lowest to the highest vertebrate species; but there are interruptions in this gradation," he wrote.

Thomas Huxley (1825–1895) disagreed, and a bitter dispute followed. Owen also anonymously wrote a critical review of Darwin's *On the Origin of Species,* but the scientific community soon figured out who had written it. His attempts to popularize science through such ventures as the concrete dinosaurs attracted further scorn. Prior to the Great Debate between Huxley and **Samuel Wilberforce** in Oxford in 1860, Owen coached Wilberforce.

Sir Richard Owen (knighted in 1884) must have been a difficult man. He was accused of appropriating the work of colleagues, not crediting the work of other scientists, and excluding younger competitors from societies. He was undoubtedly brilliant and has been described as "more right than wrong"; for his work on paleontology and comparative anatomy, science should be grateful to him. His greatest error was his unwavering rejection of Darwin's theories. Others of his generation were able to change their minds. Some authors have asserted that privately Owen partly accepted Darwin's ideas, but, because he was a favorite of Queen Victoria, giving talks on natural history to the royal children and late in life living in a small house in Richmond Park, and because the Queen detested Darwinism, he might have felt he could not openly recant.

FURTHER READING

Owen, The Reverend Richard. 1894. *The Life of Richard Owen.* London: J. Murray.
Rupke, Nicolaas. 1994. *Richard Owen: Victorian Naturalist.* New Haven, CT: Yale University Press.

P

Pacific Ocean

The largest ocean; its traverse during the latter part of the voyage of the *Beagle* was formative in the intellectual development of Charles Darwin.

The Pacific Ocean, bounded by North and South America, Asia, Australia, and Antarctica occupies approximately one third of the planet and has an area of about 63,690,000 square miles (about 165,000,000 square kilometers) including its peripheral seas. It is the deepest ocean and is sprinkled with many thousands of islands.

HMS *Beagle,* with the seasick Darwin aboard, entered the open waters of the Pacific on the morning of June 12, 1834, and departed **Tasmania** for Western Australia on February 16, 1836. He thus spent about 20 months within the confines of the Pacific Basin. He explored the west coast of the mainland of South America thoroughly, calling at a number of points in Chile and Peru. He examined the island of **Chiloé** carefully and landed on several of the islands in the Chronos group. The sojourn in the **Galapagos Islands** archipelago is well known but is probably overrated. He glimpsed several coral atolls from the mast of the *Beagle* as the ship cut its her way across before the trade winds. He spent several days in **Tahiti,** from where he glimpsed Eimeo (Moorea) from a high point, before proceeding to the **Bay of Islands** in North Island, **New Zealand,** probably sighting other islets on the way. Several weeks in **New South Wales** on the Australian Pacific coast were followed by a brief visit to Tasmania.

In addition to the continental environments of the Andes in South America and the Blue Mountains in Australia, he inspected islands large and small; tropical and cool temperate; and formed of continental rocks, from coral growth, and through volcanic activity. These combined experiences were immensely significant. By the time he entered the Pacific, he was largely converted to the theories of **Charles Lyell,** understanding that the features of the Earth were formed by the long-continued, gradual application of processes at present in operation. Although he was affected by an earthquake and saw the damage wrought by a tsunami on the Chilean coast, he was becoming a uniformitarian rather than a catastrophist. He had trained himself, after two years voyaging, to seek the *vera causa,* or the bold theory or guiding principle.

On the South American coast, Darwin thought he had found evidence of major rises in the land relative to sea level, and, for the remainder of his voyage, he was on the lookout for evidence of changes in sea level, particularly evidence for subsidence that in some way might compensate for the rises elsewhere. Several times he thought he had found it. He saw atolls, barrier and fringing reefs, and, while he was sailing between Tahiti and New Zealand, developed his coral atoll theory explaining the origin of these through subsidence. He saw both very young volcanic islands in the Galapagos and those that were older and much eroded at Tahiti and began to experiment with ideas on volcanic isles that were in some ways analogous. Despite the apparent luxuriance of the tropical forest of Tahiti, he noted that it was species poor: plants and animals on the island must have made the journey to the island from elsewhere. He compared the appearance and customs of the Chilotans, the Polynesians on Tahiti, and the Maoris in New Zealand. He met Aborigines in New South Wales and heard of the sad decline of the Tasmanian Aboriginal people while he was in Hobart. He experienced both what he considered the beneficial influences of Christian missionary activity and the deleterious effects of the clash of European civilization and settlement with the traditional ways of life of indigenous people. He went for long journeys through the Australian bush, contrasting the strikingly different ecological communities he saw with the environments he had encountered in other parts of the world. Had there been two creations?, he wondered for a moment while sitting on a grassy bank in New South Wales. Specimens he collected (especially those from the several islands of the Galapagos) were important when he started to develop his evolutionary ideas after his return (probably about March 1837). All these experiences were of enormous import.

Interestingly, several of his most important supporters, friends, and correspondents in later life had had broadly similar Pacific experiences. James Clark Ross, leader of an early antarctic expedition between 1839 and 1843, had stated that he wanted such a person as Darwin on the voyage. And **Joseph Hooker** secured the position of assistant surgeon on HMS *Erebus,* which together with the *Terror,* explored the Southern Ocean, reaching as far south as 78° 17' S. The expedition crossed the southern part of the Pacific, and Hooker collected plants from Australia and New Zealand.

Thomas Huxley also obtained a position of ship's doctor on the *Rattlesnake*, which, like the *Beagle*, was engaged on a voyage of hydrographic survey (1846–1850). The *Rattlesnake* visited Australia, calling at Sydney and sailing along much of the Pacific coast of Australia to the Torres Strait and New Guinea. Studies were made of coral forms and of the customs of native peoples.

Hooker and Huxley were Darwin's fervent supporters and dearest friends. **James Dwight Dana** never met Darwin, but there are many analogies in their lives and work. Dana was a scientist on the U.S. Exploring Expedition (1838–1842), largely confirmed (and extended) Darwin's work on **coral and coral reefs,** and, like Darwin studied Pacific volcanic islands. Dana visited Hawaii and Fiji (rather than Tahiti and the Galapagos), but both called at New Zealand, touched at Sydney, and undertook geological fieldwork in New South Wales, visiting some of the same locations.

The effect of the strong commonality of the experience of these naturalists with Darwin is difficult to estimate but was probably considerable. Having visited some of the same places, had similar experiences, and worked in much the same way must have meant that they understood Darwin more than many of his desk-bound contemporaries.

FURTHER READING

MacLeod, R. and P. E. Rehbock, eds. 1994. *Darwin's Laboratory: Evolutionary Theory and Natural History in the Pacific.* Honolulu: University of Hawaii Press.
Viola, J. V. and C. Margolis, eds. 1985. *Magnificent Voyagers: The US Exploring Expedition, 1838–1842.* Washington, DC: Smithsonian Institution Press.

Paley, William (1743–1805)

Clergyman and theologian; propounder of the doctrine of natural theology, he had an important early influence on Charles Darwin.

Darwin wrote in his *Autobiography*, late in life:

> In order to pass the B.A. examination, it was, also, necessary to get up Paley's *Evidences of Christianity*, and his *Moral Philosophy*. . . . The logic of this book and as I may add of his *Natural Theology* gave me as much delight as did Euclid. The careful study of these works, without attempting to learn any part by rote, was the only part of the Academical Course which, as I then felt and as I still believe, was of the least use to me in the education of my mind. I did not at that time trouble myself about Paley's premises; and taking these on trust. I was charmed and convinced of the long line of argumentation. (*Autobiography*, edited by F. Darwin, 1887, 41)

William Paley was born in the cathedral city of Peterborough, in Northamptonshire, in the English Midlands. Like Darwin, he was an undergraduate at Christ's College, Cambridge, being later appointed a fellow of the college and tutor (1766–1776). (Darwin at one stage lived in the college rooms that Paley had used, and today portraits of the two men share the same wall of the college dining hall.) He was later archdeacon of Carlisle, a position he held until his death in May 1805; he was buried in Carlisle Cathedral. He also held a position at Lincoln Cathedral from 1795.

His first book, *Principles of Moral and Political Philosophy* (1785), was based on his teaching of ethics at Cambridge. It expounded what has become known as utilitarianism, which can be summarized in the dictum "what is expedient is right." His *Horae Paulinae* attempted to demonstrate the truth of the New Testament by showing a correlation between the Epistles of St. Paul and Acts. This is generally considered his most original work, although others were more popular. His *View of the Evidences for Christianity* (1794) was written as an answer to attacks on Christianity by Edward Gibbon and David Hume.

Probably his most influential work was *Natural Theology: Or, Evidences of the Existence and Attributes of the Deity, Collected from the Appearances of Nature,* originally published in 1802 but running into many editions throughout the nineteenth century. Here Paley set out the doctrine of natural theology, the notion that the living world and the universe could provide insights to the nature of God the creator. He introduced one of the best-remembered metaphors in the philosophy of science: the image of the watchmaker. If one were to stroll over a heath and find a stone, one might believe that it had always been there; but if a watch were to be found, the finder might reason that it had been designed and made by someone. Design implies a designer, he argued:

> [W]hen we come to inspect the watch, we perceive . . . that its several parts are . . . put together for a purpose, e.g. that they are so formed and adjusted as to produce motion, and that motion so regulated as to point out the hour of the day; that if the different parts had been differently shaped from what they are, or placed after any other manner or in any other order than that in which they are placed, either no motion at all would have been carried on in the machine, or none which would have answered the use that is now served by it. . . . the inference . . . is inevitable, that the watch must have had a maker—that there must have existed, at some time and at some place or other, an artificer or artificers who formed it for the purpose which we find it actually to answer, who comprehended its construction and designed its use. (*Natural Theology,* 1807 edition, 2–3)

Living organisms, he argued, were far more complex than a watch, to "a degree that defies computation." Moreover, each organism is adapted intricately to its environment and way of life. This, he argued, implies intelligent design, just as only an intelligent designer could have made the watch.

A single quotation form Paley's book illustrates the argument:

> The air-bladder also of a *fish* affords a plain and direct instance, not only of contrivance. . . . The principle of the contrivance is clear; the application of

the principle is also clear. The use of the organ to sustain, and . . . to elevate, the body of the fish in the water, is proved by observing, what has been tried, that, when the bladder is burst, the fish grovels at the bottom; and also, that flounders, soles, skates, which are without the air-bladder, seldom rise in the water, and that with effort. The manner in which the purpose is attained, and the suitableness of the means to the end, are not difficult to be apprehended. The rising and sinking of a fish in water, so far as it is independent of the stroke of the fins and tail, can only be regulated by the specific gravity of the body. When the bladder, contained in the body of the fish, is contracted, . . . the bulk of the fish is contracted along with it; whereby, since the absolute weight remains the same, the specific gravity, which is the sinking force, is increased, and the fish descends: on the contrary, when, in consequence of the relaxation of the muscles, the elasticity of the inclosed and now compressed air, restores the dimensions of the bladder, the tendency downwards becomes proportionably less than it was before, or is turned into a contrary tendency. (*Natural Theology*, 1807 edition, 243–245)

The structure and behavior of the organism are intricately adapted to the creature's habitat and way of life. The individual parts of the organism appear to accord with an overall plan. Paley went on to argue that if God had taken such care in designing even the most insignificant creatures, how much more must God care for humanity.

In every nature, and in every portion of nature . . . we find attention bestowed upon even the minutest arts. The hinges in the wings of an *earwig*, and the joints of its antennæ, are as highly wrought, as if the Creator had nothing else to finish. We see no signs of diminution of care by multiplicity of objects, or of distraction of thought by variety. We have no reason to fear, therefore, our being forgotten, or overlooked, or neglected (*Natural Theology*, 1807 edition, 541–542)

Paley derived much of his argument from John Ray (1627–1705), although Paley makes little acknowledgment of him. Charles Darwin took from his reading of his predecessor at Christ's College the notion of adaptation. The idea that every organism is adapted to its environment—its habitat and way of life—not only in its morphology or shape but in its behavior was a component of Darwin's theory of evolution through natural selection, just as it was of Paley's natural theology. And although Darwin departed from a literalist interpretation of the creation accounts of the book of Genesis, he did not reject the possibility of the existence of God. "I deserve to be called a Theist," Darwin stated late in life. There is also some similarity between the literary style and method of argumentation of Paley and Darwin. Indeed, it has been suggested that *On the Origin of Species* could be described as the last of the works on natural theology as well as the first of evolutionary biology.

William Paley was familiar with the writings of Thomas Malthus. For example:

The order of generation proceeds by something like a geometrical progression. The increase of provision, under circumstances even the most advantageous, can only assume the form of an arithmetic series. Whence it follows, that the population will always overtake the provision, will pass beyond the line of plenty, and will continue to increase till checked by the difficulty of procuring subsistence. Such difficulty therefore, along with its attendant circumstances, *must* be found in every old country: and these circumstances constitute what we call poverty, which, necessarily, imposes labour, servitude, restraint. . . . Nature has a strong tendency to equalization. (*Natural Theology,* 1807 edition, 505–507)

Paley adds a note, "See this subject stated in a late treatise on population," obviously Malthus's *Essay on Population*. Paley seems to be stating that the mechanisms of population control are part of some great plan on part of a deity. A little earlier he stated:

What further shows, that the system of destruction amongst animals holds an express relation to the system of fecundity; that they are parts indeed of one compensatory scheme; is, that, in each species, the fecundity bears a proportion to the smallness of the animal, to the weakness, to the shortness of its natural term of life, and to the dangers and enemies by which it is surrounded. An elephant produces but one calf; a butterfly lays six hundred eggs. Birds of prey seldom produce more than two eggs: the sparrow tribe, and the duck tribe, frequently sit upon a dozen. In the rivers, we meet with a thousand minnows for one pike; in the sea, a million of herrings for a single shark. Compensation obtains throughout. Defencelessness and devastation are repaired by fecundity. (*Natural Theology,* 1807 edition, 480–481)

It is possible that Darwin first came across Malthus's theories while reading Paley as an undergraduate. A number of entries in his notes from the *Beagle* period indicate that he was perceptive of the problem of animal numbers, but none of Paley's writings was aboard the *Beagle*.

The Paleyan arguments from natural theology have a long tradition. They have been the mainstay of Creationists, or, as they sometimes prefer to be called, Creation Scientists. In the years after 2000 they have reemerged in a slightly different form with the label intelligent design, particularly among those who argue that the idea of independent divine creation should be taught alongside evolution in science classes in schools.

One of the difficulties with natural theology is the problem of explaining the many cases of pain, waste, destruction, and cruelty in the living world. Why would a benevolent designer have made cats play with their prey before killing and eating them? Or create parasites that eat their hosts from the inside, causing their hosts enormous pain? Paley (and many others) struggled to reconcile the apparent cruelty and indifference of nature with his belief in a benevolent God, and he finally concluded simply that the joys of life outweigh the negativity of its pains and sorrows. Paley wrote much about the delight and joy to be found in all nature in the final pages of *Natural Theology*.

Even in his own day Paley came under criticism from some evangelical Christians who felt that Paley emphasized reason at the expense of revelation and Scripture in his writing. Closer to our own time, the "watchmaker" argument has come under attack, most recently and stridently from Oxford zoologist **Richard Dawkins** in *The Blind Watchmaker* (1986). In this book, Dawkins argues that there is no need to seek an intelligence or a designer to explain the complexity and diversity of life. Random mutations, changes in the DNA of organisms, plus the effect of natural selection are sufficient.

FURTHER READING

Dawkins, Richard. 1986. *The Blind Watchmaker.* London: Longmans.
Paley, William. 1802. *Natural Theology; or, Evidences of the Existence and Attributes of the Deity.* London: F.C. and J. Rivington.

Patagonia

The low plateau that constitutes the southern portion of what is now southern Argentina, approximately from Bahia Blanca, 1,250 miles (2,000 kilometers) south to the Strait of Magellan; extensively toured by Darwin.

The land of Patagonia rises, through several terraces, eastward to the Andes. To the north, the region merges with the pampas, the temperate grasslands around the Rio de la Plata. Darwin explored several portions of the Patagonian region between 1832 and 1834. Because the Andes Mountains shield the region from the moist westerly winds, the climate of parts of Patagonia is arid or semiarid, with a vegetation of tussac grass and shrubs. There are salt lakes. Glacial deposits occur in the west, close to the foothills of the Andes. The plateau is cut into by a series of west-to-east trending valleys—those of the Rio Colorado, Rio Negro, and Santa Cruz—several of which Darwin, sometimes in the company of other members of the *Beagle*'s crew, explored. Coastal sites visited included Patagones and Port Desire, where the ship spent Christmas Day 1833. Darwin described the landscape of the region in the following terms:

> I thought I had seen some desert looking country near B[ahia] Blanca; but the land in this neighbourhood so far exceeds it in sterility, that this alone deserves the name of a desert. The plain is composed of gravel and not a drop of water. In the valleys there is some little but it is very brackish. (*Diary,* December 24, 1833)

Today, parts of Patagonia are sheep-rearing country, but in Darwin's day it was very wild frontier land. To secure passage to sites he wished to visit, Darwin had to negotiate with General Juan Manuel de Rosas, who Darwin descried as "a perfect gaucho," with a gaudy shawl and poncho. His despotic nature was legendary, and he had been sent with "a villainous, banditi-like army" to exterminate the Indians who lived in the area, with a view to opening the land for cattle ranching. Darwin shook a hand that was covered in blood.

Darwin enjoyed exploring the open country on horseback, often with parties of gauchos; he studied the geology of the area intensively and collected a number of vertebrate fossils, including some that were later important in the development of his ideas. Important among these was the **Megatherium,** a huge ground-living relative of the sloth. He saw armadillos and several dozen large flightless birds he calls ostriches but which were, in fact, **rheas,** a distinctive South American bird related to the African ostrich. The gauchos hunted them with their *bolas,* large balls attached to ropes. On one occasion, Darwin found a nest containing 27 eggs and surmised that this represented the clutches of several females. These giant birds were of great importance to him; there were two species, and Darwin speculated about their possible relationship and origin. Indeed, some his first writings that can definitely be declared to be evolutionary in character were concerning the two species of "ostriches"—included in some jottings in a small red notebook and probably written after the return to England, perhaps in early 1837.

Peppered Moth

Species of insect found in Britain that has been held to illustrate the occurrence of the process natural selection within a living species.

The common form of the peppered moth, *Biston betularia,* until the middle of the nineteenth century, was of a speckled gray color that provided excellent camouflage when resting on the trunks of lichen-covered trees: the name *typica* was given to this form. From about 1848 onward, near Manchester, in northern England's industrial belt, a dark form *carbonaria* began appearing and soon was also reported from the coalfield areas of Yorkshire and adjoining counties. By 1895, 98 percent of the peppered moths collected near Manchester were of the *carbonaria* form; by the 1950s, the *carbonaria* form was found throughout the industrial areas of northern England. Populations of moths from eastern England (i.e., downwind from the industrial heartlands) also contained a proportion the dark or *melanic* form. H.B.P. Kettlewell performed a series of experiments in the 1950s and demonstrated to his own satisfaction that birds differentially preyed on the dark forms when they were placed on the trunks of lichen-covered trees and on the lighter forms when placed on dark backgrounds, such as tree trunks devoid of lichens and darkened by industrial pollution. He suggested that bird predation constituted the principle mechanism for natural selection. He argued that the conspicuous light form moths tended to be removed from the population in industrial, sooty districts favoring the melanic form. Kettlewell wrote that if he were alive, Darwin would accept this as proof of his theory of evolution through natural selection, and vindication of his work. Other scientists received the work appreciatively: population geneticist Sewall Wright called it in 1978 "the clearest case in which a conspicuous evolutionary process has actually been observed."

Further support for Kettlewell appeared when, following the passage of the United Kingdom's Clean Air Acts of 1956 and 1968, which reduced pollution, lichens were allowed to recolonize areas from which they had been virtually eliminated. The number of dark moths then declined in the 1980s, and *typica* reemerged as the dominant form in some areas.

However, in recent decades, Kettlewell's work has been heavily criticized. It was pointed out that peppered moths are night-flying, resting during the day on the undersides of branches rather than on exposed tree trunks, and thus the 1950s experiments were "unnatural." Moreover, although *typica* forms may appear almost invisible on lichen-covered trees to humans, birds make greater use of ultraviolet and may see things differently. In Wales, a relatively unpolluted area, melanic forms were recorded more frequently than one might expect: on the other hand, in some places, the light forms started returning before lichens returned to the tree trunks. Among other criticisms leveled was that some of the experiments were done in the unnatural conditions of aviaries.

These and other criticisms led some to claim that Kettlewell's work was flawed, or even faked. Headings of popular magazine articles began to appear that called the peppered moth study a hoax. Creationist groups gleefully seized on the flaws in Kettlewell's work as disproof of Darwin's theories on evolution by natural selection.

The considered view from more than 60 years later is that, although there may have been defects in some of Kettlewell's methods and that he may, for example, have underestimated the role of movement and migration in the peppered moth populations, on the whole, he was a competent and careful scientist, and his conclusions were at least partially valid. Industrial melanism in the peppered moth does provide an example of natural selection (but not perhaps of evolution), but the whole process may be much more complex than he envisaged. Other processes may be at work. One who reviewed the work carefully was Cambridge geneticist M.E.N. Majerus, who, although he pointed out some defects in Kettlewell's studies, summarized:

> Differential bird predation of the *typica* and *carbonaria* forms, in habitats affected by industrial pollution to different degrees, is the primary influence on the evolution of melanism in the peppered moth. (*Melanism: Evolution in Action*, 1998, New York: Oxford University Press, 116)

FURTHER READING

Jones, J. S. 1982. "More to Melanism than Meets the Eye." *Nature* 300: 109–110.

Kettlewell, H.B.D. 1955. "Selection Experiments on Industrial Melanism in the Lepidoptera." *Heredity* 9: 323–342.

Kettlewell, H.B.D. 1956. "Further Selection Experiments on Industrial Melanism in the Lepidoptera." *Heredity* 10: 287–301.

Kettlewell, H.B.D. 1973. *The Evolution of Melanism.* Oxford, England: Clarendon Press.

Majerus, M.E.N. 1998. *Melanism: Evolution in Action.* Oxford, England: Oxford University Press.

Planaria

Simple organisms belonging to the phylum Platyhelminthes; varying in length from 3 to 12 millimeters, they have three layers of cells but no body cavity. They are also known as flatworms and occur in freshwater and some damp terrestrial environments. Darwin discovered specimens in several parts of the world on the *Beagle* voyage and was very interested in them; his observations are significant for several reasons.

Although common, for example, among weeds in freshwater bodies, Darwin describes finding 12 terrestrial species of planaria during the course of the voyage of the *Beagle.*

> Two in the forests of Brazil; three on the open grassy country northward of the Rio Plata; one on the arid hills near Valparaiso in Chile, and three in the damp wooded country southward of central Chile the most southern location was at lat. 460' S. I also found one species in New Zealand (which I lost), another in Van Diemen's Land [Tasmania], and a third at the Mauritius; the latter I had not time to examine. Hence it appears that the terrestrial section of this genus is widely diffused; but as far as is at present known, only in the southern hemisphere. (*Annals and Magazine of Natural History,* 1844, Vol. 14: 241–251)

Darwin wrote toward the end of the voyage: "the habit of comparison leads to generalization." He was constantly comparing the organisms of one location with those of another. He was especially interested in Southern Hemisphere distributions, and he draws attention to a number of groups that have distributions that include the southern part of South America, Tierra del Fuego, New Zealand, and Tasmania in his writings. In doing so, he prepared the way for writers, such as Joseph Hooker, who sought to explain these southern hemisphere links by land bridges, and much later for those who sought evidence for the movement of the crustal plates. It is not correct that terrestrial planarians are confined to the south—there are a number in North America—but Darwin, like us all, made mistakes. And he admitted that his Tasmanian specimens perished "through neglect."

Darwin is often thought of as being an observational scientist and a theorizer rather than an experimentalist. But, in fact, he undertook detailed experiments on the planaria he found in the abundant rotting wood of Tasmanian forests. He described their reaction to light (they "disliked" it and immediately crawled beneath fragments of wood) and other stimuli such as touch. He also bisected one and observed the organism's ability to regenerate from a fragment. But a over a month later, as the *Beagle* entered the tropics, "they gradually sickened and died." He prepared extremely detailed notes on his experiments. Some of these experiments had been conducted before, but his insistence in repeating them for himself is notable. Moreover, this work provides an early example of his interest in the behavior of organisms. In the paper he wrote on the planaria he collected on the voyage—full of observational detail—some emphasis is placed on the behavior and irritability of these lowly creatures, as well as their ecology.

> The species which live under stones, both in the grassy undulating land of northern La Plata, and on the arid, rocky hills of central Chile, generally inhabit small sinuous chambers, like those frequented by earth-worms, in which they lie coiled and knotted up. They are often found in pairs; and I once found a pair attached together by their lower surfaces, apparently in copulation. . . . [T]hey progress by a regular wave-like movement of the foot, like that of a gastropod [snail], using the anterior [front] extremity, which is raised from the ground, as a feeler. ("Brief Description of Terrestrial Planariae, *Annals and Magazine of Natural History*, 1844, Vol. 14: 141–151)

Here is fine observational detail and a linking of the form, behavior, and ecology of the organism, showing the integration so often displayed in Darwin's writing.

Punctuated Equilibrium

The theory that evolution, rather than being very slow, gradual, and continuous, is characterized by long periods of virtual standstill (equilibrium), punctuated by episodes of rapid development of new forms. The theory is particularly associated with scientists **Stephen Jay Gould** and Neil Eldredge. In one of their early papers, they claimed:

(1) New species arise by the splitting of lineages.
(2) New species develop rapidly.
(3) A small subpopulation of the ancestral form gives rise to the new species.
(4) The new species originates in a very small part of the ancestral species' geographic extent—in an isolated area at the periphery of the range.

These four statements entail two important consequences:

(1) In any local section containing ancestral species, the fossil record for the descendant's origin should consist of a sharp morphological break between the two forms. . . . we will rarely discover the actual event in the fossil record.
(2) Many breaks in the fossil record are real; they express the way in which evolution occurs, not the fragments of an imperfect record. (Eldredge and Gould, 1972)

In other words, new species arise quite quickly, in a small area—the term peripheral isolate is often used—but then spread from that area rapidly. It is, therefore, in this view not surprising that intermediates between species are seldom found. The gaps are real and not solely the result of the imperfections of the geological record.

These ideas are sometimes set in opposition to the phyletic gradualism or very slow change espoused by Darwin. In fact, Darwin freely acknowledged that evolution would vary considerably in its speed. In the first edition of *On the Origin of Species,* in discussing a branching diagram that summarized his idea of evolution, he acknowledged:

> But I must here remark that I do not suppose that the process ever goes on so regularly as is represented in the diagram, though in itself made somewhat irregular. (*On the Origin of Species,* chapter 4, "Natural Selection")

In later editions, he was more definite:

> It is a more important consideration, leading to the same result, . . . namely, that the period during which each species underwent modification, though long as measured by years, was probably short in comparison with that during which it remained without undergoing any change. (*On the Origin of Species,* 1872 edition, chapter 9, "On the Imperfection of the Geological Record")

He admitted that the sudden arrival of new species, or indeed whole biological groups in the fossil record, posed problems:

> The abrupt manner in which whole groups suddenly appear in certain formations, has been urged by several palaeontologists . . . as a fatal objection to the belief in the transmutation of species. (*On the Origin of Species,* 1859 edition, chapter 9, "On the Imperfection of the Geological Record")

He answered this by speculating that the initial differentiation might take place in a limited region of the world, but later expansion into new areas might take place quite rapidly: in many parts of the range, therefore, a particular form or group of forms might appear in the geological record very suddenly. This idea is quite analogous to Eldredge and Gould's concept of a peripheral isolate.

But he also accepted that the actual rate of evolution might vary widely. Here is one example he gives in the first edition of *On the Origin:*

> [I]t might require a long succession of ages to adapt an organism to some new and peculiar line of life, for instance to fly through the air; but that when this had been effected, and a few species had thus acquired a great advantage over other organisms, a comparatively short time would be necessary to produce many divergent forms, which would be able to spread rapidly and widely

throughout the world. (*On the Origin of Species,* 1859 edition, chapter 9, "On the Imperfection of the Geological Record")

Another frequently quoted instance of suddenness in the fossil record is the apparent abrupt appearance of many different biological groups quite early in the record. This is discussed in the article on the **Cambrian Big Bang.**

FURTHER READING

Eldredge, N. and S. J. Gould. 1972. "Punctuated Equilibria: An Alternative to Phyletic Gradualism." In *Models in Paleobiology,* ed. T.J.M. Schopf, 82–112. San Francisco: Freeman, Cooper.

Gould, S. J. and N. Eldredge. 1977. "Punctuated Equilibria: The Tempo and Mode of Evolution Reconsidered." *Paleobiology* 3: 115–151.

R

Raverat, Gwen (1885–1957)

Granddaughter of Charles Darwin, artist, associate of the Bloomsbury Group of writers, chronicler of the Darwin family, and eccentric.

Of the many distinguished and talented descendants of Charles Darwin, Gwen Raverat stands out as one of the most extraordinary. She is best known for her charming and perceptive portrait of late Victorian and Edwardian Cambridge, published in 1952 as *Period Piece: A Cambridge Childhood*. She was also an artist of international repute. The daughter of Charles's most distinguished son, **George Darwin** (1842–1912), the Cambridge mathematician and astronomer, and Maud du Puy of Philadelphia, Gwen studied at the Slade School of Fine Art in London. She admired the wood engravings of Thomas Bewick (1753–1828), and became one of the leading exponents of the craft of the woodcut. She thus represents a confluence of two important streams of English intellectual life: the academic Cambridge Darwins and the London group of artists and writers associated with Bloomsbury. She knew the writers Virginia Woolf and Rupert Brooke well. She married the eccentric, volatile, and allegedly bisexual French artist Jacques Raverat. Frances Darwin, writing to Rupert Brooke, said that "to find two people answer each other from the top to the bottom of the piano like Gwen and Jacques is the rarest and most splendid thing." Both were passionate and intense. They lived for some years in Venice and in France, and many of Gwen's earlier woodcuts are of the French countryside and French provincial life. But Jacques's father George became involved in a financial scandal and lost a large part of his fortune. Gwen is reported to have found this liberating. Rupert Brooke and many of their Cambridge associates perished in the Great War (1914–1918): this too affected her greatly.

Jacques was diagnosed with multiple sclerosis, a disease that was, in the early decades of the twentieth century, little understood. As well as caring for two young children, Gwen nursed her deteriorating husband for several years. In the end, a kind of Darwinian logic took hold of her, and, as one biographer has put it, Gwen "seized a pillow and terminated his suffering" (Spalding, 2001, 308).

No legal consequences seem to have followed, and she moved back to England, where she continued her work as an artist and writer. She designed stage sets and costumes, and she was art critic for the important literary magazine *Time and Tide* from 1928 to 1939. During World War II, she was a draughtswoman for British Naval Intelligence. She illustrated dozens of books, particularly books for children. In later life she returned to her roots, living in a house known as the Old Granary adjacent to her childhood home. Some of her best engravings are of Cambridge life and townscapes. There is, perhaps, something of her grandfather's power of observation in the detail of some of her work. She resembled some of the older Darwins in other respects, too—for example, in her agnostic, and at some times almost militantly atheistic, views. Yet at other times she flirted with Catholicism, and some of her engravings were of religious subjects.

She had a stroke and was confined to a wheelchair in her last years; to this she had a easel attached and in the 1950s was a familiar figure in Cambridge as she painted scenes along the River Cam. (This was the manner in which the present author glimpsed her in his Cambridge childhood in the 1940s and 1950s.) She was in a great deal of pain. Eventually, perhaps in some strange way seeking a symmetry with the killing of her husband over three decades earlier, she took her own life, consuming a large number of aspirin tablets. "This seems the simplest plan for everyone," were her final, utterly unsentimental, words. Her work is held in the British Museum, and the Fitzwilliam Museum in Cambridge and in many private collections.

FURTHER READING

Raverat, Gwen. 1952. *Period Piece: A Cambridge Childhood*. London: Faber.
Spalding, Frances. 2001. *Gwen Raverat: Friends, Family and Affections*. London: Harvill.

Ray, John (1627–1705)

English clergyman, pioneer botanist, geologist, and polymath.

It has been said that it is John Ray who "initiated the true adventure of modern science" (Raven, 1942, 452). He represents a sharp break with the confusion of anecdote, superstition, and allegory that was much of natural history as it was inherited from the monastic period of the Middle Ages. He provided a rich lode that was mined by Gilbert White (1720–1793) and **William Paley** (1743–1805). The former wrote of the "excellent Mr Ray" in *The Natural History of Selborne* (a book that Darwin enjoyed); the latter borrowed extensively from Ray for his *Natural Theology* (without full acknowledgment), one of the few books that Darwin read while at Cambridge that he felt was of use to him in his subsequent scientific work. There is thus an almost direct line of influence from the thought of Ray to that of Darwin.

John Ray was a man of humble origins: he was the son of a blacksmith from the village of Black Notley in Essex, in rural eastern England. His first mentor was the local herb woman. He went to Catherine Hall, Cambridge, but later moved to Trinity College. He was ordained to the Church of England priesthood in 1662. He became a fellow of his college but resigned his fellowship in the years of religious dispute around the time of the Act of Uniformity of 1662 (which established certain doctrines and practices of the Church of England).

His first publication of note (1660) was a *Catalogue of Plants of the Cambridge Area,* which established high standards for descriptive botany, emphasizing order and classification, in contrast to the somewhat unstructured accounts of some earlier publications. He described 558 plants he had seen personally, often describing the structure of the plant in considerable detail, mentioning its habitat, and sometimes mentioning localities where it was to be found. Later (1670) he compiled a catalogue of the plants of the whole of England, and then wrote extensively on fossils, birds, and language. But by far his most important book was *The Wisdom of God Manifested in the Works of Creation*, first published in 1690, and going through 20 editions over the next century and a half. It has been described as "breathtaking in its scope," and as "the ancestor of the *Origin of Species*" (Raven, 1942, 452) taking in the solar system, geology, animals, and plants together with their adaptation to

John Ray: "The Excellent Mr Ray" (Gilbert White), "with whom the adventure of modern science begins" (Charles Raven). From an eighteenth-century print.

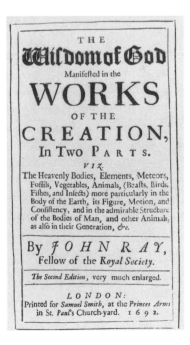

Title page of John Ray's *The Wisdom of God*, 1692.

environment, behavior and instinct, and human physiology and anatomy. It contains fine observational detail. Taking as its starting point the words of Psalm 104, "How manifold are thy works O Lord: In wisdom hast thou made them all," Ray sees the beauty and complexity of the world, living creatures, and the universe as evidence for a divine creator and the exquisite adaptability of plants and animals to their environment as evidence for the creator's wisdom. Animals show an "exact fitness of the parts of their bodies to their nature and manner of living." To take a single example, woodpeckers

> have a tongue which they can shoot forth to a very great length, ending in a sharp stiff bony tip, dented on each side; and at pleasure thrust it deep into the holes, clefts and crannies of trees to stab and draw out insects lurking there. . . . [Also] they have short, but very strong legs, and their toes stand two forwards, two backwards, which disposition Nature, or the Wisdom of the Creator, hath granted to Woodpeckers, because it is very convenient for the climbing of trees. (*Wisdom of God*, 1692 edition, 132)

FURTHER READING

Raven, Charles E. 1942. *John Ray: Naturalist*. Cambridge, England: Cambridge University Press.

Recapitulation

The doctrine that the life history of an individual organism repeats or recapitulates the phylogeny or evolutionary history.

The notion was put forward in the nineteenth century by Ernst Haeckel (1834–1919). A mammal, for example, starts out as a single cell (the zygote or fertilized ovum) resembling its protozoan ancestor; it then becomes a two-layered embryo, recalling a coelenterate ancestor (the group that includes the sea anemones and corals), and later develops gill slits like a fish. Darwin discussed embryology in *On the Origin of Species,* but mainly to show that similarities in the embryos of different species might provide clues to their classification. Nevertheless, Darwin adopted a similar theory in some of his later work. The idea is not now emphasized as much as it was formerly, except insofar as evidence suggests that there is sometimes a closer resemblance between the embryos of animals of different species and biological groups than between the adult forms.

Reconciliation

The term often used for the attempts made by some seventeenth-, eighteenth-, and nineteenth-century scholars to reconcile or harmonize the Book of Moses (the Old Testament accounts of the creation) with the Book of the Rocks. See article on **Darwinism and theology.**

Red Notebook

One of a series of small notebooks kept by Charles Darwin during and immediately after the voyage of HMS *Beagle*. It contains ideas, thoughts, speculations, and references rather than detailed field observations. It is important because it seems to include Darwin's first known writings on evolution.

Physically, the notebook is ordinary enough— it is well made, with a red leather cover, enclosing about 90 leaves (i.e., about 180 sides or pages) of good quality paper, some of which have been completely or partly removed (most, but not all of these excised pages have been found among Darwin's papers in the Cambridge University Library, which now holds the notebook). The cover bears the ironic phrase "Nothing for any purpose" in Darwin's handwriting, in ink. Annotations on the first 113 pages are mainly written in pencil and were, without doubt, written aboard the *Beagle*. The latter pages are in ink and were written after Darwin's return to England in October 1836. Many of the entries are struck through with a single line; this was Darwin's custom with his notes when he had made use of material, perhaps in a publication.

The first four pages are missing, so it is difficult to place an exact date on the opening of the notebook, but there is circumstantial evidence that this was around the time of Darwin's departure from **Australia** in March 1836. Page 5 (the first extant page) mentions "Marine confervae": this was the term Darwin used for marine phytoplankton, possibly blue-green algae. Elsewhere Darwin had written a detailed note on the mass of these organisms that the *Beagle* encountered on March 18, 1836, off Cape Leuwin, the most southwesterly point of Australia. There is also a note on "Granite nodules in Gneiss"; Darwin had made extensive observations of what he referred to as the "gneiss-granite" landscape of King George's Sound (visited March 6–13, 1836). Page 6 mentions a reference to the geology of Australia; page 7 mentions "dikes" (dykes, linear igneous intrusions that he had seen and described several times on his short visit to southwestern Australia). Entries on pages 8 and 9 suggest Darwin that had been reading Dampier's account of his voyage to New Holland, the old name for Australia. If the mid- to late March 1836 date is correct, then the departure from Australia represented a critical point for Darwin. From then on, he was homeward bound. Although a good deal of sound observation and collecting took place in the period April to September 1836 (in the **Cocos (Keeling) islands,** South Africa, **St. Helena and Ascension Island,** for example), there is evidence that at some of the ports of call (**Mauritius** and the **Azores**) his work was somewhat half-hearted. It is as though after Australia the time of detailed observation was ending and the period of sorting, evaluation, and theorizing was beginning.

Be that as it may, the first two-thirds of the book mentions many of the places visited in the last six months of the voyage: the **Cape of Good Hope,** St. Helena, Ascension Island, the **Cape Verde Islands,** and the **Azores.**

Entries in the latter part of the notebook—the part written in ink—can be dated partly on the basis of the names of people Darwin met in London to the first few months of 1837. The words "one species does change into another" appear on page 130 of the notebook. This is consistent with the suggestion that Charles Darwin, as acknowledged in his own writings, was converted to an evolutionary point of view in mid- or late March 1837 (although vague ideas were probably in his mind previously).

The material in the latter part of the book has a strong relationship to the development of Darwin's notion of the transmutability of species; it includes references, brief memoranda, and ideas touching on the geographical distribution of organisms, long-distance dispersal, the plants and animals found on remote islands, and the reproductive methods of organisms—all of which were picked up in his later evolutionary writings. There were also a number of reference to volcanoes, earth movements, and changes in the relative levels of land and sea. These are themes that were followed up in the *Geology of the Voyage of the Beagle,* particularly the volumes on *Coral Islands* and *Volcanic Islands.*

Of the annotations that have a strongly evolutionary flavor, a few examples may be given:

127. Speculate on neutral ground of 2 ostriches; bigger one encroaches on smaller:—change not progressive: produced at one blow.
129. Should urge that extinct Llama owed its death not to change of circumstances.
130. The same kind of relation that the common ostrich bears to (Pettisse . . .): extinct Guanaco to recent: in former case position, in latter time. (or changes consequent on lapse) being the relation.—As in first case distinct species inosculate, so must we believe ancient ones: not gradual change or degeneration. from circumstances: if one species does change into another it must be per saltum—or species may perish. = This [inosculation] representation of species important, each its own limit & represented.

All this is somewhat difficult to decode. Darwin is suggesting that the relationship between the "common ostrich" (i.e., the greater or common **rhea**, *Rhea americana*) and the "petisse" (lesser rhea, Darwin's rhea, *Pterocnemia pennata,* formerly *Rhea darwinii*), which had two distinct distributions in South America, is in some ways analogous to that between the extinct llama or "guanaco" to the modern form. (Darwin had taken back bones of the extinct form which had been identified and described by **Richard Owen.**) In both cases, Darwin seems to be hypothesizing that they might have a common ancestor: he uses the word inosculate, which is a medical term (perhaps picked up in his Edinburgh Medical School days) used for the joining or branching of blood vessels. However, he seems to be thinking in terms of a sudden or saltatory change because he uses the words per saltum (by a leap or in fits and starts) and "produced at one blow." At this early stage in Darwin's development, his notion of evolution seems to be closer to the **punctuated equilibrium** theory of **Stephen Jay**

Gould nearly 150 years later (the term **saltatory evolution** is sometimes used). Darwin's gradualist approach to evolution strengthened later.

Possibly the Red Notebook was filled by about May 1837; some of the themes he develops in it are taken up by later notebooks in the period 1837 to 1839. Notebook A followed up some of the geological themes; in Notebook B (followed by C, D, and E), he continued to record his thoughts and speculations on the species question. Notebook M (possibly opened mid-1838) and N, which followed it, included speculations on behavior. Darwin believed that adaptive change in some cases might be first manifest in the behavior of animals rather than their form and appearance.

The Red Notebook, therefore, opened while aboard the *Beagle,* perhaps within sight of Australia, the land that often has been used to illustrate evolutionary concepts, stands as a the first milestone on the road that led—over 20 years later and through many drafts—to the publication of *On the Origin of Species.* It is, therefore, one of the most important documents in the history of science.

FURTHER READING

Herbert, Sandra. 1980. *The Red Notebook of Charles Darwin.* London: British Museum (Natural History).

Religion in the Life of Charles Darwin

Darwin wrote relatively little on the subject of religion, and some of what he wrote is difficult to interpret. His views changed over time, and, although he certainly felt that evolution presented a set of ideas incompatible with the acceptance of parts of the Bible as the literal truth, he maintained that he was never an atheist.

Although his father Robert has been described as an agnostic or atheist who did not widely advertise his views, Charles's early life was somewhat conventional from a religious point of view. It would not have done for the family of a leading doctor and prominent member of the Shrewsbury gentry to attract too much attention. The young Charles was baptized in St. Chad's Anglican Church, Shrewsbury (Church of England). Susannah, his mother, however was a Unitarian and took her children to the Unitarian chapel: he went for a couple of years to a school run by the Unitarian minister. However, his mother died when he was eight, and the Unitarian influence probably waned. The headmaster of Shrews-

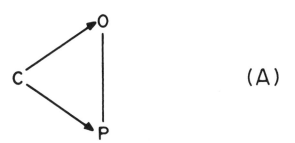

(A)

An attempt to depict some of Charles Darwin's changing views in diagrammatic form, after Howard Gruber. A. 1832 and before. The Creator (C) made the organic world (O) and the physical world (P). O is perfectly adapted to P: Natural Theology.

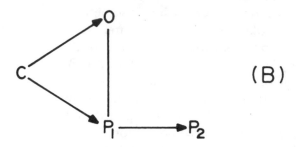

1832–1834. During geological explorations in South America, the early *Beagle* voyage. The physical world undergoes continuous physical change, in accordance with natural laws summarized in Charles Lyell's *Principles of Geology*.

(B)

bury School, where he was sent when he was a few years older, was Samuel Butler—a Church of England clergyman with a traditional outlook.

In **Edinburgh,** the young Darwin was exposed to the free-thinking Dr. Grant and to nonconformity of various forms. But studies at Edinburgh medical school were not a success, and Charles left unqualified. He was then dispatched to Christ's College, Cambridge—the heart of the Anglican establishment, as many of the University's teachers were clergy—so that he might train to be a Church of England priest. There is every reason to suppose that his views while at Cambridge were entirely conventional. He attended King's College Chapel evensong, much enjoying the singing. He studied some theology and Greek. He read (and was impressed by) **William Paley**'s *Natural Theology.* His cousin **William Darwin Fox,** to whom he was very close, went into the Church of England priesthood, and the *Beagle* voyage was originally intended to be an extended intermission between undergraduate study and commencing work in a parish.

While on the *Beagle,* Darwin had a reputation for being rather traditional in his religious views among the officers, although he was not as fervent as the evangelical captain, **Robert FitzRoy.** He attended divine service when it was held on board and had a Greek New Testament in his possession. He proudly asserted his Protestant identity when discussing religious matters with Catholics in South America. He strongly approved of the work of the missionaries he encountered in **Tahiti** and **New Zealand,** and, in discussing their work among the **Maori** on New Zealand, wrote of the way in which these people had been affected by "the excellence of the Christian religion."

However, the die was cast and he became set on a career in science rather than in the Church, while on the voyage. As early as September 1833, his sister Catherine, hearing of his exploits, wrote to him:

> I have great fears how far you will stand the quiet clerical life you used to say you would return to.

Doubts grew as he developed his evolutionary ideas while living in London and Cambridge in the early 1840s. There were a number of people in the intellectual salons of the time (including Darwin's brother **Erasmus**) who professed atheistic, or what would now be called agnostic, views. Some of his developing thoughts can be traced in the terse statements in his notebooks such as, "Mine is a bold theory" and "Origin of man now proved.

Metaphysic must flourish.—He who understands baboon would do more towards metaphysics than Locke." As he struggled with these ideas, he was clearly realizing the religious and philosophical significance of his notions. If his explanations of the development of life on Earth were correct, the accounts of the creation in the book of Genesis must be mythical.

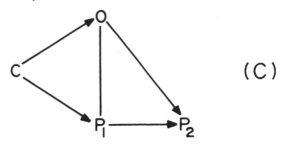

(C)

1835. Across the Pacific. The activities of organisms, as exemplified by corals in coral reefs, contribute to changes in the physical world.

His interest in psychology and in **animal behavior** sometime led him in similar directions. Humans, like many animals, are social beings, and many aspects of human behavior, including morality, were instinctive and had survival value. He reflected that moral acts by humans were as instinctive as a deer's bark warning the rest of the herd of the advance of a predator.

Could it be, he wondered, that the basic Christian precepts such as thou shalt love thy neighbor as thyself and the Golden Rule to do to others as you would have them do to you were the result of "sexual, parental and social instincts"? At one stage, he enigmatically noted "Zoology itself is now purely theological." Perhaps "theology is purely zoological" might have been a more accurate expression of his position, but one catches the drift.

He knew he was treading on dangerous ground and that too loud an exposition of these ideas might have implications for his personal happiness. He was courting his cousin Emma Wedgwood, who was a devout young woman and who worried about his strange notions. In his *Autobiography*, Charles notes that his father cautioned him "to conceal carefully doubts" that he might have. Charles obviously ignored his advice. She wrote to him shortly before they were married (November 21–22, 1838) a loving letter:

> My dear Charles . . . When I am with you I think all melancholy thoughts keep out of my head but since you are gone some sad ones have forced themselves in, of fear that our opinions on the most important subject should differ widely. My reason tells me that honest & conscientious doubts cannot be a sin, but I feel it would be a painful void between us. I thank you from my heart for your openness with me & I should dread the feeling you were concealing your opinions from me from fear of giving me pain. It is perhaps foolish of me to say this much but, my own dear Charley, we now do belong to each other & I cannot help being open with you. Will you do me a favour? Yes I am sure you will; it is to read our Saviour's farewell discourse to his disciples which begins at the end of the 13th Chap of John. It is so full of love and devotion & every beautiful feeling. It is the part of the New Testament I love best. This is a whim of mine; it would give me great pleasure, though I can hardly tell why. (*Correspondence of Charles Darwin*, Vol. 2, 123, Cambridge University Library, Darwin Archive; punctuation slightly edited)

Although Charles's reply to Emma's letter is lost, it is clear from subsequent correspondence that he complied with her request, and his responses were satisfactory to her: "I believe I agree with every word you say." Anyway they were married, according to Anglican rites, slightly modified to cope with Unitarian susceptibilities, by their cousin, the Reverend Allen Wedgwood, at St. Peter's Church, close to Emma's home at Maer, on January 29, 1839.

Nevertheless, uneasiness on both sides persisted. In what Charles described as a "beautiful letter" about a month after their marriage, Emma wrote that she knew that he was "acting conscientiously & sincerely . . . trying to learn the truth" but felt that his opinion was not yet fully formed. She was concerned that the fact that his elder brother Erasmus had gone before into religious skepticism might be having an influence on Charles. She went on:

> May not the habit in scientific pursuits of believing nothing till it is proved, influence your mind to much in other things that cannot be proved in the same way, & which if true are likely to be above our comprehension? (*Correspondence of Charles Darwin,* Vol. 2, 172, Cambridge University Library, Darwin Archive)

On matters of morality and conduct to others, they were in complete agreement.

A little later, deeply concerned for the well-being of her husband's immortal soul, Emma wrote:

> Everything that concerns you concerns me & I should be most unhappy if I thought we did not belong to each other forever.

Darwin's belief in Christianity as divine revelation withered gradually; one aspect that particularly troubled him. The New Testament, he wrote, toward the end of his life, asserted that those who did not believe, "and this would include my Father, Brother and almost all my best friends, will be everlastingly punished." This, he thought, a "damnable doctrine." On another occasion, he suggested that the remnants of Christianity remained with him until he was 40. He was ambivalent in some ways. He supported the local Sunday school and contributed to a fund for the rebuilding of the vicarage. He had no objection to members of his family attending the village church in Downe; sometimes he accompanied them but did not enter himself. When directly questioned on religious matters in later

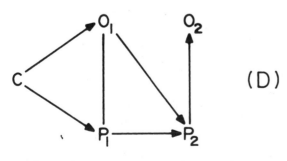

1835 to early 1837. The voyage home and immediately after. Changes in the organic world imply changes in the physical world, if adaptation is to be maintained; the physical environment induces appropriate biological adaptations.

life, he was sometimes evasive, saying something like every man must judge for himself. In one letter, he stated that a person could be "An ardent theist and an evolutionist." He wrote also that he had "never been an atheist ... denying the existence of a God." He felt that the term agnostic (a term invented by his friend **Thomas Huxley**) "would be a more correct description" of the state of his mind. In 1870, he admitted that his religious views were "a muddle"; on one hand, he found no evidence for *beneficent* design in nature: he felt that the struggle for existence was blind,

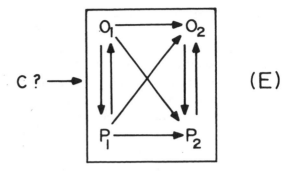

(E)

March 1837 and later. The physical and organic worlds are continuously evolving and interacting. The Creator (assuming he exists) may have set all natural systems into being, but does not intervene in their operation. Drawn at Geography Department, University of Western Australia.

wasteful, and cruel. On the other hand, in letters to his American friend **Asa Gray,** he felt the universe could not have resulted from pure chance. There are signs that at times he felt that the initial creation of life in the remote past might have been through some creative intervention.

Many urged him to be more forthright in opposition to religion, but he always demurred. The country gentleman and squire within him saw established religion as a force for social cohesion and stability. He had no wish to upset Emma, and many of his friends, acquaintances, and scientific correspondents were Anglican clergy, as were some of his and Emma's relatives.

Some say that his long delay in publishing *On the Origin* was due to his not wishing to upset his wife; this may be so, but the need to collect massive evidence, to establish his scientific reputation through other work, and the years spent on his definitive work on barnacles provide other possible explanations.

Darwin was a complex character: this complexity is reflected in his religious views and in much else in his life and work.

See also: Darwin Emma; Darwinism and Theology; Darwin's Death and Westminster Abbey Funeral

Rheas

A group of large flightless birds found in South America; they are ratites and are thus related to the ostrich in Africa, the emus and cassowaries of Australia, the kiwis and extinct moas of New Zealand, and the extinct elephant birds of Madagascar. The ratites' southern distribution provides evidence for the former existence of a continuous southern continent, Gondwana. Darwin encountered rheas in South America; he collected specimens and wrote at some length on their form, habits, and distribution—both at the time and subsequently.

Two species occur in the southern part of South America: the greater or common rhea (*Rhea americana*) and the lesser or Darwin's rhea (*Pterocnemia pennata*). The former is around 6 feet (180 centimeters) in height, the latter little over half that size. The Andean form of the smaller species is considered by some ornithologists to be a distinct species—*Pterocnemia garleppi*.

The significance of rheas in a consideration of Darwin's work is twofold. First, he described their behavior in some detail—their social structures, nesting habits, and vocalizations. He devoted more attention to their behavior than he does to many other species he encountered on the *Beagle* voyage. In emphasizing behavior of animals (mammals, reptiles, birds, insects, and fish) he was ahead of his time; this had important implications for his later work, both on evolution and more generally on psychology. Second, his observations on the distribution of the two species and their similarity of form led him to speculate that they might have had a common ancestor. Some of Darwin's earliest evolutionary writing thus concerns rheas. Many of his writings refer to ostriches, although the African ostrich is appreciably different.

John Gould, when compiling the Birds volume of ***The Zoology of the Voyage of the Beagle,*** named the smaller species *Rhea darwinii* not realizing that an earlier (and therefore priority) scientific name existed. Nevertheless, the eponym Darwin's rhea has stuck.

> This species . . . differs in many respects from the Rhea americana. It is smaller, and the general tinge of the plumage is a light brown in place of grey; each feather being conspicuously tipped with white. The bill is considerably smaller and especially less broad at its base. (*The Zoology of the Voyage of the Beagle, Part III: Birds,* 1842. London: Smith, Elder & Co., 123)

There is much further detail on the structure of the difference between the two species, particularly the legs and feet.

Here follow a few extracts from Darwin's diary of his encounters with rheas on the plains of the pampas in 1833 and 1834.

> They [a group of gauchos] gave us an Ostrich egg, & before we left them they found another nest or rather depository in which there were 24 of the great eggs. [a few days later he found a nest with 27.] It is an undoubted fact that many female Ostriches lay in the same spot, thus forming one of their collections. (*Diary,* September 8, 1834)
>
> I saw some deer & Ostriches; the latter made an odd deep noise. (*Diary,* September 10, 1834)
>
> At this time of year, the eggs of the ostrich are their [the gauchos'] chief prize. In this one day they found 64—out of which 44 were in two nests, the rest scattered about in ones or twos. (*Diary,* September 15, 1834)
>
> I came quite close to an Ostrich on her nest; but did not see her till she rose up & stretched across the country. (*Diary,* September 25, 1834)
>
> We crossed some fine plains abounding with cattle; here also were many Ostriches. I saw several flocks of between 20 & 30. When seen on the brow

of a hill against the clear sky they form a fine spectacle. Some of them are very tame; if, after approaching close, you suddenly gallop in pursuit, it is beautiful to see them, as a sailor would express it "up with their helm" and make all sail, by expanding their wings right down the wind. (*Diary*, May 11, 1833)

Although Darwin is appreciating the aesthetic appeal of these creatures, within the anecdotes are perceptive notes on their locomotion, display, breeding, and group behavior that he used later.

For further comment on the significance of the rheas in the development of Darwin's evolutionary ideas, see the article on the **Red Notebook.**

River Plate

River on the east coast of South America. The name is also used for the district surrounding the estuary.

The *Beagle* visited both Monte Video (Uruguay) and Buenos Aires (Argentina) on the north and south sides of the estuary of the River Plate several times in July and August 1832. Both countries had gained their independence from Spanish rule less than two decades previously (1825 and 1816, respectively), and both capitals had experienced a succession of revolutions and were in a highly disturbed state. Darwin recorded that a few years previously in Buenos Aires (Darwin often wrote Buenos Ayres), "they had 14 revolutions in 12 months." The government in Monte Video was "a military usurpation." The crackle of muskets was heard, and, on entering Buenos Aires, the *Beagle* was fired on (it was alleged by the local authorities that this was a signal that the ship should pause for a quarantine inspection). When he was allowed on shore, Darwin thought the landscape was uninteresting; it reminded him of the flat country of eastern England. On climbing Monte Video, he recorded:

The view . . . is one of the most uninteresting I ever beheld. Not a tree or a . . . trace of cultivation give cheerfulness to the scene. An undulating green plain and large herds of cattle [are to be seen]. Whoever has seen Cambridgeshire [one of the flattest parts of England and a region Darwin knew well], if in his mind he changes arable into pasture and roots out every tree, may say he has seen Monte Video. Although . . . there is a charm in the unconfined feeling of walking over the boundless turf plain.

Daisies, thistles, and rushes broke the monotony of the turf, which was browsed by cattle. Then, as now, an important economic activity of the country was raising livestock.

Darwin recorded:

The navigation of the Plata is difficult, owing to there being no landmarks, the water generally shoal [i.e., shallow] and running in currents, and the number of banks in the whole course. We saw several old wrecks which now serve as buoys to guide other ships.

But, then, hydrographic survey was the mission of the voyage.

Royal Navy in the Nineteenth Century

Of the British armed services, the navy is the oldest is therefore often referred to as the Senior Service. From the early eighteenth century until 1956, it was the largest and most powerful naval force in the world, playing a leading role in the establishment of the British Empire as a dominant power in the late eighteenth, nineteenth, and early twentieth centuries. Even at the start of the twenty-first century, despite stringent economies, the Royal Navy claimed to be the world's second largest navy (the U.S. Navy being the largest).

King Alfred the Great has traditionally been identified as the founder of the British navy, for in A.D. 897, he had a number of ships built to counter Viking raids along the east and south coasts of England. However, the establishment was not a permanent one, and, for the next seven or eight centuries, naval forces were raised and organized on a more-or-less ad hoc basis in times of need, usually to deal with threats of invasion from or other rivalries with France, Spain, or The Netherlands.

A permanent British Naval Service did not exist until the middle of the seventeenth century, when the Fleet Royal was taken under the control of Parliament with the defeat, and eventual execution, of Charles I in the English Civil War.

In the early eighteenth century, the Royal Navy had more ships than other European navies of the time, although it suffered acute financial problems; these affected many of its operations and much of its administration. As the eighteenth century continued, however, improved means of financing the Royal Navy were developed through the issue of bonds. With much improved finances, the Royal Navy was able to develop the ability to counteract the movements of other countries' naval forces by the means of blockade, with the support of efficient naval logistics, the development of superior naval tactics and strategy, and a very high morale. Thus, the navy developed an almost unprecedented power over the oceans from 1805 to 1914. It came to be said that Britannia ruled the waves. The Napoleonic Wars saw the Royal Navy reach a peak of efficiency, dominating the naval forces of Britain's adversaries. The height of the Navy's achievements came on October 21, 1805, at the Battle of Trafalgar, where a combined fleet of French and Spanish ships was defeated by a smaller but more experienced British naval fleet under the command of Admiral Horatio Nelson.

With the defeat of France came the Pax Britannica. The role of the navy shifted to combating piracy, discouraging the slave trade, and pursuing exploration and particularly hydrography, notwithstanding occasional operations such as naval bombardments during the Crimean War.

The establishment of the Hydrographic Department within the Admiralty (the government department responsible for the navy) occurred in 1795. The work of surveying was, however, usually done by the navy's normal vessels and officers, although often with ships that were specially equipped and manned. With the expansion of the Empire, under the protection of the Royal Navy, came trade, and both trading merchant ships and the navy's own operations generated a strong demand for accurate hydrographic charts.

The first head of hydrography was Alexander Dalrymple (1737–1808), whose tenure in office seems to have been somewhat contentious. It is said he only provided charts for areas in which he was interested (for example, the East Indies) despite the urgent need for charts of areas of greater importance for trade. (Dalrymple was a geographer rather than a naval officer, as were some of his successors). On his death in 1808, he was replaced by Thomas Hurd, followed by Edward Parry (1790–1855) the arctic explorer, and then by Sir Francis Beaufort (1774–1857), who took over in 1829, retaining the office of hydrographer for 25 years. These men established the reputation of British Admiralty Chart. Captain **Robert FitzRoy,** commander of HMS *Beagle* on her second surveying voyage, reported to Beaufort, with whom he seems to have had a good rapport. Following the voyage on which FitzRoy and Darwin sailed (1831–1836), the *Beagle* sailed again under the command of their shipmate, John Lort Stokes, another brilliant hydrographic surveyor, to survey the coast of Australia—then an increasingly important location of British colonies—between 1837 and 1843.

At the beginning of the nineteenth century, the Royal Navy consisted of sailing ships, although the development of the screw propeller allowed the direct application of steam power to the naval ships, and the navy's first screw-driven steamship, HMS *Arrogant,* was launched in April 1848. Captain FitzRoy was put in command of *Arrogant* in March 1849, holding the appointment for a year. This could be seen as an important early step in the development of a modern, mechanized navy.

FURTHER READING

Hordern, Marsden. 1989. *Mariners Are Warned! John Lort Stokes and H.M.S. Beagle in Australia 1837–1843.* Melbourne, Australia: Melbourne University Publishing.

Mellersh, H.E.L. 1968. *FitzRoy of the Beagle.* London: Rupert Hart-Davis.

Royal Society

Founded in 1660, the Royal Society describes itself as the independent scientific academy of the United Kingdom, dedicated to promoting excellence in science. The granting of a fellowship by the Royal Society is considered the highest scientific honor in Britain (and the British Commonwealth).

The origins of the Royal Society are to be found in a group of natural philosophers who began meeting in the 1640s to discuss the ideas of Francis Bacon (1561–1626), statesman, philosopher, and the father of inductive reasoning. Its official foundation date is November 28, 1660, when a group of 12 met at Gresham College in London after a lecture by Christopher Wren, the architect and astronomer, and decided to found "a Colledge [*sic*] for the Promoting of Physico-Mathematicall Experimentall Learning." This group included Wren, physicist Robert Boyle, John Wilkins (clergyman, astronomer, and mathematician), Sir Robert Moray (soldier, chemist); all were men of brilliance, and the assembly constituted an extraordinary group of polymaths.

The Society met regularly to witness experiments and discuss what would now be called scientific topics. The first "curator of experiments" was physicist Robert Hooke. It was Robert Moray (the first president) who informed the King, Charles II, of the venture and secured his approval and strong encouragement. The name Royal Society first appears in print in 1661, and in the second Royal Charter of 1663, the Society is referred to as The Royal Society of London for Improving Natural Knowledge.

Traditionally the Society played (and still plays) an extremely important and influential role in national and international science policy. The core of the Society has always been its fellows. In the early years of the Society, the conditions for obtaining a fellowship were somewhat vague. Sir Joseph Banks, Captain James Cook's botanist, become president in 1778, and remained in the position for over 40 years until his death in 1820; he was in favor of maintaining a mixture among the fellowship of working scientists and wealthy amateurs who might become their financial backers. This approach fell away as the nineteenth century wore on, and in 1847 the Society decided that from then on fellows would be elected solely on the merit of their scientific work. The criteria for elevation to a fellowship of the Royal Society have been, since then, extremely high, and thus the Society has included the scientific elite of Britain (and also the British Commonwealth, for there have been, and still are, Australian and New Zealand fellows, although those countries have developed their own scientific academies).

The Royal Society has always attached importance to scientific publication. In 1665, the first issue of *Philosophical Transactions* was edited by Henry Oldenburg, the Society's secretary. The Society took over publication some years later, and *Philosophical Transactions of the Royal Society* is now the oldest scientific journal in continuous publication, maintaining a very high reputation.

The history of the Darwin family is intimately associated with the Royal Society. The following Darwins were elected to fellowships.

Erasmus Darwin (1731–1802): elected 1761
Robert Waring Darwin (1766–1848): elected 1788
Charles Robert Darwin (1809–1882): elected 1839
Sir George Howard Darwin (1845–1912): elected 1879
Sir Francis Darwin (1848–1925): elected 1882
Sir Horace Darwin (1851–1928): elected 1903
Sir Charles Galton Darwin (1887–1962): elected 1922

Although the criteria for admission were different in the eighteenth century, there was at least one fellow of the Royal Society in each generation of the Darwin family for five generations; in one generation, there were three. There was at least one Darwin who was a fellow, without a break, for 200 years; their specialties included botany, zoology, geology, medicine, astronomy, mathematics, engineering, and physics. Their achievements within the society were also considerable. Charles Darwin was awarded the Society's Royal Medal in 1853 and the Copley Medal in 1864. His grandson, Sir Charles Galton Darwin, received the Royal Medal in 1935. Son Francis received the Darwin Medal, named after his father, in 1912, and another son replicated his father's achievements, receiving the Royal Medal in 1884 and the Copley Medal 1911. Several members of the family took important roles in the governance of the Society. Charles was vice president 1854 to 1856; son George held the position 1908 to 1909; and grandson Charles did likewise 1939 to 1941. This constitutes a combined family record that is unique.

FURTHER READING

Gribbin, J. 2005. *The Fellowship: The Story of a Revolution*. London: Allen Lane/Penguin.

Lomax, R. 2002. *The Invisible College: The Royal Society, Freemasonry and the Birth of Modern Science*. London: Headline.

Lynch, W. T. 2002. *Solomon's Child: Method in the Early Royal Society of London*. Stanford, CA: Stanford University Press.

S

Sedgwick, Adam (1785–1873)

Pioneer geologist, **Cambridge University** professor, evangelical clergyman, teacher, and friend of Charles Darwin.

There were, until the first half of the twentieth century, families in which for many generations all the sons became clergymen of the Church of England, and the daughters married into parsonages. Clerical families thus comprised a tight network, held together by the bonds of kinship and marriage. This network, in the Victorian period, held a close grip on England's intellectual life. Adam Sedgwick was in many ways a typical product of this network. He was the son of a country clergyman, the vicar of Dent, in Yorkshire, in northern England. As a boy, he wandered through the Yorkshire countryside, collecting natural history specimens. He attended school in the nearby town of Sedbergh and then proceeded to Trinity College, Cambridge. He became a fellow of the College (i.e., a member of its governing body) in 1810, and became an ordained clergyman in 1817. He was appointed Woodwardian Professor of Geology in 1818. He had no special knowledge of geology, and he is said to have remarked at the time: "Hitherto I have never turned a stone; henceforth I shall leave no stone unturned." And so it was. He was a giant of what has been called the Heroic Age of geology, a period when the main geological time periods were defined and named, and fundamental concepts underlying the subject were established. Sedgwick was responsible for describing the Cambrian system (from Cambria, the Latin name for Wales, where most of the fieldwork was done)—the series of rocks containing fossils of some of the oldest and most primitive forms of life. This work led to a painful dispute with another pioneer geologist Roderick Impey Murchison, who, based largely on the fossil content of the rocks (Sedgwick had concentrated on rock types), had identified the Silurian (named after an ancient Welsh Borderland tribe, the Silures). Muchison's Silurian overlapped with parts of Sedgwick's Cambrian. The dispute became heated and took years to resolve. An eventual solution was achieved when Charles Lapworth described the disputed series of rocks as comprising the Ordovician (named after another ancient tribe, the Ordovices).

While these researches were proceeding, Sedgwick and the young Charles Darwin became friends; **John Stevens Henslow** encouraged this friendship, and, in the summer of 1831, Sedgwick spent the night at the Darwin family home in **Shrewsbury,** before taking Darwin on a geological tour through **North Wales,** providing him with an excellent grounding in field geology—the basis for much of Darwin's geological work while he was on the *Beagle* voyage. While Darwin was voyaging, crates of rock and fossil specimens were sent back by ship, and Sedgwick was able to view these. He wrote to Darwin's family: "He is doing admirably in S. America, & has already sent home a collection above all praise." Darwin was ever-after grateful for this training and support.

The Reverend Professor Adam Sedgwick, Darwin's mentor who taught him almost all the geology he ever knew in two weeks in North Wales but later read *On the Origin* "with pain." National Portrait Gallery, London.

Sedgwick was elected a canon of Norwich Cathedral (Norwich is a cathedral city approximately 60 miles [about 100 kilometers] northeast of Cambridge) and remained an active clergyman. Some geologists sought to marry their Christian faith with their scientific outlook through the doctrine of catastrophism—the notion that the history of the Earth was best understood in terms of occasional cataclysmic events, each of which destroyed much of the Earth's life, before a new assemblage of creatures was brought into existence. Some even saw biblical events such as the flood, the destruction of the Walls of Jericho and of the cities of Sodom and Gomorrah as events in this series of catastrophes. While Sedgwick might not have completely embraced the views of French anatomist and geologist **Georges Cuvier** (1769–1832), who strongly promoted these views, he at least initially opposed the ideas of **Charles Lyell** (1797–

1875), who emphasized gradual change, gradualism or uniformitarianism. In Sedgwick's earlier career, he might have been described as a diluvialist— one who attributed some of the Earth's features to the biblical flood—but he abandoned these ideas as he came to appreciate the immense age of the Earth.

Despite their long friendship, he wrote in an outspoken manner to Charles Darwin after the publication of *On the Origin of Species* in November 1859. In a long letter, he wrote of how much he admired the "great knowledge; store of facts; capital views of the correlations of various parts of nature; admirable hints about the diffusions, thro' wide regions, of nearly related organic beings" that the book revealed, but that he had:

> read your book with more pain than pleasure. Parts of it I admired greatly; parts of it I laughed at till my sides were almost sore; other parts I read with absolute sorrow, because I think them utterly false and mischievous—You have deserted—after a start in that tram-road of solid physical truth—the true path of induction.

It was the materialist nature of the theory of natural selection that distressed Sedgwick most, because he thought that it neglected humanity's spiritual dimension. He continued:

> There is a moral or metaphysical part of nature as well as a physical. A man who denies this is deep in the mire of folly.

It obviously grieved Sedgwick to disagree with his friend and former student so fundamentally. He wrote in such a forthright way only because he thought that Darwin was "a good-tempered & truth loving man." (*Correspondence*, Vol 7, 396–398; Cambridge University Library, Darwin Archive)

Adam Sedgwick was an inspiring and brilliant lecturer and teacher; he pioneered field-teaching with students. Some of his excursions took place on horseback. Groups of up to seventy mounted undergraduates would gallop across the Cambridgeshire countryside, listening, in the course of a day, to several lectures. The last was given from the roof of Ely Cathedral, where a wide view of the landscape could be obtained. At one stage in his career, Sedgwick stated: "I cannot promise to teach you all geology, I can only fire your imaginations."

And so he did. He held the chair of geology for 55 years (until his death); his legacy was enormous and, in some ways, it still continues. Generations of geologists (and other scientists) were trained by him, including notables such as **Charles Kingsley** (1818–1875).

Adam Sedgwick, although a creationist, believed in the existence of extremely long stretches of geological time. He understood the importance of fossils for correlation of geological strata. He pioneered fieldwork and treasured his students. A superb lecturer, he opened his lectures to women (an innovation in mid-Victorian England). He was president of the **Geological Society of London** (1829–1831). In 1845, he became vice master of Trinity College (Cambridge's wealthiest and most prestigious college). From this influential position he campaigned for the admission of non-Anglicans to Cambridge (a brave posture for a priest of the Church of England) and for the modernization of the university's academic programs. His importance and influence is remembered in the naming of the Cambridge University geological collection the Sedgwick Museum of Geology.

Sedimentary Rocks

Rocks formed from lithified or consolidated sediments, particles formed by the disintegration of preexisting rocks and their redeposition or as the result of biological activity.

Sedimentary rocks are one of the three great classes of rocks—the others being **igneous rocks** and **metamorphic rocks**—and are formed in three main ways: by the deposition (through the action of water, wind, or ice) of the weathered remains of other rocks (clastic sedimentary rocks); by the deposition of the results of the activities of organisms (such as corals); and by precipitation from solutions. Examples of sedimentary rocks include common types such as conglomerate, sandstone, shales, chalk, and limestone. Sedimentary rocks cover about three-quarters of the Earth's surface, and they constitute about 5 percent of the volume of the Earth's crust. The structures (such as ripple marks) and the fossils that sedimentary rocks contain provide evidence of the nature of the geological past. Darwin had been instructed in the interpretation of this geological evidence in the summer of 1831, by professors John Henslow and Adam Sedgwick, particularly in a fortnight's tour in North Wales with Sedgwick. Darwin obviously enjoyed this instruction and put it to good use. The young Darwin wrote to Henslow in March 1834, not long after leaving Tierra del Fuego:

> I am quite charmed with Geology but like the wise animal between the two bundles of hay, I do not know which to like the best, the old crystalline group of rocks [i.e., igneous and metamorphic rocks] or the softer & fossiliferous beds. (*Correspondence,* Vol. 1, 365, original in Royal Botanic Gardens, Kew)

A single example of Darwin's powers of observation and a description of sedimentary rocks must suffice. Here he is on the "softer and fossiliferous" sedimentaries, examined intensively when he landed on San Sebastian's Bay, on the eastern shore of Tierra del Fuego. The remarks are based on his notes but were polished for publication:

> along the eastern coast of Tierra del Fuego . . . [the rock] probably belongs to the great Patagonian Tertiary formation. . . . The cliffs in Sebastian's Bay are

200 feet in height, are composed of fine sandstones often in curvilinear layers, including hard concretions of calcareous sandstone, and layers of gravel. In these beds there are fragments of wood, legs of crabs, barnacles encrusted with corallines still partially retaining their colour, imperfect fragments of Pholas distinct from any known species, and of a Venus. . . . Leaves of trees are numerous between the laminae of muddy sandstone. (*Geology of the Voyage of the Beagle,* Vol. 3, 117–118; *Pholas* and *Venus* are types of shells)

A modern geological map shows that this area is indeed underlain largely by Tertiary rocks (i.e., rocks up to about 65 million years old).

Shrewsbury

Market town in Shropshire, on the border between England and Wales; birthplace and childhood home of Charles Darwin.

Shrewsbury is a picturesque and historic town built on a defensive site on a tight bend in the River Severn at the bridging point on a major route between England and Wales (there is an English Bridge and a Welsh Bridge). Traditionally, Shrewsbury has supported light industries such as brewing and tanning that linked the town to the surrounding farmlands. A conspicuous red sandstone eleventh-century castle contributes to the town's distinctive character, as do the winding medieval streets lined by the historic churches and the multitude of Elizabethan half-timbered houses.

Today the town owes much of its comfortable prosperity to its historical and literary associations, which have contributed to an important tourist trade. East of town a short walk across the English Bridge stands Shrewsbury Abbey—Benedictine Abbey of St. Peter and St. Paul—which, although founded in 1083, has more recently found worldwide fame as the home of Ellis Peters's fictional character Brother Cadfael, whose chronicles (detective stories with a medieval setting) are set in, and were inspired by, the town of Shrewsbury. St. Chad's Church, rebuilt in 1788 after the collapse of the tower of the original 1,000-year-old building was where the infant Charles Darwin was baptized. The Mount (a large red brick house overlooking the River Severn) was built by Charles's wealthy doctor and businessman father in about 1800, and was the naturalist's birthplace. It is currently used by the local tax authorities. In the High Street is the Unitarian Chapel, attended by the young Darwin and his mother.

Shrewsbury School (one of England's most famous public schools) was founded in 1552; it was attended by such notables as Sir Philip Sidney, Elizabethan poet and diplomat; Admiral John Benbow; Samuel Butler, satirist and poet; and Charles Darwin, of whom a bronze statue was erected in 1897 outside the old school building. A younger Darwin, Galapagos iguanas at his feet, was erected in the grounds of the new set of school buildings on the outskirts of the town in 2000. The Bell stone is to be seen in the precincts of Morris Hall. This large boulder is a glacial erratic brought to its present position by an ice sheet in the ice age. It was shown to the school-boy Darwin by a Mr. Cotton and is said to be Darwin's introduction to geology.

The town has a population of about 100,000; its importance as a destination for visitors has been enhanced recently by the establishment of an annual Darwin Festival of exhibitions, lectures, and other events. Nevertheless, the character of parts of the town remains much as it did when members of the Darwin family walked its streets 200 years ago.

Sketch of 1842

Darwin's first coherent outline of his evolutionary ideas.

Darwin probably became converted to an evolutionary outlook in the first few months of 1837 and was working on his theories, as well as proceeding with other important projects, in the months and years that followed. In late May and June 1842, almost certainly simply to bring together and clarify his own ideas, he wrote a brief outline while staying at Maer (his wife's family home) and at **Shrewsbury** (his father's home). It is written with a soft pencil on poor-quality paper. It was written rapidly and is almost illegible in places: words are left out or incomplete. There are many erasures and corrections in the 35 pages. He probably never envisaged it being read by anyone but himself. The original is held in the Darwin Archive in Cambridge University Library.

The apparent division of the manuscript into sections, its structure, some of the headings, and some of the phrasing render it a precursor to his later evolutionary writings (e.g., the **Essay of 1844,** the 1858 presentation to the **Linnean Society of London,** and *On the Origin of Species* itself). The sketch commences with a section "On variation under domestication and on the principles of selection," in which he discusses variation in organisms and its inheritance. He then continues with "On variation in a state of nature and on the natural means of selection," in which the term natural selection is introduced, and examples are given; possible objections to the theory of selection are mentioned. He notes that "instincts and other mental attributes" vary as well as external features. He then considers the geological (and paleontological evidence), admitting it to be very incomplete, together with that from the geographical distribution of organisms. He noted the distinctiveness of **Australia,** at present as well as in the past, and the biological poverty of remote **islands:** "How unlike [are] these islands in nature to neighbouring lands." He sees a pattern that may reflect evolutionary history in the similarities between the great classes of organisms and refers to the idea that the development of the individual may reflect its evolutionary history:

> This general unity of type in the great groups of organisms . . . displays itself in a most striking manner in the stages through which the foetus passes. In

early stage[s], the wing of bat, hoof, hand paddle are not to be distinguished. At a still earlier stage there is no difference between fish, bird, etc., and mammal.

Acknowledging the essential cruelty of nature, he remarks toward the conclusion of the sketch the importance of competition and conflict to evolution:

> From death, famine, rapine and the concealed war of nature we can see that the highest good, which we can conceive, the creation of the higher animals has directly come.

At the conclusion, Darwin states:

> There is a simple grandeur in the view of life with its powers of growth, assimilation and reproduction, being originally breathed into matter under one or a few forms, and that whilst this our planet has gone circling on according to fixed laws, and land and water, in a cycle of change, have gone on replacing each other, that from so simple an origin, through the process of gradual selection of infinitesimal changes, endless forms most beautiful and most wonderful have been evolved.

This remarkable sentence, almost mystical in its tone, is almost identical to that which concludes the final chapter of the first edition of *On the Origin of Species*, remaining almost unchanged in subsequent editions.

The Sketch of 1842, written quickly in the early summer of that year, thus contains all the principle components of the full theory, published in full detail over seventeen years later. It is a remarkable document in the evolution of evolutionary theory.

FURTHER READING

de Beer, Gavin, ed. 1958. *Evolution by Natural Selection*. Cambridge, England: Cambridge University Press. This contains the text of the Sketch in full at pp. 41–88.

Smith, Adam (1723–1790)

Moral philosopher and economist, founder of the Scottish School of political economy. His writings are a possible source of some of Darwin's ideas on natural selection.

Born in Kirkcaldy, Fife, Scotland, Adam Smith studied at Glasgow and Oxford Universities. He became professor of logic at Glasgow in 1751, moving to the chair of moral philosophy the following year. In 1776, he moved to London and published *An Enquiry into the Nature and Causes of the Wealth of Nations*. (He moved back to Scotland, to an administrative post in Edinburgh, in 1778.) The *Wealth of Nations* examined the consequences of economic freedom, including competition, the division of labor (specialization), and the implications of a laissez-faire economy.

There are similarities between Darwin's theory of **evolution through natural selection**—the suggestion that the environment selects those organisms fittest to survive, enabling them to pass on their characteristics to later generations—and Adam Smith's doctrine of the invisible hand that promotes order in the world of laissez-faire capitalism and competition. A businessman has no intention of promoting the public interest in such a world. "He intends only his own gain, and he is in this . . . led by an invisible hand to promote an end which was not part of his intention." Just as in Darwin's theory, competition, predation, disease, and environmental extremes select individual organisms in a population that have the characteristics that favor survival, so Adam Smith's invisible hand of competition in the marketplace favors the business enterprises that are most efficient.

The extent to which Darwin was influenced by Smith is much discussed. It is possible that Darwin read Smith's *Wealth of Nations* in **Edinburgh** in the 1820s; or he may have come across his ideas in another way, in Edinburgh or later. **William Paley**'s *Natural Theology* (which Darwin read at Cambridge) uses the same metaphor to describe a bird held to its nest while incubating eggs by an invisible hand, even though such a posture is "repugnant . . . to her organisation [and] her habits"; the sacrifice, in the long run, is beneficial. There are other possible routes through which Darwin might have been influenced by Smith. Harriet Martineau acted as a publicist for and popularizer of Adam Smith and moved in the same circles as Darwin in London in the late 1830s; indeed, her name was linked to that of Charles's brother Erasmus for a time. **Thomas Malthus** was influenced by Adam Smith's writings, and his *Essay on Population* provided Darwin with a critical key idea in the development of the notion of natural selection. Suffice it to say that Adam Smith, Thomas Malthus, Harriet Martineau, and William Paley were writing at approximately the same time and certainly influenced one another, and several of them are acknowledged influences on Darwin. There is a commonality of ideas that can be distinguished: order emerging from the apparent disorder of competition; the importance of whole populations rather than individuals; the environment (whatever it might be) providing an invisible hand or a directionality to change; and the idea of a dialogue between a population and its environment. These ideas can be seen in the writings of all these thinkers. Whatever the chain of influence, Adam Smith was one of the first to use these ideas, and Darwin the most important.

Spencer, Herbert (1820–1903)

British philosopher and sociologist who attempted to apply Darwinian evolutionary concepts to philosophy, psychology, and the study of society. He is the originator of what has become known as social Darwinism.

Herbert Spencer was an important influence on nineteenth-century thought, although many of his ideas no longer find favor, and indeed have been dubbed racist. Today he is remembered for political thought, especially his defense of the idea of natural rights.

He was born in Derby, in north-central England, to a schoolteacher's family; he was the eldest of nine children, although the only one to reach adulthood. The family was unconventional, subscribing to the dissenting (i.e., non-Church of England) tradition and had radical political views. Training initially as an engineer, Spencer soon switched to journalism, working for *The Economist* 1848 to 1853 and coming into contact with such writers as Thomas Carlyle, **Thomas Huxley,** and Mary Ann Evans (George Eliot). An inheritance in 1853 allowed him to devote himself full-time to writing.

Social Statics, or the Conditions Essential to Human Happiness (1851) presents Spencer's interpretation of the development of human freedoms and a defense of individual liberty based on a somewhat Lamarckian evolutionary theory. *Principles of Psychology* followed in 1855, emphasizing the close link between body and mind.

Spencer then began to develop (apparently mainly psychological) health problems, which led him to seek seclusion and prevented him from writing for more than a few hours each day. Nevertheless, he embarked on a writing project that occupied a substantial part of the rest of his life: the nine-volume *A System of Synthetic Philosophy* was published over the period 1863 to 1893. This work attempted to integrate his views on biology, ethics, politics, and sociology, placing the material into an evolutionary framework. He was at pains to show that the evidence and concepts from one science could be applied to others.

In the first volume of *System,* Spencer maintained that all phenomena could be explained in terms of evolutionary theory. There was a principle of continuity: homogeneous organisms were unstable, and there was a broad trend in organic evolution from simple to complex and from homogeneity to heterogeneity. Hence the variation that is fundamental to Darwin's theories. It was, in fact, Spencer who introduced the term survival of the fittest; Darwin liked it and used it in some of the later editions of *On the Origin.* Darwin had a good deal of respect for Spencer (and vice versa; Spencer attended Darwin's funeral in 1882, breaking his own rule that he would never enter a church). However, Spencer's view was partly Lamarckian in tone: he believed in the inheritance of acquired characteristics and stressed the influence of the external environment on an organism's development. He also argued that there was a trend in nature toward specialization and individuation. Human nature—"the aggregate of men's instincts and sentiments"—over time became adapted to a social existence.

Paradoxically, perhaps, he argued that this development of individuation would contribute to the development of society; there was an inclination in all beings to comport themselves in ways that would ensure their survival.

In humans, rational self-interest had led to their coming together into so-cieties for protection against war and violence.

Despite this emphasis on the importance of the individual, Spencer held an organic view of society: social life was an extension of the life of the natural organism, and societies obeyed the same evolutionary principles as did organisms. Over time, therefore, human natures would become adapted to the societies around them. There was thus a unity of mind, body, and society: they evolved—more or less in a Larmarckian manner—through time and in relationship to one another. Some societies were thus "supe-rior" to others.

Much of Spencer's work had an ethical dimension. As individual humans become aware of their individuality, they become aware of the individuality of others. In the *Law of Equal Freedom,* Herbert Spencer held that "Every man has freedom to do all that he wills, provided he infringes not the equal freedom of any other man." Thus, although there was an egoist theme in Spencer's philosophy, he maintained that rational egoists—individuals seek-ing to maximize their own advantage—would not seek deliberately to do what conflicted with the rights of others. Nevertheless, to spend resources on someone who has no direct relation to oneself—for example, support-ing the unemployed—is not only contrary to one's own interests but en-courages laziness and works against evolution. Social inequity was thus, to some extent, justified on evolutionary principles. Egalitarianism ignored the just deserts of individuals and biological needs and efficiency. He was opposed to authoritarian governments imposing notions of what was good on the populations under their control.

Herbert Spencer was offered many honors, including being nominated for the Nobel Prize for Literature in 1902, but he accepted few of them. His works sold over a million copies within his own life time and were translated into French, German, Spanish, Russian, and Italian. His views were especially popular in France and the United States. William Graham Sumner (1840–1910), a professor at Yale University, enthusiastically pro-claimed similar views on social Darwinism and the freedom of the individual in defense of laissez-faire capitalism. He asserted that interference by the state in the economy and society was contrary to evolutionary principles. These ideas brought him into serious conflict with the university's presi-dent Noah Porter (1811–1892). It was also claimed, as late as 1896, that three justices of the United States Supreme Court were Spencerians.

Spencer's reputation was at its peak in the 1870s and 1880s, and it de-clined, as did his health, in his last decades (he may have been dependant on morphine and opium). While many still support his emphasis on the free-dom of the individual, the idea that societies are close analogues of organ-isms and populations of species does not now find favor, and the notion that the same principles apply to both organic evolution and the development of societies has been displaced. Spencer died in relative obscurity on December 8, 1903.

FURTHER READING

Gray, T. S. 1996. *The Political Philosophy of Herbert Spencer.* Aldershot, England: Avebury.

Jones, G. 1980. *Social Darwinism and English Thought: The Interaction between Biological and Social Theory.* Brighton, England: Harvester Press.

Kennedy, James G. 1978. *Herbert Spencer.* Boston: Twayne Publishers.

St. Helena and Ascension Island

Two small islands in the tropical south Atlantic Ocean; both are British possessions.

One of Charles Darwin's shipmates declaimed "The folk of St Helena have a saying: 'We know we live on a rock, but the poor people of Ascension live on a cinder.' " After visiting the two remote islets of the southern Atlantic Ocean, Darwin felt "The distinction is in truth very just." (*Diary,* June 20, 1836)

Both small islands are in the tropical South Atlantic, both are volcanic in origin and associated with what is referred to as the Mid-Atlantic Ridge; both have long been British possessions. They are about 750 miles (1,200 kilometers) apart. Darwin visited each of them—for just under a week in each case with a few days between the two visits—in mid-July 1836.

Darwin, in his Diary, compared both islands with fortified sites.

July 8th. In the morning arrived at St Helena. This island, the forbidding aspect of which has so often been described, rises like a huge castle from the ocean. A great wall, built of successive streams of black lava, forms around its whole circuit, a bold coast. . . . [T]here is one striking view; an irregular castle perched on the summit of a lofty hill . . . boldly projects against the sky.

Darwin extended the comparison of both islands to well-defended castles to the function of the two islands, sometimes mingling the two. After the description of the isle of St. Helena as "like a huge castle," he continues:

Near to the town, as if in aid of the natural defences, small forts & guns are everywhere built up & mingled with the ragged rocks.

And later:

There are alarm houses and alarm guns on every peak . . . [and] forts and picket houses on the line leading down to Prosperous Bay.

Ascension Island was, until 1922, administered by the Admiralty, the population consisting almost entirely of marines: "there is not a private person on the island," Darwin wrote. "The whole Island may be compared to [a] huge ship," he continued. It was not much more than "a mere fortress in the ocean." Both islands were significant provisioning stations for the Royal Navy, but the main reason for the extensive fortification of the islands in the early nineteenth century was that St. Helena was used as a place of detention of Napoleon after his defeat in 1815. Ascension Island was garrisoned to discourage an attempt to release him.

Napoleon had died in 1821 and was buried on St. Helena (Darwin wrote that, for the period July 9–13, he "obtained lodgings in a cottage within a stone's throw of Napoleon's tomb"), although the emperor's body was later removed to France. Much of the infrastructure remained, although in decline.

Although he noted the plants and animals on the two islands, Darwin's main concern on both of them was with the volcanic history; he referred to the existence on St. Helena of "a remnant of a great crater," describing how a "wall or parapet" was similar to those he had seen surmounting several of the craters in the Galapagos Islands.

In his chapter on the geology of St. Helena, in volume 2 (chapter 4) of the *Geology of the Voyage of the Beagle,* Darwin is at his comparative best:

> There is much resemblance in structure and in geological history between St Helena, St Jago [in the Cape Verde Islands] and Mauritius. All three islands are bounded (at least in the parts I was able to examine) by a ring of basaltic mountains, now much broken, but evidently once continuous. These mountains had, or apparently once had, their escarpments steep towards the interior of the island, and their strata dip outwards. . . . I feel however that . . . their average inclination is greater than that, which they could have acquired, considering their thickness and compactness, by flowing down a sloping surface. At St Helena, and at St Jago, the basaltic strata rest on older and probably submarine beds of different composition. At all three islands, deluges of more recent lavas have flowed from the centre of the island, towards and between the basaltic mountains; and at St Helena, the central platform has been filled up by them. All three islands have been raised in mass. . . . In these three islands, but especially at St Jago and Mauritius, when standing on the summit of one of the old basaltic mountains, one looks in vain towards the centre of the island—the point at which the strata beneath one's feet and of the mountains on each side rudely converge—for a source whence these strata could have been erupted; but one sees only a vast hollow platform stretched beneath, or piles of matter of more recent origin.

Darwin's explanation was that uplift, volcanic eruptions, and denudation continue contemporaneously.

In the same chapter, Darwin offers a brief comparison with the geology of Ascension Island:

> The contrast in the superficial state of St Helena, compared with the nearest island, namely, Ascension, is very striking. At Ascension, the surface of the lava-streams are glossy, as if just poured fourth, their boundaries are well defined, and they can be traced to perfect craters whence they erupted; in the

course of many long walks I did not observe a single dike. . . . On the other hand, at St Helena, the course of no stream of lava can be traced, either by the state of its boundaries or superfices . . . but the surface of some of the highest hills, are interlaced by worn-down dikes.

The implication of all this was that Ascension was a much more recently formed volcanic island than St. Helena. He described the "singularly convoluted forms" of the surface of the Ascension Island lava flows, and the "conical red-coloured hills, scattered over the northern and western borders of the island." Standing on the central mountain, he counted "between twenty and thirty of these cones of eruption." He noted that they all sloped toward the southeast, the ejected fragments and ashes being blown by the trade wind. A further indication of the recency and violence of the volcanic eruptions were the volcanic bombs, varying in size from that of an apple to that of a man's body, that occurred in great numbers, some of them at a distance from points of eruption. They had a coarsely cellular "scoriacious" interior surrounded by a layer of compact lava and a cracked outer crust. These were formed by masses of viscous material being expelled during an eruption with considerable force. The secret of Darwin's success was due to his habit of comparison.

St. Paul's Rocks

A tiny cluster of rocks, uninhabited, in the equatorial Atlantic Ocean.

A week after leaving St. Jago in the **Cape Verde Islands** (on February 15, 1832), the *Beagle* was within sight of the tiny cluster of rocks known as St. Paul's. They are almost on the equator (0° 58' N, 29° 15' W) about 540 miles (870 kilometers) from the shore of South America. The highest point is about 60 feet (18.3 meters) above the sea; the total area exposed is a little more than a few hundred square meters. The islets are now under Brazilian sovereignty.

Two boats went ashore; Darwin was in one of them and set about with his geological hammer slaughtering seabirds. There were boobies (a species of gannet) and noddies (a species of tern). These creatures were completely unaccustomed to humans and did not move. Darwin was already beginning to think ecologically, and he noted the extreme biological simplicity of the island's biota: there was a fly, a beetle, a woodlouse, and spiders, as well as parasites on the seabirds. These species, he reasoned, were associated with the seabird nests (made out of seaweed), dung, and feathers. There were also crabs that emerged from crevices when the birds left their nests to take the fish left nearby. Offshore were many species of fish that were caught, but the difficulty was that, as soon as a smaller fish was hooked, the "voracious sharks" took it. There were also many species of seaweed in the surrounding sea, but ashore there was "not a single plant, not even a lichen" on the dung-whitened rock. Like naturalists visiting remote islands since, Darwin

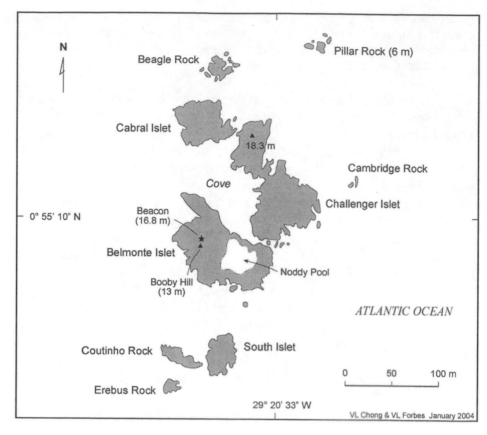

N

Beagle Rock

Pillar Rock (6 m)

Cabral Islet

18.3 m

Cambridge Rock

Cove

Challenger Islet

Beacon
(16.8 m)

0° 55' 10" N

Belmonte Islet

Noddy Pool

Booby Hill
(13 m)

ATLANTIC OCEAN

Coutinho Rock

South Islet

0   50   100 m

Erebus Rock

29° 20' 33" W

VL Chong & VL Forbes January 2004

Map of the tiny group of rocks in the tropical Atlantic Ocean. Map drawn at Geography Department, University of Western Australia.

understood this ecological poverty, the product, perhaps, of the extreme remoteness. But he also appreciated it. The simple ecological community was easier to understand, and the relationships within it were clearer.

Darwin also used his hammer for its proper purpose and took samples of the dark green rock of which the islets are composed. Today the olivine-rich rocks are identified as peridotites, and it is suggested that the material may have come from the Earth's mantle, deep below the Earth's crust, ripped up during some movement of the crustal plates tens of millions of years ago. Darwin knew nothing of plate tectonics or of the inner Earth, but he did describe the characteristic mineralogy of the rocks and stated that they were definitely not composed of ordinary volcanic materials. In a few hours, he executed a remarkably complete scientific study.

Sulivan, Bartholomew James (1810—1890)

Naval officer and hydrographer. Good friend of Charles Darwin on HMS *Beagle* and subsequently.

Sulivan was one of Darwin's closest friends from the *Beagle* days and one of the officers with whom he went on shore excursions, seeking geological and other specimens (for example, in the Falkland Islands and at the Cape of Good Hope). When, after the voyage, Darwin was confused about the origins of some of his specimens from the **Galapagos Islands,** Sulivan let him examine some of his specimens.

Captain FitzRoy seems to have had a special regard for the abilities of Bartholomew Sulivan, because, for example, on April 17, 1834, he was put in charge of the *Beagle* while FitzRoy, Darwin, some of the officers, and about twenty other crew members started out on a three-week expedition in three whale boats up the Rio Santa Cruz in Patagonia. Eighteen months later, FitzRoy named a small islet in the Galapagos Islands Bartholomew (now, Bartolomé) Island in honor of his officer.

Sulivan went on to have a distinguished career in the Royal Navy. After serving as lieutenant on the *Beagle* from 1831 to 1836, he surveyed the Falkland Islands in HMS *Arrow* 1838 to 1839. He commanded the *Philomel* 1842 to 1846, after which he resided in the Falkland Islands, attempting to farm there 1848 to 1851. He then commanded *Lightning* in the Baltic 1854 to 1855, before being appointed a naval officer in the Marine Department of the Board of Trade, 1856 to 1865. He was promoted to admiral in 1877 and was knighted in 1869.

Sulivan remained a lifelong friend and correspondent of Darwin; his letters on feral animals and plant material thrown up onto the coasts of the Falkland Islands were of particular value in Darwin's work on domestic animals, his species theory, and long-distance dispersal. One of Sulivan's letters contained suggestions for medical treatment. He and a couple of other former officers from the *Beagle* visited Darwin at **Down House** at the end of October 1862.

T

Tahiti

Group or archipelago of islands surrounded by coral reefs in the South
Pacific.

Tahiti—or Oetahiti, as it was sometimes called in Darwin's day—is a
group of (extinct) volcanic islands, surrounded by coral reefs in the South
Pacific Ocean (17° 30' S, 149° 30' W), now under French administration
(as part of French Polynesia). The main island has an area of 400 square
miles (about 1,000 square kilometers), and the highest mountain, Mt.
Orohena, is 7,350 feet (2,241 meters) in height. The island is intensely
beautiful, although today parts of the northern coast are affected by tourist
and residential development. Much of the largest island remains forested,
as it was in the early nineteenth century. Tropical crops including bread-
fruit, vanilla, coconuts, pineapples, and avocado are produced.

Darwin only visited the main island, although he glimpsed others from
afar. He liked Tahiti and the Tahitians from the start. He refers to "the
delights of the first impression provided by a new country" (*Diary*,
November 15, 1835), of "charming Tahiti," and the "merry faces of the
people," as well as "an intelligence that shows they are advancing in civilisation." The men were the fittest Darwin ever beheld—they were tall, ath-
letic, well-proportioned, their dusky skins were "pleasing," and most of them
were tattooed—the decorations, he recorded, "so gracefully follow the
body that they have a graceful & pleasing effect." The land appeared pro-

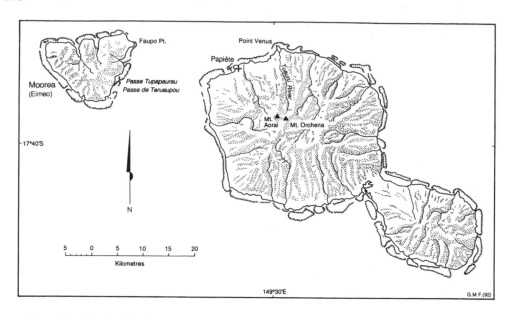

Map of the Islands of Tahiti. Darwin's view of the Isle of Eimeo (now Moorea) with its barrier reef, from the hills not far from the modern Papiéte, gave him important clues for his theory of coral reefs. Map drawn at Geography Department, University of Western Australia.

ductive; the low ground close to the shore—alluvial land at the foot of the mountains—was covered by a "beautiful orchard of Tropical plants . . . bananas, orange, cocoa-nut & breadfruits." There were also yams, sugar cane, guavas, and pineapples. The winding paths leading to the scattered houses were another source of delight. *Beagle* captain Robert FitzRoy, too, was impressed by much of what he saw, especially by the bright sunshine, which he felt "heightened the vivid and ever-varying tints of a rich verdure." Not all was perfect, however. Both Darwin and FitzRoy thought that the women were less attractive than the men, some of the houses were not as clean as they might have been, and both deplored the ragged and sometimes dirty European-style clothes worn in place of the traditional costume. Both felt there had been a decline in Tahitian society since the days of Captain Cook and other early explorers.

Darwin explored part of the northern coast of the main island and penetrated some miles inland along the valley of the River Tuaura. Darwin's descriptions of the Tahitian landscape are evocative and, to some extent, ring true for the modern visitor. He noted the altitudinal zones of plant communities. Above the "beautiful orchard of tropical plants" along the coast, as one rose into the hills:

> The vegetation is singular, consisting almost exclusively of small dwarf fern, mingled higher up with coarse grass. . . . At the highest point which I reached trees again . . . appeared, tree ferns having replaced the Cocoa nut. (*Diary,* November 17, 1835)

He described the cool dampness of the thick forest and noted how the vegetation clung to tiny inaccessible ledges in the ravines. Darwin was impressed by the deepness of these valleys, cut into the volcanic rocks, understanding correctly that they had been cut by "running water through a long succession of ages."

The principal component of the biophysical environment that interested him was the fringe of coral reefs that surrounded the island. He noted that the limit of coral growth was 25 to 35 fathoms in depth. He marveled at the variety of coral forms. He was particularly impressed by the view from the mountains above the point where the *Beagle* lay—of the beautiful island of Eimeo (now called Moorea) with its surrounding lagoon and, a little further from the shore, the barrier reef. This sight profoundly influenced his thinking on **corals and coral reefs** and atolls, and indeed his thinking about living things in relation to their environment.

Darwin encountered Christian missionaries at a number of places during his voyage, and, although he disapproved of the zeal with which, in Tahiti, they discouraged indigenous music and dancing, on the whole

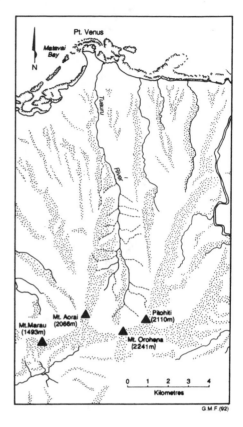

Map of Tuauru Valley, Tahiti, explored by Darwin. Map drawn at Geography Department, University of Western Australia.

he approved of their activities and considered them a benign influence, especially in their opposition to liquor. He uses such phrases as "sensible agreeable gentlemen," "high and respectable character," and "unpretending excellent merit" to describe the missionaries he met in Tahiti.

Tasmania

The large, generally temperate island south of the mainland of Australia. Visited by Darwin in February 1836.

The crossing to Tasmania from Sydney took six days, and the weather was bad some of the time; when the vessel entered Storm Bay, "the weather justified this awful name." Nevertheless, Darwin was on deck, making observations on the rock formations as the ship made its way up, late on February 6, 1836. His first impression was that Hobart was inferior to Sydney, for "the latter might be called a city, this only a town" (*Diary*, February 5, 1836). Admittedly, around the cove were some "fine warehouses" (they still

Tuauru Valley, Tahiti. Photo: Patrick Armstrong.

Coast near Point Venus, Tahiti, mountains composed of volcanic rocks in the background.
Photo: Patrick Armstrong.

stand), but Battery Point did not impress him. The defenses were "contemptible" compared to the fortifications of some of the places he had visited in South America. But despite these initial impressions, Darwin seems to have preferred Hobart to Sydney, stating that he would certainly select Tasmania in preference to New South Wales were he compelled to emigrate. The shops, he said, "appeared good," and there was a good water supply—"a thing much wanted in Sydney." Some of the farms were "very nice"; others were "very tempting."

The lower parts of the surrounding hills had been cleared, and agriculture flourished. There were "bright yellow fields of corn and dark green ones of potatoes" (it was late summer). The upper slopes of Mount Wellington, a flat-topped mountain behind the town, were covered with "a light wood" and were crisscrossed with a network of field-boundaries, which probably reminded him of parts of the English and Welsh countryside with which he was familiar. The climate was more moist, Darwin noted, and he thought the soils more fertile than those of New South Wales. "The cultivated fields look well," he wrote, "and the gardens abound with thriving vegetable and fruit trees." But the greatest difference was in Hobart's "society," which he felt was infinitely to be preferred to that of Sydney: he thought the difference might be due to the lack of well-to-do former convicts. He also seems to have been impressed with the level of engineering and scientific expertise in the small community. Of one of his geological excursions he later wrote:

> I took a long walk on the side of the bay opposite to the town: I crossed in a steam-boat, two of which are constantly plying backwards and forwards. The machinery of one of these vessels was entirely manufactured in this colony, which, from its very foundation, then numbered only three and thirty years! (*Voyage of the Beagle,* chapter 19)

More controversial, perhaps, is his comment that the island enjoyed "the great advantage of being free from a native population." Darwin had had ample opportunity—in New Zealand, New South Wales, on Chiloé, Tahiti, and Tierra del Fuego—of seeing that contact between Europeans and indigenous people usually resulted in the degradation of the latter, the deterioration of their social structures, and conflict with the newcomers. He considered that the removal of the small remnant of the Tasmanian native population to an isolated location was probably in its best interests. There had been terrible conflict with the settlers—robberies, burnings, and murders. Darwin understood very clearly, however, where the blame lay:

> I fear there is no doubt that this train of evil and its consequences, originated in the infamous conduct of some of our own countrymen. (*Voyage of the Beagle,* chapter 19)

Darwin had no personal experience of the Tasmanian Aborigines, but he made careful enquiries about their fate, both while on the island and subsequently. He later described the manner in which an attempt was made to round up the remaining individuals.

> The plan adopted was nearly similar to that of the great hunting-matches of India: a line was formed reaching across the island, with the intention of driving the natives into a *cul-de-sac* on Tasman's peninsula. The attempt failed; the natives, having tied up their dogs, stole one night through the lines. (*Voyage of the Beagle*, chapter 19)

Eventually, however, most of the Tasmanians did surrender and, through the offices of a Mr. Robinson, "an active and benevolent man," were taken to an island in the Bass Strait "where food and clothes were provided them." Darwin predicted the extinction of the race, and he was more or less right. The last full-blood Tasmanian died in 1876, although many persons who claim part of their descent through Tasmanian Aborigines still constitute a vocal group in Tasmanian affairs. Darwin compared the situation with that on mainland Australia, where many Aborigines had had little contact with whites, and where families "swarm with children." Nevertheless, he had noted some signs of decline in their social structures.

Darwin's observations on the natural vegetation of Tasmania are mainly based on his ascent of Mount Wellington. Darwin estimated its height at 3,100 feet (945 meters); modern maps show it at 1,271 meters. He described the mountain as high but without picturesque beauty.

He attempted to ascend the mountain on February 10, but, as he put it: "I failed in a first attempt, from the thickness of the wood." He tried again the following day, this time taking a guide with him. Darwin complained that the guide:

> was a stupid fellow, and conducted us to the southern and damp side of the mountain, where the vegetation was very luxuriant; and where the labour of the ascent, from the number of rotten trunks, was almost as great as on a mountain in Tierra del Fuego or in Chiloé. It cost us five and a half hours of hard climbing before we reached the summit. In many parts the Eucalypti grew to a great size, and composed a noble forest. In some of the dampest ravines, tree-ferns flourished in an extraordinary manner; I saw one which was at least twenty feet [6.1 meters] to the base of the fronds, and was in girth exactly six feet [1.8 meters]. The fronds forming the most elegant of parasols, produced a gloomy shade, like that of the first hour of the night. (*Voyage of the Beagle*, chapter 19)

The damp forest, with its ferns and tangled undergrowth was in marked contrast to the low, shrubby plant community at the summit of Mount Wellington, which was described as "broad and flat, and is composed of huge angular masses of naked greenstone [dolerite]."

Darwin, as he did in Tahiti and elsewhere, clearly understood the zonation of plant communities with altitude. But Darwin's real focus of interest when he was in Tasmania was geology. He had the advantage of exploring with **George Frankland,** the surveyor general of the colony, but, even allowing for this, his grasp of the geological structure of the rocks of the Hobart area after only a few days in the field was remarkable. By studying the relationships between the rock masses—which overlaid which, which igneous rocks intruded which sediments—he was able to reconstruct the geological history of the region supremely well (see article on **metamorphic rocks**).

For much of his voyage, Darwin had been interested in changes in the relative heights of land and sea. Just a few weeks earlier, partly on the basis of what he had seen in Tahiti, he had drafted his theory of coral reefs, which depended on changes in the seal level relative to the land. After his visit to Tasmania, he wrote:

> I now come to a subject which I have so frequently discussed in my Geological Memoranda, viz recent movements in the level of the land. On both sides of the Bay, & along nearly the whole line of coast broken shells are found on the land to the height of 30 & 40 ft [10 to 12 meters]. (*Geological Notes,* Cambridge University Library, Darwin Archive)

It has been suggested that these accumulations of shells so far above the tide line were middens—masses of material abandoned by the Aboriginal inhabitants of the area, rather than firm evidence for recent shorelines at exactly this height. Moreover, Storm Bay, the Derwent River Estuary, and the complicated tangle of islands and promontories within them were produced by a geologically recent (i.e., post–Ice Age) rise in sea level relative to the land rather than the opposite—a fact that Darwin did not realize. Possibly there have been some movements in both directions (up and down) over the last few thousand years. But, as far as Darwin was concerned, he saw evidence that changes in sea level were confirming the general theme of his work on the coral reefs in the Pacific. In its simplest form, his idea was that there were some places where the sea level was falling, compensating for the rises in other places (such as in the Pacific) where the rise was causing fringing reefs to pass into barrier reefs and eventually atolls.

Teilhard de Chardin, Pierre (1881—1955)

French Jesuit priest, paleontologist-geologist, evolutionist, and mystic. Teilhard attempted to reconcile Darwin's evolutionary thought with Christianity in the twentieth century, as did Charles Kingsley, for example, in the nineteenth.

Teilhard was the product of an extraordinarily caring and insightful family background. His mother, Berthe-Adele, was the great-grandniece of Voltaire, and of her Teilhard wrote, "To her I owe the best part of my soul." His father, Emmanuel, was a graduate of the École des Chartres and had a special interest in the landscape and history of the province of Auvergne; he encouraged members of his family to collect natural history and geological specimens and to try to understand the beautiful, young, volcanic landscape of the district.

> Auvergne moulded me . . . [and] served me both as a museum and as a wild-life preserve. Sarcenat in Auvergne gave me the first taste of the joys of discovery . . . my delight in nature . . . my most precious possessions: a collection of . . . rocks still to be found there. . . . I was interested in Mineralogy and biological observation. I used to love to follow the course of the clouds, and I knew the stars by their names. . . . To my father I owe a certain balance, on which all the rest is built, along with a taste for the exact sciences. (Quoted by C. Cuénot, *Tielhard de Chardin: A Biographical Study.* Baltimore, MD: Helicon Press, 1965, 3)

Several years at a Jesuit secondary school (where he did well but was not outstanding) were followed by a year free from much formal study, occasioned by health problems. He studied mathematics and went on field trips searching for mineral specimens. Two years of study with the Jesuits at Aix-en-Provence in southern France were followed by a period of university training at Caen, in the north. Then, in 1902, when the Jesuits were temporarily expelled from France, he lived and studied for four years on the Isle of Jersey in the British Channel Isles. Again Teilhard displayed his enthusiasm for geology in making a map of the island's geological structure. He published a brief note on mineralogy and geology in the bulletin of the local geological society. His attraction to the great forces of nature, formed in his childhood and developed while in Jersey, awoke in him "a vibrant cosmic consciousness," and, through nature, as he put it, "He learned to feel the hand of God." This was the basis of his later ideas. He saw the life and work of Jesus as a manifestation of the evolutionary process.

In 1905, Teilhard began three years of teaching science at a Jesuit College in Cairo, Egypt; geological and paleontological interests were furthered by excursions to collect fossils from the North African deserts. In 1908, he was moved by his superiors to Ore Place, near Hastings in southern England, for four years of rigorous theological training. Here he came under the influence of the writings John Henry Newman (1801–1890), the distinguished English theologian and mystic, originally Anglican (Church of England), later Catholic. Teilhard saw a congruence between Newman's notion of theological development and Darwinian evolutionary ideas. In 1911, he was ordained priest, and after a final year of theological studies he was interviewed by the distinguished geologist and vertebrate paleontologist, Professor Marcelline Boule, in Paris. This interview, he later recalled, set the direction of much of his later life. While based in Paris at this time, Teilhard undertook a course on paleontology at the Paris Natural History Museum and undertook fieldwork, excavating caves at Santander and Altamira in Spain.

The final stage of his training started in Canterbury, in southern England, in 1914. But very soon he was conscripted into the French army as a medical orderly and stretcher bearer. At his own request, he served with a regiment of mainly Muslim North African troops during some of the fiercest battles of World War I in northern France. At one stage, Teilhard was asked to serve as chaplain (with the rank of captain); he asked to remain with his men in the ranks, where he thought he could do more good. He was heavily decorated for great bravery. Two of his brothers were killed in the conflict (three other siblings had died before the war). While serving at the front, he wrote a number of important essays on religious and philosophical subjects, which he forwarded to his cousin, Marguerite Teilhard-Chambon, to whom he was extremely devoted.

The years after the war were occupied with further studies of science, particularly paleontology, including the preparation of a doctoral thesis, which he defended in March 1922. He was briefly appointed to a teaching position at the Institute Catholique in Paris, but it was terminated (while he was en route to China). A draft of a paper he had prepared on the significance of (then) modern ideas on Darwinism, and particularly **human evolution,** for Catholic doctrine—and, in particular, the notion of original sin—was stolen from his desk and forwarded to Rome. Much of the next 25 years was spent in China, although there were occasional periods of home leave, and he also visited other parts of Asia, including India, Indonesia, Burma, and Mongolia, as well as the United States and Ethiopia. Such were his views that his superiors wished to keep him at a distance. Although usually living in Catholic institutions, he undertook an enormous amount of scientific work, excavating fossil remains, particularly those of fossil humans (e.g., *Sinanthropus*) in many countries. He was appointed an adviser to the Chinese Geological Service. His research, sometimes funded by U.S. foundations, on paleontology—including human and vertebrate paleontology—was of the highest order. In 1931, he took part in an expedition to the Gobi Desert, supported by and using experimental vehicles provided by Citroën, that lasted for many months and that penetrated areas that had had no serious scientific evaluation. Besides his extensive geological writings and those on evolution, Teilhard also wrote on theological topics. He was at pains to link the two streams of thought. One Jesuit thinker summarized by saying that Teilhard attempted:

> To rethink within his own distinctive evolutionary system the data of Christian revelation concerning the person of Christ. . . . [Teilhard] believed that Christ as God Incarnate, revealed in himself not only the mystery of God but also the meaning of man, and therefore the ultimate meaning of that evolutionary process of which God is the cause and man the culmination. (C. F. Mooney, *Teilhard de Chardin and the Mystery of Christ*. New York: Harper and Row, 1964, 7)

The evolution of the cosmos, the "building of the earth" (a phrase much used by Teilhard), the evolution of life on Earth, the development of humanity, and humanity's spiritual progress were seen as a single unified process—a movement toward the "Omega-point." There is a mysticism about Teilhard's ideas.

> [E]verything in the universe is in fact ultimately moving towards Christ-Omega: because cosmogenesis, moving in its totality through anthropogenesis, ultimately shows itself to be a Christogenesis. . . . We have seen that Christ, by reason of his opposition as Omega of the world represents a focus toward whom and in whom everything converges. (P. Teilhard de Chardin, *Super-humanité, super-Christ, super-charité,* 1943; quoted by Mooney, 1964, 161)

Later he summarized his views more directly: "Evolution, which offers a passage that escapes total death, is the hand of God drawing us to himself." From about mid-1938 onward, Teilhard was working "a page or two a day" on *Le Phénomène humain,* a compilation of his philosophical, theological, and evolutionary views. The work was mostly completed by 1940; however, Teilhard was isolated in China throughout the war. Although he was working hard in the fields of geology and paleontology, as well doing church work, publication was impossible.

Shortly after his return to France from China at the end of World War II, Teilhard planned to visit South Africa, where important human and prehuman fossils had been found. A heart attack followed by a long convalescence prevented him from making the trip. However, the opportunity came again in 1951, and he spent several months in South Africa. He was able to visit Sterkfontein and Makapan in the Transvaal and Taungs in the Orange Free State, where *Australopithecus* and other significant material had been found. A second visit to Africa in 1953 enabled him to travel more widely. Following this, at a lecture in New York, he said, presciently: "It seems surprising that Africa was not immediately identified as the only region of the world where the first traces of the human species could be sought with any changes of success."

In 1948, Teilhard de Chardin traveled to Rome to seek permission from the Roman Catholic Church for his *Le Phénomène humain* to be published. He met with courteous but firm refusal. It was not to be published until after his death on Easter Day (April 10) 1955. Publication in English of *The Phenomenon of Man* followed in 1959.

A ban on the publication of Teilhard's greatest work was accompanied by other restrictions on his publishing and seeking teaching appointments. He obtained a research position in New York, and, apart from a short visit to France in the summer of 1954, when he was able to visit his birthplace at Sarcenat in the Auvergne for the last time, he lived in that city until his death.

Other ideas important to Teilhard need to be briefly mentioned, because they have had a particular valence with late twentieth-century and twenty-first-century thought. The mystical side of his thinking emphasized the profoundly ecological idea that everything is connected to everything else; plants, animals, rocks, and humans all formed an integrated whole—a notion akin to that of *Gaia,* the modern suggestion that the Earth and all its processes constitute a sort of super-organism. In one of his essays from his early days in the French army, he asserted that "everything formed a single limpid mass in which no division between things could be seen."

Finally, he advocated the idea of a "thinking earth"; in the 1920s, he referred to an *anthroposphere,* and in 1925 introduced the term *noosphere.* It was a key element in his vision. Just as there existed a geosphere or lithosphere consisting of the rocks of the Earth's crust; a hydrosphere including the waters of the oceans, rivers, and lakes; an atmosphere; and a biosphere, so too there was a "thinking" layer of mind and spirit that surrounded the globe. The emergence of the noosphere was an important step in becoming human, of evolving humanity, or "hominization." Some devotees of Teilhard have suggested that this notion predicted the modern Internet or worldwide computer network.

Theologian, geologist, paleontologist, priest, and mystic, Teilhard de Cardin's writings (originally largely in French) are difficult, and his ideas are controversial. They are too mystical for some scientists and too scientific for some theologians. He was isolated and reviled by his own Church in his own day (although views have moderated). Yet more, perhaps, than any other, he sought to bring evolutionary and religious views into a single framework.

FURTHER READING

Cruéot, C. 1965. *Teilhard de Chardin.* London: Burns and Oats.

King, Ursula. 1998. *Spirit of Fire: The Life and Vision of Teilhard de Chardin.* Maryknoll, NY: Orbis Books.

Teilhard de Chardin, Pierre. 1959. *The Phenomenon of Man,* ed. and trans. B. Wall. London: Collins. Published in French as *Le Phénomène humain* in 1955.

Teilhard de Chardin, Pierre. 1960. *The Divine Milieu.* London: Collins. Published in French as *Le Milieu Divin.*

Tenerife

A small volcanic isle, the largest of the Canary Islands, 795 square miles (2,059 square kilometers) at 28° 15″ N, 16° 30″ W, a short distance from the shore of North Africa. The archipelago is governed by Spain. The peak rises steeply 12,195 feet (3,718 meters), but the subtropical climate allows the land at lower altitudes to be used for growing fruit and vegetables. Even in Darwin's day oranges were exported.

During Darwin's final few weeks in Cambridge, in the spring and early summer of 1831, his friend and teacher, **John Henslow** loaned Darwin a copy of the English translation (by Helen Maria Williams) of **Alexander von Humboldt**'s *Personal Narrative of a Voyage to the Equinoctial Regions of a New Continent, 1799–1804*. This book made a tremendous impression on Darwin (Henslow, in fact, some weeks later, gave a copy to Darwin, which he had with him on the *Beagle*). Darwin later wrote that he read the work "with care and profound interest" (*Autobiography,* 1887 edition, 47). It may be that Darwin learned from Humboldt his sense of integration—of the network of subtle relationships among rocks, land forms, vegetation, animal life, climate, and human activities—that can be seen in Darwin's writing. Darwin went on to say that this was one of the books that stirred in him "a burning zeal to add even the most humble contribution to the noble structure of natural science." In his autobiography, written late in life, he noted that he "Copied out from Humboldt, long passages about Teneriffe, and read them aloud."

These readings seem to have occurred during the course of excursions into the Cambridgeshire countryside with Henslow and other young Cambridge academics. Possibly the young Darwin slightly overwhelmed his older friends with his enthusiasm:

> I . . . talked about the glories of Teneriffe, and some of the party declared that they would go there; but I think they were only half in earnest. I was, however, quite in earnest.

His letters of this period to friends and relations confirm his near obsession with Humboldt's detailed account of the Island of Tenerife. In a letter to his sister Caroline, written from Cambridge on April 28, 1831, he writes:

> I will never be easy till I see the peak of Teneriffe and the great Dragon tree; . . . I am working regularly at Spanish . . . I have written myself into a Tropical glow.

Humboldt's description of the dragon tree seems to have been a particularly powerful influence. Here is the account (in Helen Williams's translation):

> Although we were acquainted, from the narratives of so many travellers, with the dragon tree . . . we were not the less struck with its enormous magnitude. We were told, that the trunk of this tree, which is mentioned in several very ancient documents as marking the boundaries of a field, was as gigantic in the fifteenth century. Its height appeared to be about 50 or 60 feet; its circumference near the roots is 45 feet. . . . The trunk has a great number of branches, which rise to form a candelabrum, and are terminated by tufts of leaves. [It] bears still every year both flowers and fruit. Its aspect feelingly recalls to mind "the eternal youth

of nature," which is an inexhaustible source of motion and life. (H. M. Williams, *Personal Narrative of a Voyage to the Equinoctial Regions of a New Content, 1799–1804,* a translation into English of Alexander von Humboldt's 1816 work. London: Longman Rees, Orme, Brown and Green, 1818)

The scientific name of the dragon tree is *Dracoena draco;* the specimen described by Humboldt and mentioned by Darwin blew down in 1868; its trunk had a girth of 45 feet (approximately 14 meters) and a height of 70 feet (about 22 meters).

Humboldt's account included a note on the plant's limited distribution on the Atlantic islands and its affinity with Asia, hinting at a distribution by humans from there. There was much in the description to excite the young potential traveler. In the *Picturesque Atlas* accompanying the text, a picture of the dragon tree is included, based on a sketch made in 1776. It is not

Darwin never got to see the dragon tree on Tenerife. It was, however, Humboldt's descriptions of the island and particularly the tree that fired Darwin, in the summer of 1831, to see something of the world and make a contribution to science. From: "Picturesque Atlas" accompanying Humboldt's *Personal Narrative of a Voyage to the Equinoctial Regions of a New Continent,* 1814–1825.

clear whether Darwin had access to the *Atlas* with this illustration, but in view of his extraordinary interest in the tree and his mention of it in several letters, it seems probable.

However, as Darwin later put it, the expedition to Tenerife was "knocked on the head by the voyage of the *Beagle*"; for, after his brief geological excursion through **North Wales** with Adam Sedgwick (August 5–29, 1831), the letter from Henslow with the suggestion that he join Captain **Robert FitzRoy**'s voyage awaited him in Shrewsbury. It was as if a trigger had been pulled. If it had not been for the reading and rereading of Humboldt in the spring and summer of 1831, Darwin might never have developed his enthusiasm for remote islands, strange plants, and the brilliant light of the tropics. He might not have spent as much of that summer teaching himself geology (with Sedgwick's help), or picking up sufficient Spanish to be useful in South America.

On January 5, 1832, the voyage of the *Beagle* was just nine days old. Darwin had been unwell as the ship tossed its way across the Bay of Biscay: he records that he experienced "great and unceasing suffering . . . [and] . . . very nearly fainted from exhaustion." By daybreak on the 6th, however, the ship was within sight of Tenerife, and he felt better. "Everything," he wrote, "had a beautiful appearance." He continued:

> the colours are so rich & soft. The peak of sugar loaf has just shown itself above the clouds. It towers in the sky twice as high as I should have dreamed of looking for it. A dense bank of clouds entirely separates the snowy top from its rugged base. (*Diary*, January 6, 1832)

He goes on to describe the "coloured houses of white, yellow & red"; the tangle of masts of the vessels in the harbor against the background of dark volcanic rock; the patches of dark green vegetation; the "oriental-looking churches"; and the low, dark fortifications with the bright Spanish flag waving above. The scene was very picturesque and exciting.

Alas, Darwin was not to set foot on what he called "this long wished for object of my ambition." He was within sight of Tenerife, but

> Oh misery, misery, we were just preparing to drop anchor within half a mile of Santa Cruz, when a boat came alongside, bringing our death-warrant. The consul declared we must perform a rigorous quarantine of twelve days. Those who have never experienced it can sparely conceive what a gloom it cast on every one. (*Diary*, January 6, 1832)

Captain FitzRoy was not going to have his ship languish offshore for 12 wasted days, and at once ordered sails to be set for the Cape Verde Islands. The effect on Darwin was profound, and there was an immediate change in his style of writing. Because the visit to Tenerife was eagerly anticipated, he used the present tense in his descriptions: "Everything *has* a beautiful appearance: the colours *are* rich and soft." After the devastating news was given, he moves to the past tense: "The . . . vallies [*sic*] . . . *were* spotted with patches of a light green vegetation." He tried to console himself in a desultory way: "I suppose Volcanic islands under the same zone have much the same character." "It is past," he wrote, and "we have left perhaps one of the most interesting places in the world, just at the moment when we were near enough for every object to create without satisfying our utmost curiosity."

But the young naturalist's morale soon improved. The weather was warm, skies were blue, and it was relatively calm. Darwin read Humboldt and at sea found much of interest as he made a net and trawled for marine organisms. Yet on January 13, he wrote: "I cannot help much regretting that we were unable to stay in Teneriffe."

Tenerife, that long-hoped-for island was never visited by Darwin; yet the hoping and the planning, and the reading and rereading of Humboldt, fired Darwin with enthusiasm for islands, the tropical environment, and for travel.

Tierra del Fuego

Group of islands at the southern extremity of South America.

This island—or rather group of islands and promontories—at the southern extremity of South America (approximately 52° 15' to 56° 00' S and 65° to 72° W), separated from the mainland by the Strait of Magellan, is today (and has been since 1881) divided between Argentina and Chile, but in Darwin's day there was no established lawful authority whatsoever and no European settlement. The total area is 19,000 square miles (30,600 square kilometers). There are high, snow-capped mountains in the west and south—a continuation of the Andean mountain system. The mountainous western portion has been glaciated (glaciers still exist) and deeply dissected by a complex network of fjords with high rocky walls. The northern part of the main island is a flat scrubland. To the south, although the high ground is treeless (and snow-covered for part of the year), along the Beagle Channel, for example, that separates Navarin Island from the mainland, there are forests dominated by the several species of **southern or antarctic beech** (*Nothofagus*).

Captain **Robert FitzRoy**'s seizure of a small party of Fuegians as hostages against a stolen boat and his subsequent decision to transport them to England for education was part of the motivation for the *Beagle*'s visit to the island. The intention to establish a missionary station among the Fuegians at the so-called the end of the earth with the young missionary, Richard Matthews, in charge was not successfully completed. After a few weeks, Matthews was attacked, his property stolen, and the building and gardens constructed by the *Beagle*'s crew destroyed. (Matthews was eventually taken to join relatives in New Zealand.)

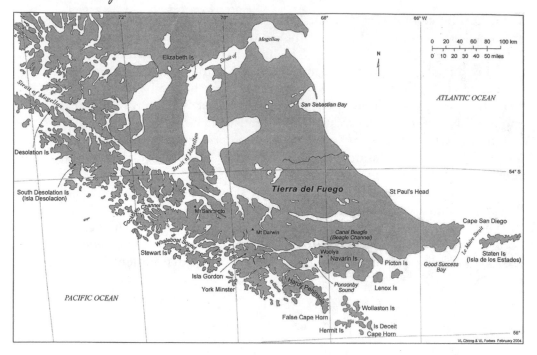

Map of Tierra del Fuego. Map drawn at Geography Department, University of Western Australia.

On the voyage that carried Charles Darwin around the world, HMS *Beagle* first reached the coast of Tierra del Fuego on December 16, 1832, just to the south of Cape St. Sebastian. The local people lit fires just as they had done on the arrival of Magellan nearly 300 years previously: the name Tierra del Fuego means Land of Fire.

The ship remained in Tierra del Fuego waters for a couple of months. This was real exploration, for the region was very little known. Charts were prepared, and Darwin undertook a good deal of scientific work, collecting fossil and rock specimens, climbing mountains, and obtaining specimens of insects (especially beetles), birds, mammals, and fish. The *Beagle* then left for the **Falkland Islands** and further work along the east coast of South America, returning a year later, in early 1834, again spending several weeks in the area. A final glimpse was provided by the traverse of the Magellan Strait in June 1834: this was in the middle of the Southern Hemisphere winter, and temperatures were often below freezing; it sometimes snowed.

Despite the piecemeal nature of his explorations of Tierra del Fuego, Darwin was able to combine them into remarkably integrated accounts. He appreciated the distinction between the low plateau in the northern part of the island made up of geologically relatively recent (Tertiary period) sedimentary rocks and full of fossils and the old, crystalline metamorphic (slates, schists, and gneisses) and igneous rocks of the south and west. The latter had a strong west-east trend and were upfolded into high mountains by earth movement.

The East coast from the St of Magellan . . . to St Polycarp's Bay, is formed of horizontal tertiary strata, bounded some way towards the interior by a mountainous band of clay-slate. This great clay-slate formation from St Le Mairie westward for 140 miles, along both sides of the Beagle Channel. (*Geology of the Voyage*, part 3, *South America*, 151)

Darwin's accounts of the plants and animals of the island were equally integrated. He made a special study of the forests, with their beech trees laden with mosses and lichens; he commented on the admixture of these *Nothofagus* with "winter's green" (*Drimys winterii*).

He discovered a fungus, apparently new to science and now known as **Darwin's fungus** (*Cyttaria darwinii*) growing on the beech trees, along with the mosses and lichens.

But Darwin's most important observations from Tierra del Fuego were those of the native inhabitants. He comments on their food, clothing (or lack of it), simple weapons, and basic forms of shelter. His approach is generally to compare (unfavorably) their primitiveness with civilized, Western humanity. Words such as "savage," "hostile," and "wretched" occur in his descriptions.

The Beagle Channel, looking south. The snow-capped mountains are on Navarin Island. Photo: Patrick Armstrong.

I never saw more miserable creatures; stunted in their growth, their hideous faces bedaubed with white pint and quite naked. . . . Their red skin filthy and greasy, their hair entangled, their voices discordant, their gesticulation violent and without any dignity. . . . How little can the higher powers come into play? (*Diary*, February 25, 1834)

To the modern ear, this passage is racist and inappropriate. But Darwin's words must be considered within the context of his background and times. In fact, Darwin was extremely tolerant of all races and nationalities. He had had almost no previous experience of tribal, non-European people, and the Fuegians were a shock to him. Later he encountered many different races in Chile, the Pacific Islands, New Zealand, Australia, and Africa, and he compared these groups, using his insights in his later evolutionary works such as *Descent of Man*.

Only a handful of individuals with true Fuegian blood survive. Western diseases accounted for many deaths among the native inhabitants of Tierra del Fuego, and their way of life has completely disappeared. Today, Tierra del Fuego produces oil, and factories attracted by remote area subsidies in towns such as Usuaria produce electronic components; tourism plays an important role in the area's economy.

Tiktaalik

Fossil organism apparently intermediate between fish and land animals found in Devonian rocks in the Canadian arctic.

One of the objections often raised to Darwinian evolutionary theory is the rarity of forms that are intermediate between the major biological groups. To some extent, the problem of the gap between the reptiles and birds was filled by the discovery of **Archaeopteryx** in the middle of the nineteenth century.

The transition between the fish and the land vertebrates was, perhaps, an even greater mystery. A discovery published early in 2006 has gone some way to its solution. Several fossils of a creature called *Tiktaalik roseae* (the name Tiktaalik means large shallow-water fish in the Inuit language) were found in deposits laid down in a tropical river delta in the Devonian period (417 to 354 million years ago) in Ellesmere Island, in arctic Canada. It was about 9 feet (2.75 meters) in length and probably somewhat resembled a crocodile. The organism had bony scales and fins, but the front fins have some limblike characteristics; they have the internal skeleton structure of an arm with wrists and elbows, but with fins instead of separate fingers. The lower jaw and palate are also similar to those in primitive lobe-finned fish (sacopterygians). The animal had a structure on its head that resembles a gill-slit, that might be described as a partly formed ear and an elongated snout that would have served to catch prey on land. It probably lived in warm, shallow water.

See also: Transitional Forms.

FURTHER READING

Daeschler E. B., N. H. Shubin, and F. A. Jenkins, Jr. 2006. "A Devonian Tetrapod-like Fish and the Evolution of the Tetrapod Body Plan." *Nature* 440: 757–763.

Toponyms

Place names. A number of geographical features and settlements have been named after Charles Darwin. The first was Mount Darwin, a mountain 7,997 feet (2,438 meters) high at 54° 44' S, 69° 21' W, in **Tierra del Fuego** (now in Chile). This name was suggested by HMS *Beagle* captain **Robert FitzRoy** after Darwin helped save the expedition's boats when they were about to be overwhelmed by a great wave formed when ice from a glacier collapsed into the Beagle Channel in January 1833. On East Falkland, a small sheep farming settlement is named Darwin (51° 47' S, 58° 59' W). This is close to the furthermost point that Darwin reached on his overland exploration of the **Falkland Islands** while the *Beagle* was anchored in Berkeley Sound in March 1834 (it was the scene of fierce fighting in the Falklands War in 1982). There is also a small settlement called Darwin on the Rio Negro in Argentina (39° 12' S, 65° 45' W). A Canal Darwin (approximately 45° S, 74° W) separates two islands in the Chonos archipelago, just south of the Isle of **Chiloé** on the Chilean coast. The name Darwin Island has also been used for Culpepper Island, a tiny islet in the **Galapagos Islands** group, but the name Volcán Darwin (Darwin Volcano) on Isla Isabella in the Galapagos (0° 19' S, 91° 17' W) is well established: it rises to 4,200 feet (1,280 meters). Away from the South American realm, the region where the influence of Darwin (and his shipmates) on toponyms was strongest is Australasia. In the high mountains of South Island, New Zealand, is another Mt. Darwin; it is about 9,715 feet (2,961 meters). Not far away is the Darwin Glacier. See the separate article on the **City of Darwin,** the capital of the Northern Territory, Australia, situated on a broad embayment known as Port Darwin, into which feeds the Darwin River.

Transitional Forms

Organisms, usually fossilized, that illustrate an evolutionary transition. They may possess certain primitive or pleisiomorphic characteristics compared with their more derived or highly evolved biological relatives. The phrase "missing link" is a popular phrase sometimes used for a transitional form.

According to evolutionary theory, all populations of organisms are in transition, so a transitional form is an artificial construct, although it may vividly represent a particular evolutionary stage.

When Darwin published ***On the Origin of Species*** in 1859, the fossil record of many parts of the world was very poorly known, and the claim that there were very few transitional **fossils** was eminently reasonable. Darwin freely admitted this and acknowledged that this absence was a most "formidable objection" to the theory (*On the Origin,* chapter 10) of evolution through natural selection that he espoused. However, the discovery in Germany a couple of years later of *Archaeopteryx*—a fossil that apparently represented a transitional form between reptiles and birds— was seen as a triumph for Darwin's notion of common descent. Enormous gaps remain in the fossil record, despite the increase in knowledge since Darwin's day. While it is sometimes maintained that this is a significant problem for evolutionary theory, most scientists accept that the rarity of fossils means that many extinct plants and animals will remain unknown. **Stephen Jay Gould**'s idea of **punctuated equilibrium** is one mechanism that has been suggested to explain the rarity of transitional forms in the fossil record.

Othniel Charles Marsh (1831–1899), a pioneer American paleontologist arranged known fossils of the horse and its relatives into a schema that showed a single directional lineage with many transitional types, which he thought accurately represented the **evolution of the horse** from *Eohippus* to the modern animal. This model has been criticized: modern evolutionists prefer a branching, multistemmed, treelike model with numerous dead ends.

Other specimens mentioned as transitional forms include the "walking whale" *Ambulocetus,* recently found in Pakistan—which, although it had limbs, also had shared a number of adaptations to an underwater life-style with the true whales; the recently discovered lobe-finned fish **Tiktaalik** from the Canadian arctic, which had many tetrapod (four-legged) characteristics; and various early hominids such as *Australopithecus* (from Africa), which may be considered transitional between an apelike ancestor and modern humans.

See also: Human Evolution.

Tristram, Henry Baker (1822–1906)

English parson-naturalist, distinguished zoologist, and one of the first to adopt Darwin's evolutionary ideas in his work.

Although some Church of England clergy, such as **Francis Orpen Morris,** remained resolutely opposed to Darwin's views, there were also a number who saw no incompatibility between evolutionary ideas and the Christian message. Henry Tristram was such a man.

Henry Tristram was the son of a clergyman and was born in the vicarage at Eglingham, near the small town of Alnwick in England's northernmost county, Northumberland. He studied at Durham School and then at Lincoln College, Oxford. In 1846, he became a priest, but he suffered from respiratory problems and spent some years abroad for the benefit of his health. He traveled extensively in North Africa and the Middle East, writing a number of books on the natural history of these regions, as well as attempting to identify sites mentioned in the Bible. He became canon of Durham Cathedral in 1873. His travels and contacts enabled him to accumulate an extensive collection of bird skins, and he was known at one time as "the great gun of Durham." Later in life he converted to the conservation approach and was an active campaigner for the protection of birds. Tristram was a elected a fellow of the **Royal Society** for his ornithological work in 1868.

He may have been the first zoologist to make use of Darwin's evolutionary ideas in his work, even before *On the Origin of Species* was published. He noticed Darwin and Wallace's brief paper in the **Linnean Society of London**'s journal and, within months, he quoted it in a paper on the birds of North Africa. "Writing with a series of about 100 Larks of various species in front of me," he wrote, "I cannot help feeling convinced of the views set forth by Messrs Darwin and Wallace." He accepted at once that change from one species to another had occurred, and was "possibly occurring still" (H. B. Tristram, 1858, "On the Ornithology of North Africa," Part 3, The Sahara, *The Ibis*, 1: 415–435). However, he may not have been completely converted; he does not entirely exclude the possibility of some independent creation.

U

Uniformitarianism

The idea that the natural processes operating in the past are identical to those observed in the present. The concept is frequently summed up in the statement: "The present is the key to the past" and is sometimes said to be the opposite of **catastrophism**; the term "actualism" is occasionally used.

Until the eighteenth century, it was widely (but not universally) believed that the Earth had had a comparatively short history, albeit one punctuated by a number of spectacular changes, possibly very different from those that could be witnessed today. Some theologians saw the events described in the Old Testament in this context: the creation, the flood, and the destruction of Sodom and Gomorrah were interpreted as catastrophic events without a modern parallel.

Although the essential principle of uniformitarianism is an ancient one, the notion was developed and publicized by James Hutton (1726–1797) in *The Theory of the Earth* in 1795. He described, for example, what became known as Hutton's Unconformity in layers of sedimentary rocks on the Scottish coast at Siccar Point, some 30 miles (50 kilometers) east of Edinburgh. At this locality, the lower portion of the cliff reveals layers of shale tilted into an almost vertical orientation; immediately above this, in the upper part of the cliff, there are more or less horizontal layers of red sandstone. Hutton argued that there must have been a number of cycles, each involving deposition of sediments on a sea floor, uplift, tilting, and erosion, followed by further subsidence for additional layers of material to be deposited. This sequence could have been repeated many times during a very long Earth history. At Siccar Point in about 1786, Hutton is said to have remarked "that we find no vestige of a beginning, no prospect of an end."

The notion was further popularized by **Charles Lyell** (1797–1875), who applied the concept extensively to geological science in his book *The Principles of Geology*, published in three volumes 1830 to 1833. This was the vehicle through which uniformitarianism, and indeed the whole notion of **gradualism** (which emphasizes the role of gradual change in relation to many phenomena), reached Charles Darwin. Darwin read Lyell's volumes on the *Beagle* voyage, and the ideas therein had a profound effect on him.

In the twentieth century, there was an attempt to reconcile the concepts of uniformitarianism and catastrophism. Catastrophic, dramatic, sudden events such as earthquakes, tsunamis, landslides, volcanic eruptions, and meteoritic impacts do occur and have profound effects on the Earth. It is widely held that a meteorite hitting the Earth was responsible for the extinction of the dinosaurs. It can be argued that these events have occurred throughout geological time at approximately the same—albeit possibly low—frequency and thus are part of the normal range of processes that affect the planet's surface.

V

Vestiges

The abbreviated title of *Vestiges of the Natural History of Creation,* originally published anonymously in 1844 by **Robert Chambers** (1802–1871). An early Victorian evolutionary tract read by Darwin.

Victoria (1819–1901; sovereign 1837–1901)

British Queen and Empress of India, one of England's six queens regnant (ruling in her own right), reigning and living longer than any other English monarch. Her presence dominated the period during which Charles Darwin lived and worked.

Because she was a woman of enormous personal strength and character; because she was the last British monarch to reign before the country became a true democracy; because she ruled as Queen-Empress over a great empire; and because she oversaw a period of enormous industrial, political, and scientific development, her reign was of enormous importance.

She was in no sense an intellectual and believed that good character, experience, and sound common sense were of greater importance than academic achievement or brilliance. Her opposition to such ideas as women's suffrage, democracy, socialism, or, it seems, Darwinism, was based on ignorance and, as such, probably coincided with the views of the average person. Her last prime minister, Lord Salisbury, stated that if he knew what view the Queen had on a particular policy, he knew what opinion her subjects would hold. Nevertheless, she was lively and curious about a great range of subjects. As a child, she spoke English with a German accent (because of the influence of her German mother, her German governess, and others close to her upbringing), but the accent disappeared over time. She also spoke French and Italian quite well. She was a competent painter and sketcher. She had a simple personal Christian piety and was tolerant in matters of religion, respecting the views of others.

Her father died when she was very young, and it was thus under the dominating influence of her mother that she grew up; she later described her childhood as "rather melancholy" and isolated. She knew, from the age of 13, that she was likely to become queen. She attained her majority at the age of 18, and four weeks later, on the death of her uncle, King William IV, ascended to the throne. A few hours after being woken early in the morning of June 20, 1837, she received the prime minister and confirmed him in office and then met the Privy Council, which contained the government ministers and other leaders. This must have been an enormous ordeal for the young girl, but she conducted the proceedings with a composure that amazed those present. She at once asked for the bed to be removed from her mother's room, and that night for the first time wrote in her journal without the supervision of her mother or governess. She wrote:

> Since it has pleased Providence to place me in this station, I shall do my utmost to fulfill my duty towards my country; I am very young, and perhaps in many, though not in all things, inexperienced, but I am sure that very few have more real good will and more real desire to do what is fit and right than I have. (Viscount Esher, *The Girlhood of Queen Victoria, a Selection from Her Majesty's Diaries, 1832–1840*, Vol. 1. London: John Murray, 1912, 196)

The dignity and resolution she displayed during the first few hours of her reign was to characterize the rest of her life.

Victoria was crowned on June 28, 1838, and her confidence grew as she undertook her duties. She was fortunate that she had the guidance and support of Prime Minister Lord Melbourne (1779–1848), who supported her in an almost fatherly manner; she referred to him often as "My excellent Lord Melbourne." She was also in frequent correspondence with her uncle Leopold, King of the Belgians, who also offered the teenage queen advice, which she often took.

Inexperience led to some difficulties. Her close relationship—some describe it almost as a flirtation—with Melbourne tended to lead to accusations of her favoring the Whig party over the Tories. Later in life she developed a preference for the Conservative Benjamin Disraeli over the Liberal **William Ewart Gladstone** (1808–1898), who, she said, tended to speak to her as though he were "addressing a public meeting." A constitutional monarch has to be politically impartial, and occasionally she deviated from this ideal.

She gained the support and love of her people both in Britain and throughout the Empire, and she aspired to very high standards in her personal and family life. Her predecessors as monarch, George IV and William IV, had been less than exemplary in their lives; their drinking, womanizing, and gambling had been the cause of comment. Victoria sought to redeem the reputation of the royal family. Nevertheless, at times, she and her family were subjected to vitriolic satire and lampooning. The media were becoming a force to be reckoned with.

A lady at Victoria's court, a few months into her reign, as she gained in confidence, worried that her fault might be that she tended to become too reliant on herself and a little obstinate. The close link with Melbourne was causing comment. There were those who felt that the spirited young queen needed to marry and settle down. The choice of possible suitable husbands was narrow. For legal reasons (the Act of Settlement), he had to be Protestant; by convention he had to be of royal blood or at least of aristocratic background; and he had to be personally acceptable. Uncle Leopold took charge: two of his young nephews, princes of Saxe-Coburg, were cousins of the Queen. Ernest and Albert had already visited England and were known to Victoria; on the second visit of the young princes in 1839, her feelings became clear. Victoria's personal diary for October 15, 1839 records:

> At about 1/2 p. 12 I sent for Albert; he came to the closet where I was alone, and after a few minutes I said to him, that I thought he must be aware why I wished them to come here,—and that it would make me too happy if he would consent . . . to marry me. We embraced each other, and he was so affectionate . . . I felt it was the happiest brightest moment of my life . . . I then told him the necessity of keeping it a secret, except for his father and Uncle Leopold. . . . I then told him to fetch Ernest, which he did and he congratulated us both and seemed very happy. (Esher, Vol. 11, 268–269)

Victoria took the initiative because she felt that it was unfair to expect Albert to propose marriage to the British Queen. They were married four months later on February 10, 1840. The match was not universally popular. Albert was regarded by some as an obscure foreigner. To Victoria's chagrin, Parliament would not allow him the title of King-Consort (there was and is no such position), and his grant of income was reduced from £50,000 per annum to £30,000.

Although Albert was closely related to Victoria and very close in age, he differed in significant ways: he was handsome, she was regarded as rather plain; he had a fine intellect and was interested in the arts, the sciences, and technology; and he was patient while Victoria was impulsive. Yet his sense of duty was as solid as hers. Nevertheless, he was sometimes misunderstood by those close to the royal couple: Albert's German sense of correctness made him appear cold and stiff; his attention to detail and concern for form, efficiency, and protocol was described by the English aristocracy as priggish. Albert made determined attempts to master the intricacies of

British politics, while the aristocrats around him treated politics with about the same degree of seriousness as they did fox-hunting or horse-racing.

Albert served his adopted country with great devotion; his character and skills complimented Victoria's, and he increased the respect afforded the royal family. Nevertheless, there were early difficulties. Victoria, despite her early wish that Albert become King-Consort (Parliament would not allow the title of Prince Consort until 1857), had definitely married a husband, not a co-sovereign. Having been prepared for a career close to the center of power, Albert did not relish the isolated position in which he initially found himself (to begin with, he was not allowed to see official papers). Gradually, the position improved, and, as Victoria became more mature and occupied with matters of family as well as those of state, she deferred to him more and more. Although ultimate decisions remained hers, he became her political secretary and personal advisor. His industry, efficiency, and political skills enabled her to rule consistently without the element of arbitrariness that could be detected in some of her earlier decisions. The marriage was supremely happy.

A single example must suffice to demonstrate the importance of Albert's benign influence. Officially, in the matter of the American Civil War of 1861 to 1865, Great Britain was neutral, but many of Victoria's aristocratic politicians tended to favor the southern Confederacy, and they did not prevent the Confederates from obtaining weapons from Britain. There were protests from the federal government in Washington, and tension mounted to a dangerous extent, particularly over the *Trent* affair, in which a British ship carrying southern envoys to Europe had been intercepted by northern forces. In almost the last act of his life—he was dangerously ill with a fever at the time—Albert redrafted a British Foreign Office dispatch that otherwise might have led to a serious breach.

Victoria presided over an enormous expansion of British economic, industrial, military, and political power. Telegraphs and railways expanded (there were only 200 miles of rail in Britain in the year of Victoria's coronation). Britain's industrial might—based on coal, iron, steel, and textiles—increased apace. Raw materials were obtained from across an expanding empire, and manufactured products were exported to distant British colonies. Later in her reign, cables began to link the overseas territories of the Empire. The penny postage came in the year of Victoria's marriage and enormously improved communications.

Imperial expansion sometimes came at a heavy price. There were wars against the Maoris in New Zealand, the Zulus in southern Africa, and the Indian Mutiny came in 1857. Toward the end of her reign, there were campaigns in the Sudan and against the Boers (Dutch settlers and farmers) in South Africa. Troubles in Europe included war against Russia in the Crimea in 1854. Victoria was always extremely concerned with the welfare of her soldiers and sailors and was a devotee of the work of Florence Nightingale among the wounded soldiers of Crimea.

At home, the British government was faced with Ireland's desire for self-determination. Agitation was led by Daniel O'Connell but collapsed in 1843, and, before it could revive, there occurred the disastrous potato famine of 1845 to 1848; blight (a type of fungus) destroyed several potato harvests. Estimates of the number of deaths vary, but may have numbered millions. Millions also emigrated to England, to the United States, and to Australia. Victoria showed token solidarity in rationing bread at Buckingham Palace and personally contributing to relief funds. In 1849, she (with Albert) paid her first visit to Ireland and was well received. She visited again in 1853, 1861, and 1900, but her visits were seen as insufficient. Victoria never had the affection for Ireland that she did for Scotland; in this her attitude reflected that of many of her English subjects. Ireland remained a festering sore.

Alongside the Irish situation were questions about the condition of England. Rapid, uncontrolled urban and industrial growth became associated with appalling conditions of housing and employment; rising population (over 14 percent in 10 years in an early period of her reign) aggravated the problems of unemployment. There was much suffering, and the working class, sometimes supported by the middle classes, became increasingly militant, and rioting was occasionally put down by force. The main expression of the discontent was in the People's Charter, a program of parliamentary and other reform that was designed to transform the government of the country to a democracy. Between 1839 and 1848, the Chartists presented their program to Parliament three times in the form of a petition with many millions of signatures. It was resisted. A slogan of the time was "God save the Queen, for no one else will." The first of several attempts to assassinate the Queen (usually by those who were psychiatrically disturbed and somewhat half-hearted in character) took place. Much of the discontent was focused on the political elite's privileges, including those of Victoria and Albert. But Prime Minister Sir Robert Peel (1788–1850) handled the situation with some skill. Under the guise of attempting to relieve the poverty in Ireland, he repealed the Corn Laws that had restricted trade in grain, maintained the price at a high level, favoring the landed interests, but caused discontent in the middle and working classes. Prosperity increased with freer trade and lower prices, and agitation declined. But for a while, the monarchy was in real danger.

There were important links among the expansion of the Empire, trade, and science and technology. As the colonies of the Empire were explored, settled, and developed, they sent raw materials to the home country and purchased manufactured goods from it. Along with the wool and cotton flowed biological and geological specimens, and along with the pottery, metal goods, and textiles traveled those with a thirst for knowledge—explorers or military men, sailors, administrators, and missionaries with a penchant for science. Although by the end of Victoria's reign, in Australia, New Zealand, India, Canada, and South Africa, scientific societies, museums, libraries, and universities of note had developed, there were many in Britain (particularly England rather than Scotland and Ireland) who saw the science of the colonies as subordinate to that of the home country. The role of naturalists in the colonies was to supply specimens and information to those in London, Oxford, and Cambridge, where new theories were debated and conclusions drawn. Darwin's work fits this model well; his network of correspondents throughout the Empire and elsewhere sent him replies to his queries, barnacle specimens, and much else.

With the development of science came the development of industry and technology. Geological principles began to be applied to the search for coal and other minerals. There was feedback here, for as canals and railways were constructed to support expanding industry and commerce, geological sections were exposed and knowledge improved.

Of many of these developments Victoria knew little, but she was concerned for the well-being of her people—in Britain and throughout the Empire—and her generally benign rule encouraged industrial expansion and scientific progress.

Albert was particularly encouraging of these movements. In 1847, he was elected chancellor (titular head) of **Cambridge University**, and from this position he was able to promote the cause of science and encourage higher education.

Perhaps even more important was Albert's initiation and encouragement of the Great exhibition of 1851. In early 1850, he had proposed a "Great exhibition of the Works and Industry of All Nations." to celebrate "the unity of mankind" that was developing through scientific discovery and invention. Victoria was enthusiastic, but there were many detractors: the project would be too expensive, the exhibition building would take too long to build, it would bring in "all the vagabonds of London," it would encourage the importation of cheap, shoddy foreign goods; the tourists would bring in plagues; and it would destroy the attractiveness of the proposed site (Hyde Park). The design selected was based on the design of a garden superintendent for a conservatory; the designer, who had no training in architecture, sketched the proposed building distractedly on a piece of blotting paper at a meeting. The Crystal Palace, as it came to be known, consisted of 293,655 panes of glass held in place by steel girders. The outer shell was, remarkably, completed in about three months. Queen Victoria wrote to her uncle:

> The triumph is immense, for up to the last hour the difficulties, the opposition, and their ill-mannered attempts to annoy and to frighten, of a certain set of fashionables and Protectionists [those who felt that the encouragement of free trade was implicit in the whole project] were immense; but Albert's temper, patience, firmness and energy surmounted all. (Letter from Queen Victoria to King Leopold of the Belgians, May 3, 1851; A. C. Benson and Viscount Esher, *Letters of Queen Victoria*, Vol. 2. London: John Murray, 1908)

There were 13,937 exhibitors, of which 7,381 came from Britain and the colonies and 6,556 from foreign countries. There were four themes: raw materials, machinery and mechanical inventions, manufacture, and fine arts. The Queen opened the exhibition on May 1, 1851, and proudly visited it many times. Six million visitors, including Charles Darwin and his family, attended between May and October. It was an enormous success. Prince Albert's contribution is commemorated in the Albert Memorial, which stands near the site of the exhibition in London's Hyde Park.

The Great exhibition was seen not only as a symbol of British national progress, prosperity, and inventiveness, but as an emblem of international peace. It was hoped that trade would link countries to one another and reduce the possibility of wars. Despite her interest in the army and the welfare of the soldiery, Albert and Victoria were devoted to the cause of peace. By the end of her life, Victoria was related by blood or by marriage to most of the royal families of Europe, including Russia, Portugal, Belgium, Germany, Denmark, Spain, and Greece; this did not, however, always ensure good relations between these kingdoms.

Victoria was pregnant within weeks of getting married, and the Princess Royal was born in November and was given her mother's name. Victoria and Albert's second child, Albert or Bertie (later King Edward VII), was born the following year. Between 1840 and 1857, Victoria bore nine children, all of whom survived into adulthood and several into the middle of the twentieth century. By the time of her death, she had 80 grandchildren and great-grandchildren. Her increasing family responsibilities made her increasingly dependent on Albert in matters of state. Her status as a mother was often seen as a metaphor for her role as Mother of the Nation and Mother of the Empire. The Royal Titles Act of 1876 titled her Empress of India. Late in life, her connections and those of her children with other European heads of state could have given her the dignity of Mother of Europe. Her matriarchal status was frequently lampooned, but on the whole the royal couple remained popular.

Late in December 1861, Prince Albert caught typhoid and died. This was a blow from which Victoria never recovered. At times in her grief she almost became a recluse, spending much time at Windsor Castle and at her private homes of Balmoral (in the Scottish Highlands) and Osborne (on the Isle of Wight, off the coast of southern England). The journeys away from London that her ministers had to make to consult her did not improve relations with some of them. Although she probably shared many of his values, she disliked the "Grand Old Man" of British politics, **William Ewart Gladstone**, who was a fiercely loyal prime minister four times during the latter part of her reign. Her refusal to take part in public duties to more than a minimal extent caused much opinion to turn against her. In her grief following Albert's death, she cultivated a number of friendships that were considered unsuitable, most notably with John Brown, Scottish attendant and groom, whom she selected as her personal servant for a number of years. They went on rides together, and he was often heard to call the Queen "wumman," which particularly offended court etiquette. Gossip and rumor spread.

> She is really doing all in her power to create suspicions which I am persuaded have no foundation. Long, solitary rides, in secluded parts of the park; constant attendance on her in her room: private messages sent by him to persons of rank: avoidance of observation while he is leading her pony. . . : everything shows that she has selected this man for a . . . friendship that is unwise and unbecoming. . . . The Princesses [Victoria's daughters]—perhaps wisely— make a joke of the matter, and talk of him as "mama's lover." (Personal diary entry, March 1, 1864, quoted in John Vincent, ed., *Disraeli, Derby and the Conservative Party: The Political Journals of Edward, Lord Stanley, 1849–1869.* Sussex, England: Hassocks, 1978, 210)

Others were less charitable. The Queen was widely referred to as "Mrs. Brown." A bawdy pamphlet, *Brown on the Throne*, published in 1871, contains the following rhyme:

> There was a bonny Scotsman who lived in Waterloo
> He lifted up his petticoat [his kilt] an shewed his toodle-oo
> His toodle-oo was dirty when he shewed it to the Queen
> The Queen took soap and water and washed the bugger clean!
> (Quoted in Adrienne Munich,
> *Queen Victoria's Secrets.* New York:
> Columbia University Press, 1996, 163)

Whether there was a sexual relationship between the Queen and her servant is very doubtful, but the matter cannot be entirely settled, because diaries that might have shed some light on the question were destroyed after Brown's death. The incident confirms the idea that Victoria was a woman who knew her own mind, did not always accede to advice, and was full of contradictions.

Late in her reign, although she continued to refer to Albert's death as "an inconsolable loss," with the encouragement of Conservative Prime Minister Benjamin Disraeli (who she liked, partially because he flattered her), the Queen became somewhat less of a recluse. She celebrated her Golden Jubilee—50 years on the throne—on June 21, 1887:

> The morning was beautiful and bright with a fresh air. Troops began passing early with bands playing and . . . constant cheering. . . . The scene outside was colourful and reminded me of the [opening of the] Great exhibition, which also took place on a fine day. . . . At half-past eleven we left the Palace, I driving in a handsome gilt landaue drawn by six creams. . . . Just in front of my carriage rode the 12 Indian officers and in front of them my 3 sons, 5 sons-in-law, 9 grandsons, and grandsons in law. . . . All other Royalties went in a separate possession. George [Duke of] Cambridge rode the whole way next

to my carriage, and the Master of Horse, Equerries, etc., behind it with of course a Sovereign's escort. It really was a magnificent sight. (G. E. Buckle, ed., *A Selection from Her Majesty's Correspondence and Journal between the Years 1886–1901*, Vol. 1. 1932, 322–326)

Whereas the theme of the Golden Jubilee was the celebration of the life and times of the Mother of Nation, that of the Diamond Jubilee 10 years later was the acknowledgment of Victoria as Mother of the Empire. Indian troops were in the forefront, and, before commencing her procession, she "touched an electric button" in Buckingham Palace that telegraphed a message throughout the Empire: "From my heart I thank my beloved people, May God bless them."

The last few years and months of Victoria's reign were marred by bitter military conflicts in the Sudan and South Africa and by the Queen's inevitable decline. She died, at Osborne in the Isle of Wight in the early evening of January 22, 1901—incidentally three weeks after the Australian colonies federated into an independent Commonwealth of Australia, one of the first mileposts on the road of the transformation of the Empire into a British Commonwealth of independent nations.

The London *Times* of January 23, 1901, declared:

To write of the life of Queen Victoria is to relate the history of Great Britain during a period of great events, manifold changes and unexampled national prosperity. No reign in the annals of any country can compare with that of the late Sovereign.

A woman of enormous contradictions, she strove for peace, yet urged that "whatever happened, we must not be humiliated in S. Africa" and supported the sending out a large force. She was devoted to the prosperity of all her people and yet thought that the campaigners for women's rights were "very wicked." She cared little for the ideas of science but admired the progress of technology. She was a symbol of stability, yet she oversaw the transformation of the country from a largely rural one to an industrial powerhouse, plagued at times by fierce disputes. Many of the changes that took place in her life time were inevitable. But the perceived stability and prosperity associated with Victoria's reign allowed the expansion and development of the universities and of scientific achievement. The development of capitalism in her reign has been credited with providing the right intellectual climate for the reception of the notion of evolution through natural selection. Undoubtedly the expansion of Empire and improvement of communications allowed the speedier exchange of information between scientists in Britain with its overseas counterparts. Insofar as she had an opinion on Darwin's ideas, she seems to have opposed them, favoring those of **Richard Owen.** Yet many of the circumstances that her reign brought favored Darwin's work and the development and spread of his ideas.

FURTHER READING

There are an enormous number of biographies and critical works on the life and times of Queen Victoria. The examples below comprise a tiny selection.

Gardiner, J. 1997. *Queen Victoria*. London: Collins and Brown.

Munich, A. 1996. *Queen Victoria's Secrets*. New York: Columbia University Press.

Plunkett, J. 2003. *Queen Victoria: First Media Monarch*. Oxford, England: Oxford University Press.

St. Aubyn G. 1991. *Queen Victoria: A Portrait*. London: Sinclair-Stevenson.

Weintraub, S. 1987. *Victoria: Biography of a Queen*. London: Unwin Hyman.

Voyage of the Beagle

The published version of Charles Darwin's diary or journal from the *Beagle* voyage (1831–1836). It was considerably edited and rearranged, and the diary entries interspersed with extracts from his geological and zoological notes and other material. It was originally published as the third section of the *Narrative of the Voyages of H M Ships Adventure and Beagle*, edited by Captain Robert FitzRoy, published in 1839. It was published as a separate volume (a slightly modified edition that contains some slight hints that Darwin had by then adopted an evolutionary outlook) in 1845. This edition was called *Journal of Researches into the Natural History and Geology*, although the spine title was *A Naturalist's Voyage*. *The Voyage of the Beagle* appears as the title of the 1905 edition and is the way in which the work has been referred to ever since.

See also Beagle Diary.

Wallace, Alfred Russel (1823—1913)

Naturalist, traveler, writer, polymath. Co-originator with Charles Darwin of the theory of evolution by natural selection. Sometimes described as the father of biogeography.

Wallace was the eighth of nine children, born in the small town of Usk, Monmouthshire (now Gwent), on the border between England and Wales. The family moved to Hertford, close to London, when he was a young child, but his education was cut short after much of the family property was lost. He left school at 14 and worked for his elder brother William in his land surveying business, surveying farms and country properties along the border country between England and Wales. His father died in 1843, and he briefly (and unsuccessfully) tried schoolmastering. He took over the surveying business when his brother died in 1845.

Largely an autodidact, Wallace acquired a good knowledge of natural history while tramping with his surveyor's chain across the Welsh Borderland and South Wales. And his surveyor's training rendered him an excellent draughtsman in later life: his books and articles were well illustrated with maps and pictures. Curious about the great diversity of species in the rainforests of South America, he and another naturalist, Henry Walter Bates, left for Brazil in 1848. Part of the motivation for the expedition was commercial. They intended to collect natural history specimens to sell to museums and collectors, but this part of the venture was unsuccessful because the vessel on which they were returning to England caught fire and sank.

Between 1854 and 1862, Wallace traveled through the Malay Archipelago (now Indonesia and Malaysia), again to study natural history and anthropology and to collect specimens. He detected significant differences in the faunas across a narrow zone, suggesting the existence of a zoogeographical boundary that later became known as Wallace's line. To the north and west of this line (which passes between the Indonesian islands of Bali and Lombok and between Celebes [Sulawesi] and Borneo), he believed the animals had affinities with Asia; to the south and east, they had a stronger Australian character. Wallace later moved his line slightly, and alternatives have been suggested, because some of the lines are more appropriate for particular groups of organisms. In fact, there is a zone of transition, in which the proportions of Asian and Australian organisms change as one passes from one island to another along the archipelago. The transition zone, sometimes known as Wallacea, is now regarded as the zone of the mixing of the Australian and Asian biotas formed with the collision of the Australian and the Asian crustal places tens of millions of years ago. Wallace's book *The Malay Archipelago,* first published in 1869 (and dedicated to Charles Darwin), summarizes his eight years of travel and collecting (during which he accumulated more than 125,000 specimens) in what are now the countries of Malaysia and Indonesia. One of the objectives of his book was a desire to show how the present distributions of animals and plants can be used to reconstruct changes in the history of the Earth, and is thus regarded as a classic text in biogeography. His later book, *Island Life* (1880), discussed themes such as the dispersal of organisms, and the distinctive assemblages of plants and animals on remote islands, effectively establishing the subject of island biogeography.

But in 1855, before either of these books appeared, Wallace published a paper with the title "On the Law Which Has Regulated the Introduction of Species," in which he put forth observations on the distribution of organisms in space and time. He asserted that "Every species has come into existence coincident both in space and time with a closely allied species." Many of the ideas later taken up by Darwin are present or at least implicit in this early paper. Wallace refers to common ancestors as "antitypes" and discusses the analogy between organisms in different areas and the affinity between organisms in divergent series. Several important Darwinian themes are clearly foreshadowed by Wallace: gradualism, utility, adaptation to environment, allopatric speciation (formation of species by the separation of populations by a barrier), imperfection of the fossil record, and rudimentary organs— are present in the essay or are clearly implied. The similarities in imagery and terminology are so strong that it seems Wallace was thinking along evolutionary lines, at least to some extent, by the mid-1850s.

Wallace and Darwin had briefly met on one occasion before Wallace's departure for the East, and Wallace was one of Darwin's multitude of correspondents on whom he was reliant for information. Wallace knew that Darwin was interested in the species question and, while Wallace was still traveling in the East, sent him a copy of his draft article "On the Tendency of Varieties To Depart Indefinitely from the Original Type." The manuscript—often referred to as the "bolt from the blue"—reached Darwin on about June 18, 1858. Darwin read the pages with dismay and immediately penned a letter to his geologist friend **Charles Lyell:**

> Your words have come true with a vengeance that I shd. Be forestalled. You said this to me when I explained to you . . . my views on "natural Selection" depending on the Struggle for existence. I never saw a more striking coincidence. If Wallace had my MS sketch written out in 1842 he could not have made a better short abstract! Even his terms now stand as Heads of my chapters. (*Correspondence*, Vol. 7, 107. Original owned by American Philosophical Society, Philadelphia)

Lyell and Darwin's botanist friend **Joseph Hooker** took charge of the situation and moved fast. They assembled a joint presentation consisting of Wallace's paper, part of Darwin's **Essay of 1844,** and part of a letter Darwin had written to **Asa Gray** dated October 1857 that set out the theory of natural selection. The paper was read to the **Linnean Society of London** on July 1, 1858. Hooker and Lyell were present, but Wallace was still in the East Indies, and Darwin was at home comforting his wife and family following the death of 18-month-old Charles Waring Darwin of scarlet fever on June 28.

Although it is sometimes stated that Wallace was relegated to the status of co-discoverer, events may have turned out for the best for Wallace. He was relatively unknown compared to Cambridge-educated, well-published, fellow of the **Royal Society** Charles Darwin; the joint publication was appreciated by Wallace. The link with Darwin's name gave him an entrée into English science that he would otherwise probably not have had. The two naturalists became friends, although they often disagreed.

In 1864, before Darwin had made any public utterances on the subject, Wallace published a paper titled "The Origin of the Human Races and the Antiquity of Man Deduced from the Theory of Natural Selection," which applied evolutionary ideas to the human species. Wallace was also a pioneer ecologist. He published 24 books and several hundred scientific papers. In many ways, like **Thomas Huxley,** he championed Darwin's ideas and received high honors, including the Royal Geographical Society's Founder's Medal and the Linnean Society Gold Medal (both in 1892), a fellowship of the Royal Society (1893), the Order of Merit, the Royal Society's Copley Medal, and the Linnean Society Medal (all in 1908). He had craters on the moon and on the planet Mars named after him.

Despite these successes, Wallace sometimes disturbed his friends and scientific colleagues by his advocacy of strange ideas including spiritualism, phrenology (the assessment of personality by the study of the form of the skull), the nationalization of land, mesmerism, opposition to vaccination, and a belief in miracles. These interests have led to Wallace's work being eclipsed by the brilliance of the Darwin legacy to a greater extent than perhaps was appropriate. Some of Wallace's contemporaries described him as timid in the presence of others, and he was somewhat self-effacing; after describing the flash of insight he received in Ternate, in the East Indies, he wrote:

> [T]he idea occurred to Darwin in 1838, nearly 20 years earlier than to myself; and during the whole of that 20 years he had been laboriously collecting evidence . . . I was then [as often since] the "young man in a hurry"; he the painstaking and patient student. (A. R. Wallace, 1905)

But far from being a mere stimulus to Darwin or Darwin's "moon," Wallace developed his own distinct suite of evolutionary ideas, which often varied from those of Darwin. Darwin respected many of Wallace's views and quoted him extensively in *Descent of Man* (1869), although often to differ from him.

Never a wealthy man, Wallace, in 1881, at the end of his life, was allocated a pension by the British government in recognition of his work in science. He described himself as a complete and happy man.

FURTHER READING

Finchman, Martin. 1981. *Alfred Russel Wallace*. Boston: Twayne Publishers.

Marchant, James. 1975. *Alfred Russel Wallace: Letters and Reminiscences*. New York: Arno Press.

McKinney, H. Lewis. 1972. *Wallace and Natural Selection*. New Haven, CT: Yale University Press.

Wallace, Alfred Russel. 1905. *My Life: A Record of Events and Opinions* (2 volumes). London: Chapman & Hall.

Warrah

Falklands fox or Falklands wolf. Darwin was fascinated by islands and visited almost 40 of them during the course of the *Beagle*'s circumnavigation. He had the knack of seeing what was interesting and important about their geology, plants, and animals, and in his notes and subsequent publications frequently made comparisons between the various islands and groups of islands that he had visited. His observations on remote islands provided an important source of inspiration in his work. He appreciated the uniqueness of island biotas and speculated about the origins of the plants and animals in such places. He has a lot to say, both in the notes he made on the voyage and in the subsequent *Mammals* volume of *The Zoology of the Voyage of the Beagle*, about the distinctive warrah, or the fox or wolf of the **Falkland Islands**. Four specimens were collected during the visits in 1833 and 1834 (some are in the Natural History Museum in London). The creature is now extinct.

The animals were about a meter long, excluding the tail, which was another 30 to 35 centimeters; the fur was red-brown, long, and soft; there was white around the mouth, on the throat, and at the tip of the tail. They lived in burrows, especially by the sea, feeding on seals and birds; they had a feeble bark; and some authors described them as very social, moving in groups. About ten skulls are known to exist, and some scientists believe that they show characteristics intermediate between the foxes (*Vulpes*) and the true dogs and wolves (genus *Canis*). Darwin used the scientific name *Canis antarcticis,* but the modern name is *Dusicyon australis.*

Darwin was impressed by the warrahs' extraordinary tameness, a trait that they shared with many of the birds of the Falklands. He later compared this tameness with that of some of the creatures of the Galapagos Islands; the animals of both archipelagoes (and other islands and island groups he visited) he later realized had evolved with little or no contact with humans and so had not developed a fear of them. Fear of humans, therefore, was an adaptation that had evolved through natural selection. He also appreciated the animal's uniqueness—it was endemic to the islands, found nowhere else—and wondered how its ancestors had arrived. In his notes, Darwin wrote: "It is very curious, thus having a quadruped peculiar to so small a tract of country." Both Darwin and the *Beagle*'s captain, Robert FitzRoy, expressed the view that icebergs or icefloes might be the vehicle that carried the foxes at some time in the past from South America (where related animals live) to the islands. For example:

> The Falkland Islands . . . are inhabited by a wolf-like fox. . . . Icebergs formerly brought boulders to its western shores, and they may have transported foxes, as so frequently happens in arctic regions. (*On the Origin of Species,* chapter 12, Geographical Distribution)

Long-distance dispersal is a notion intimately connected with that of evolution. If all life on Earth had a common origin or could be traced back to a few simple forms, it follows that animals and plants on remote islands must have at some time made the journey from elsewhere. During the voyage and later, Darwin displayed a great interest in the mechanisms of dispersal.

Darwin also noted that the foxes from East Falkland were smaller, darker, and more rusty-colored than those on West Falkland. Many months later, he noted that the birds of the various islands in the Galapagos were subtly different from each other. As he ruminated over his notebooks toward the end of the voyage, he compared the two situations. If there were "the slightest foundation for these remarks," he wrote, "such facts would undermine the stability of species." Darwin was not an evolutionist while he was in the Falklands, and the idea of transmutability seems only to have passed through his mind as a possibility in the final months of the *Beagle* voyage.

PLATE IV

Canis antarcticus

The warrah, Falklands fox or Falklands wolf. From: *The Zoology of the Voyage of the Beagle*, Part 2, Mammals, 1842.

But Darwin's observations on, and speculations about, a little-known animal from the Falklands played a significant role in the development of his evolutionary theories.

But Darwin's interest in the warrah is significant for other reasons, too. The human impact on the world's environments in the first half of the nineteenth century was much less than it is today, and the conservation movement hardly existed (although by mid-century, bird protection was becoming a political issue). Darwin appreciated that the warrah was already coming under severe pressure; he noted that, because of their tameness and inquisitiveness, they were easily killed by a gaucho holding a piece of meat in one hand and a knife in the other. (The fur was valuable; there are records of pelts being stored by a fur trader in New York by the late 1830s.) Darwin observed:

> The number of these animals during the last fifty years must have been greatly reduced; already they are entirely banished from [the eastern] half of East Falkland . . . and it cannot, I think be doubted that as these islands are now becoming colonized, before the paper is decayed on which this animal is figured, it will be ranked among those species which have perished from the earth. (*Zoology of the Voyage of the Beagle,* Vol. 2, based on notes made on the voyage)

Darwin's prediction was correct. The last warrah was killed by settlers at Shallow Bay, West Falkland, in 1876, well within Darwin's life time.

Waterhouse, George Robert (1810—1888)

English naturalist who cooperated with Charles Darwin in the writing of the *Mammal* volume of *The Zoology of the Voyage of the Beagle.*

A lifelong naturalist, George Waterhouse was a founder of the Entomological Society in 1833. He was curator of the Zoological Society of London's museum 1836 to 1843. In 1843, he became assistant keeper of mineralogy and geology at the British Museum and became keeper in 1851 upon the death of Charles Konig. In 1857, the department was divided and he was made keeper of geology, remaining in this position until 1880.

Charles Darwin entrusted Waterhouse with the study of the mammals and insects collected on the voyage of the *Beagle,* because he had a high opinion of his abilities as a taxonomist. He was also the author of *A Natural History of the Mammalia* (1846–1848). Charles Darwin and George Waterhouse corresponded frequently.

Wedgwood, Josiah I (1730—1795)

Pottery manufacturer, philanthropist, scientist, political activist; founder of the Wedgwood dynasty, and grandfather to both Charles Darwin and his wife Emma.

Josiah is a prime example of a self-made man. From rather humble origins, he became a person of enormous influence. He was born into a family of 12 children (he was the last) and into a family of potters at the Churchyard Works, Burslem, Staffordshire. Apprenticed to an established potter, an abscess impeded his use of the potter's wheel, and he used available time to study science. He started work as an independent potter, renting the Ivy House Works from his kinsmen (Thomas and John Wedgwood of the Big House, also in Burslem) from May 1, 1759. Wedgwood constantly experimented with types of clay and with firing and coloring methods. The circumstances were propitious in several ways; Britain's population, which had been static for half a century, began to increase rapidly in the years following 1740. Moreover, the middle class was expanding and increasing in affluence. Further, the new availability of steam power in factories and the development of the network of turnpike roads and canals promoted mass production and distribution of goods. Josiah had a flare not only for design, but also for the marketing of his product. Through the perfection of a cream-colored earthenware material, he attracted the attention of Queen Charlotte, the wife of King George III; he manufactured for her a tea and coffee service in the new material. The Queen then allowed Wedgwood to describe himself as "Potter to Her Majesty" and to name his creamware

"Queen's Ware"—a notable marketing coup. In June 1759, he moved to a new factory at Etruria. Wedgwood and his partner, Thomas Bentley, then developed a new ornamental stoneware that was named jasper, and leading artists were employed to assist in design. This was an important innovation, and this type of product has been a mainstay of the Wedgwood company ever since.

Wedgwood was also a very competent scientist. His invention of the pyrometer, a thermometer for the measurement of the high temperatures needed for firing in the kilns gained him election to a fellowship of the **Royal Society** in January 1783. In 1786, he became a fellow of the Society for the Encouragement of Arts, Manufactures and Commerce. He was also a noted philanthropist, campaigning vigorously for the abolition of slavery. Josiah had liberal views, approving of the revolution in France and the campaign for independence by the American colonies.

Josiah Wedgwood had an entrée to the salons of some of the most influential figures in England; he was friendly with members of the House of Lords and used these contacts relentlessly to promote his business. He used diplomatic missions to make contacts with European aristocracy and royalty. He had a stylish showroom in London, and he amassed a great fortune.

Yet he had much sadness in his life; he caught smallpox as a child and was horribly disfigured. As a result of this, he insisted that his children were vaccinated as soon as infant vaccination became available. One of his children, Richard, died as the result of complications following this then-dangerous procedure. Injury and osteomyelitis caused serious trouble with one of his legs, and he had it amputated in May 1768 (of course, without anaesthesia). He recovered and continued with his business. At one stage he thought he was losing his sight, but he recovered it.

In later life, he withdrew from the business to some extent, leaving its management to his son and nephew, and he concentrated on literary and scientific activities. He was a great friend of chemist Joseph Priestly. He died after a short illness in January 1795 and is buried in Stoke-upon-Trent Church. One story has it that, racked by fever and with an infection in his jaw, he deliberately took an overdose of laudanum given to him by his friend, **Erasmus Darwin,** Charles Darwin's grandfather.

The fortune that Josiah Wedgwood I accumulated and the atmosphere of learning and enterprise he engendered in his household established him as the patriarch of one of England's most important commercial and intellectual families. The family is still associated with the pottery business, and descendants of Josiah I have held an important place in Britain's intellectual and political life for over two centuries. His daughter Susannah married Erasmus's son **Robert Darwin** (her cousin). His son, **Josiah Wedgwood II,** carried his name and tradition forward and eventually became friend and mentor to Charles Robert Darwin, encouraging him to take advantage of the offer of a place on HMS *Beagle*.

FURTHER READING

Uglow, Jenny. 2002. *The Lunar Men*. London: Faber and Faber.

Wedgwood, Josiah II (1769–1841)

Second son of Josiah Wedgwood I and partner in the family pottery business at the Etruria factory from 1790 until 1841; member of Parliament, country gentleman, and friend and mentor of Charles Darwin.

Charles Darwin's grandfather, **Erasmus Darwin,** and **Josiah Wedgwood I,** the founder of the famed pottery business, were great friends, and their children maintained that link. **Robert Darwin** and Josiah II were close associates in boyhood, and the link was maintained into the next generation, and the Darwins and Wedgwoods intermarried several times.

Josiah Wedgwood II (Jos) took a part in the family firm from a young age, although he did not always agree with his father on policy—for example, he thought that having to attend on customers at the firm's London showroom was beneath him. Nevertheless, he seems to have been quite a good salesman. In 1790, he took a copy of the Portland Vase, one of the business's most famous creations, on a promotional tour of the continent.

On the death of his father in 1795, Josiah II moved to Surrey, close to London, leaving Thomas Byerley in sole charge of both the Etruria factory and the London showroom. It was only after the death of his brother Tom in 1805 that Josiah II returned to Staffordshire to take over active management of the factory. And it was not until after Byerley's death in 1810 that Josiah II took full charge, having bought Maer Hall, Staffordshire, in 1807 and living there until his death.

Interested in public affairs and literary and philosophical matters, Jos and his brother Tom gave their friend Samuel Taylor Coleridge a life annuity of £150 per annum, hoping to free the poet from financial worries and the need to support himself by uncreative work so that he could pursue his literary activities. He was also the first member of Parliament for Stoke-on-Trent (1832–1834).

Jos Wedgwood married Elizabeth Allen in 1792; they had six children, two of whom married Darwins—Emma married Charles, and Josiah III married Charles's sister Caroline. (Emma's sister Charlotte had a bit of a crush on Charles at one stage.)

Charles's father Robert was not keen on his son taking up the *Beagle* offer; however, such was his high opinion of Josiah's judgment that he wrote asking for his unbiased opinion, stating that "if you think differently from me I shall wish him to follow your advice." "Uncle Jos" carefully answered all of Robert Darwin's objections. Charles was considering a career as a Church of England clergyman, and Josiah affirmed:

I should not think that it would be in any degree disreputable to his character as a clergyman. I should think on the contrary the offer honorable to him, and the pursuit of Natural History . . . is very suitable for a clergymen. (*Correspondence*, Vol. 1, 133–134; original in Cambridge University Library, Darwin Archives)

He concluded:

[L]ooking upon him as a man of enlarged curiosity, it affords him an opportunity of seeing men and things as happens to few.

Charles was forever grateful for Josiah's support, and there was a special affection between them.

Wilberforce, Samuel (1805–1873)

Bishop of Oxford and opponent of evolutionary ideas; nicknamed Soapy Sam.

History tends to recall Samuel Wilberforce in terms of his alleged defeat in the debate on Charles Darwin's *On the Origin of Species* at the **British Association for the Advancement of Science** meeting at Oxford in 1860, but he was a notable and distinguished churchman. He was born in London, the third son of politician and emancipator of slaves, William Wilberforce (1759–1833). He studied at Oriel College, Oxford, taking his degree in 1826 and was ordained later in that year. He worked in parishes in Hampshire, in southern England. In 1840, he became chaplain to Albert, Queen **Victoria**'s prince consort. In 1845, he was nominated to the deanery of Westminster, but in October that year became Bishop of Oxford. It was during his Oxford episcopate that the Great Debate took place, chaired by Professor **John Stevens Henslow.** In the debate, Wilberforce opposed the ideas expressed in Darwin's book, and Darwin was championed by **Thomas Huxley** (1825–1895) and botanist **Joseph Hooker.** The bishop, according to Hooker, "spouted for half an hour with inimitable spirit, ugliness, emptiness and unfairness." Huxley's account refers to the "round-mouthed, oily, special pleading of the man." Wilberforce had spent the evening before with zoologist Professor **Richard Owen,** who had coached him, but obviously not very comprehensively, and it was widely asserted that he had not read the book he ventured to criticize. After two hours of speeches in a stuffy room, the bishop attempted a little levity, asking Huxley whether it was through his grandfather or his grandmother that he was descended from an ape. Huxley retorted that he would rather have an ape as a grandfather than a man endowed with great intelligence, means, and influence, but who used his faculties and influence to introduce ridicule into a scientific discussion. It was Huxley that got the laugh. Former *Beagle* captain **Robert FitzRoy,** by now an admiral, was present, and he held up a Bible and implored the audience to believe God rather than man. He was shouted down. The debate became animated, and one woman fainted. Reading the accounts of Huxley and Hooker (from letters to Darwin, who was not present, but undergoing medical treatment at a spa) one gains the impression the "Darwin party" were convinced that they had won the day. But their accounts and other descriptions differ in detail, and there were apparently some who left the room thinking it had been an entertaining draw. Wilberforce was anything but a total ignoramus who knew nothing of science. He had attended **William Buckland**'s lectures on geology at Oxford and was a member of several scientific societies, including the **Linnean Society of London.**

Certainly the affair does not seem to have harmed Wilberforce's clerical career, for in 1869 he was transferred from Oxford to Winchester, one of the most prestigious bishoprics in the Church of England. While at Oxford, he founded Cuddeston Theological College for the training of clergy (1854), and he sponsored the revision of the King James Bible. He died, after falling from his horse in 1871. Darwin mourned, for, although their views were opposed, Wilberforce had always referred to Charles Darwin as a "capital fellow"; the naturalist had a mutual feeling, remembering how he had himself been injured in a fall from his horse Tommy.

Z

Zoology of the Voyage of the Beagle

The principal vehicle for the publication of the zoological material from the *Beagle*'s 1831–1836 voyage.

Darwin worked at editing this series of volumes, which has been described as "sumptuous" in its production, between about February 1838 and October 1843. In May 1837, with the support of a number of influential political and scientific persons, he obtained the support of the Duke of Somerset, the president of the **Linnean Society of London** for financial assistance in the publication the zoological results of the voyage. The negotiations included Darwin having an interview with the Chancellor of the Exchequer (the government treasurer) on August 16, 1838, and resulted in a grant of £1,000 toward the cost. This, however, proved to be insufficient, and other funds were advanced by the publishers, Smith, Elder and Company, and by Darwin himself.

The series was made of five parts, comprising nineteen numbers, or issues. Charles Darwin contributed a geological introduction to part 1 on fossil mammalia and a geographical introduction to part 2 on mammalia. He contributed material on distribution and habits to both the mammalia and the birds (part 3) parts, and there are notes written by him, often from his specimen labels in part 4 on fish and in part 5 on reptiles. The first number of part 1 appeared in February 1838, and the original intention was that the numbers would appear, like the issues of a magazine, on the first day of every alternate month; a number of difficulties meant that this schedule could not be adhered to.

Part 1 was written by **Richard Owen,** part 2 by **George Waterhouse,** part 3 by **John Gould,** part 4 by John Henslow's brother-in-law and clerical colleague **Leonard Jenyns,** and part 5 by Thomas Bell. Gould went to Australia in spring 1838, and George Robert Gray of the British Museum took over; Thomas Bell's portion did not appear until well into 1843. The series contains 166 lithographic plates, many colored (hence the expense). The five parts were republished as individual bound volumes (1839 to 1843).

The volumes give details of the appearance, distribution, and habits of the various vertebrate animals collected on the *Beagle* voyage. A number of the organisms described were new to science. Some, such as the **warrah** (the Falklands fox or wolf) are now extinct. Although an extremely valuable resource, the volumes' appeal was, and still is, somewhat specialized, and they have not been republished to the same extent as some of Darwin's other works, although a couple of facsimile series have appeared.

See also: Geology of the Voyage of the Beagle.

Appendix: Introduction to the Extracts from Darwin's Works

The three best-known books by Charles Darwin are *The Voyage of the Beagle, On the Origin of Species*, and *Descent of Man*. Brief extracts are included here, so that readers can glimpse Darwin's literary style and its development over several decades.

The Voyage of the Beagle was originally published in 1839 as the third part of the *Narrative of the Surveying Voyages of His Majesty's Ships Adventure and Beagle between the Years 1826 and 1836, Describing Their Examination of the Southern Shores of South America, and the Beagle's Circumnavigation of the Globe*. The first section was by Captain (later Admiral) King, commander of the first voyage by the *Adventure* and *Beagle* to South America; the second was by Captain Robert FitzRoy, describing the 1831–1836 voyage. Darwin's account was based on his journal, or diary, edited, and with the style much improved. It was subsequently published separately, some editions having the title *A Naturalist's Voyage*. The style was much influenced by that of Alexander von Humboldt's *Personal Narrative of a Journey to the Equinoctial Regions of the New Continent* (1814–1825). The diary form is largely maintained, but lengthy scientific digressions are included. Darwin's excellent descriptive ability is exemplified by his account of the first few weeks of the voyage—from Devonport to Rio. Readers can feel the young naturalist's excitement as he experiences the tropics for the first time. Also included are the final few paragraphs that summarize his thoughts in relation to the voyage as a whole.

The second extract, from *On the Origin*, was first published exactly 20 years later, in November 1859. Darwin had been working on his species theory since a few months after his return from the *Beagle* voyage; March 1837 is often cited as the date for his "conversion" to an evolutionary outlook. He was accumulating information from many sources and writing what he described as his Big Species Book. Work on this enormous book was incomplete when he received the "bolt from the blue" in the form of Alfred Russel Wallace's paper setting out ideas similar to his own in June 1858. After the joint presentation arranged by Charles Lyell and Joesph Hooker at the Linnean Society of London, including both Wallace's paper and a brief summary of Darwin's views, Charles Darwin produced an abstract of his great work in *On the Origin of Species,* published late in 1859. The original species book was not published until the 1970s. *On the Origin* has been described as "one long argument" in which Darwin leads readers persuasively from a consideration of variation, through the significance of competition in nature, to the notion of natural selection. Lines of evidence for evolution from geographical distributions, the geological record, and the study of instinct are evaluated. The sections included here are from the introduction to the argument and the conclusion, which draws the threads of the book together.

Except by way of a vague generalization in the final paragraph, Darwin says almost nothing on human evolution in *On the Origin.* Taking up the theme in *Descent of Man and Selection in Relation to Sex* in 1871, Darwin applies the same methods of analysis and argument. Chapter 1 summarizes his approach.

Finally, a few extracts from Darwin's autobiography, written for his family late in his life with no thought of publication, provide insight to his views on the directions of his life and the nature of his thought.

THE VOYAGE OF THE BEAGLE

AFTER having been twice driven back by heavy southwestern gales, Her Majesty's ship Beagle, a ten-gun brig, under the command of Captain Fitz Roy, R. N., sailed from Devonport on the 27th of December, 1831. The object of the expedition was to complete the survey of Patagonia and Tierra del Fuego, commenced under Captain King in 1826 to 1830,—to survey the shores of Chile, Peru, and of some islands in the Pacific—and to carry a chain of chronometrical measurements round the World. On the 6th of January we reached Teneriffe, but were prevented landing, by fears of our bringing the cholera: the next morning we saw the sun rise behind the rugged outline of the Grand Canary island, and suddenly illuminate the Peak of Teneriffe, whilst the lower parts were veiled in fleecy clouds. This was the first of many delightful days never to be forgotten. On the 16th of January, 1832, we anchored at Porto Praya, in St. Jago, the chief island of the Cape de Verd archipelago. The neighbourhood of Porto Praya, viewed from the sea, wears a desolate aspect. The volcanic fires of a past age, and the scorching heat of a tropical sun, have in most places rendered the soil unfit for vegetation. The country rises in successive steps of table-land, interspersed with some truncate conical hills, and the horizon is bounded by an irregular chain of more lofty mountains. The scene, as beheld through the hazy atmosphere of this climate, is one of great interest; if, indeed, a person, fresh from sea, and who has just walked, for the first time, in a grove of cocoa-nut trees, can be a judge of anything but his own happiness. The island would generally be considered as very uninteresting, but to anyone accustomed only to an English landscape, the novel aspect of an utterly sterile land possesses a grandeur which more vegetation might spoil. A single green leaf can scarcely be discovered over wide tracts of the lava plains; yet flocks of goats, together with a few cows, contrive to exist. It rains very seldom, but during a short portion of the year heavy torrents fall, and immediately afterwards a light vegetation springs out of every crevice. This soon withers; and upon such naturally formed hay the animals live. It had not now rained for an entire year. When the island was discovered, the immediate neighbourhood of Porto Praya was clothed with trees, the reckless destruction of which has caused here, as at St. Helena, and at some of the Canary islands, almost entire sterility. The broad, flat-bottomed valleys, many of which serve during a few days only in the season as water-courses, are clothed with thickets of leafless bushes. Few living creatures inhabit these valleys. The commonest bird is a kingfisher (Dacelo Iagoensis), which tamely sits on the branches of the castor-oil plant, and thence darts on grasshoppers and lizards. It is brightly coloured, but not so beautiful as the European species: in its flight, manners, and place of habitation, which is generally in the driest valley, there is also a wide difference. One day, two of the officers and myself rode to Ribeira Grande, a village a few miles eastward of Porto Praya. Until we reached the valley of St. Martin, the country presented its usual dull brown appearance; but here, a very small rill of water produces a most refreshing margin of luxuriant vegetation. In the course of an hour we arrived at Ribeira Grande, and were surprised at the sight of a large ruined fort and cathedral. This little town, before its harbour was filled up, was the principal place in the island: it now presents a melancholy, but very picturesque appearance. Having procured a black Padre for a guide, and a Spaniard who had served in the Peninsular war as an interpreter, we visited a collection of buildings, of which an ancient church formed the principal part. It is here the governors and captain-generals of the islands have been buried. Some of the tombstones recorded dates of the sixteenth century, The heraldic ornaments were the only things in this retired place that reminded us of Europe. The church or chapel formed one side of a quadrangle, in the middle of which a large clump of bananas were growing. On another side was a hospital, containing about a dozen miserable-looking inmates. We returned to the Venda to eat our dinners. A considerable number of men, women, and children, all as black as jet, collected to watch us. Our companions were extremely merry; and everything we said or did was followed by their hearty laughter. Before leaving the town we visited the cathedral. It does not appear so rich as the smaller church, but boasts of a little organ, which sent forth singularly inharmonious cries. We presented the black priest with a few shillings, and the Spaniard, patting him on the head, said, with much candour, he thought his colour made no great difference. We then returned, as fast as the ponies would go, to Porto Praya. Another day we rode to the village of St. Domingo, situated near the centre of the island. On a small plain which we crossed, a few stunted acacias were growing; their tops had been bent by the steady trade-wind, in a singular manner— some of them even at right angles to their trunks. The direction of the branches was exactly N. E. by N., and S. W. by S., and these natural vanes must indicate the prevailing direction of the force of the trade-wind. The travelling had made so little impression on the barren soil, that we here missed our track, and took that to Fuentes. This we did not find out till we arrived there; and we were afterwards glad of our mistake. Fuentes is a pretty village, with a small stream; and everything appeared to prosper well, excepting, indeed, that which ought to do so most—its inhabitants. The black children, completely naked, and looking very wretched, were carrying bundles of firewood half as big as their own bodies. Near

Fuentes we saw a large flock of guinea-fowl—probably fifty or sixty in number. They were extremely wary, and could not be approached. They avoided us, like partridges on a rainy day in September, running with their heads cocked up; and if pursued, they readily took to the wing. The scenery of St. Domingo possesses a beauty totally unexpected, from the prevalent gloomy character of the rest of the island. The village is situated at the bottom of a valley, bounded by lofty and jagged walls of stratified lava. The black rocks afford a most striking contrast with the bright green vegetation, which follows the banks of a little stream of clear water. It happened to be a grand feast-day, and the village was full of people. On our return we overtook a party of about twenty young black girls, dressed in excellent taste; their black skins and snow-white linen being set off by coloured turbans and large shawls. As soon as we approached near, they suddenly all turned round, and covering the path with their shawls, sung with great energy a wild accent song, beating time with their hands upon their legs. We threw them some vintems, which were received with screams of laughter, and we left them redoubling the noise of their song. One morning the view was singularly clear; the distant mountains being projected with the sharpest outline on a heavy bank of dark blue clouds. Judging from the appearance, and from similar cases in England, I supposed that the air was saturated with moisture. The fact, however, turned out quite the contrary. The hygrometer gave a difference of 29.6 degs., between the temperature of the air, and the point at which dew was precipitated. This difference was nearly double that which I had observed on the previous mornings. This unusual degree of atmospheric dryness was accompanied by continual flashes of lightning. Is it not an uncommon case, thus to find a remarkable degree of aerial transparency with such a state of weather? Generally the atmosphere is hazy; and this is caused by the falling of impalpably fine dust, which was found to have slightly injured the astronomical instruments. The morning before we anchored at Porto Praya, I collected a little packet of this brown-coloured fine dust, which appeared to have been filtered from the wind by the gauze of the vane at the mast-head. Mr. Lyell has also given me four packets of dust which fell on a vessel a few hundred miles northward of these islands. Professor Ehrenberg finds that this dust consists in great part of infusoria with siliceous shields, and of the siliceous tissue of plants. In five little packets which I sent him, he has ascertained no less than sixty-seven different organic forms! The infusoria, with the exception of two marine species, are all inhabitants of fresh-water. I have found no less than fifteen different accounts of dust having fallen on vessels when far out in the Atlantic. From the direction of the wind whenever it has fallen, and from its having always fallen during those months when the harmattan is known to raise clouds of dust high into the atmosphere, we may feel sure that it all comes from Africa. It is, however, a very singular fact, that, although Professor Ehrenberg knows many species of infusoria peculiar to Africa, he finds none of these in the dust which I sent him. On the other hand, he finds in it two species which hitherto he knows as living only in South America. The dust falls in such quantities as to dirty everything on board, and to hurt people's eyes; vessels even have run on shore owing to the obscurity of the atmosphere. It has often fallen on ships when several hundred, and even more than a thousand miles from the coast of Africa, and at points sixteen hundred miles distant in a north and south direction. In some dust which was collected on a vessel three hundred miles from the land, I was much surprised to find particles of stone above the thousandth of an inch square, mixed with finer matter. After this fact one need not be surprised at the diffusion of the far lighter and smaller sporules of cryptogamic plants. The geology of this island is the most interesting part of its natural history. On entering the harbour, a perfectly horizontal white band, in the face of the sea cliff, may be seen running for some miles along the coast, and at the height of about forty-five feet above the water. Upon examination this white stratum is found to consist of calcareous matter with numerous shells embedded, most or all of which now exist on the neighbouring coast. It rests on ancient volcanic rocks, and has been covered by a stream of basalt, which must have entered the sea when the white shelly bed was lying at the bottom. It is interesting to trace the changes produced by the heat of the overlying lava, on the friable mass, which in parts has been converted into a crystalline limestone, and in other parts into a compact spotted stone. Where the lime has been caught up by the scoriaceous fragments of the lower surface of the stream, it is converted into groups of beautifully radiated fibres resembling arragonite. The beds of lava rise in successive gently-sloping plains, towards the interior, whence the deluges of melted stone have originally proceeded. Within historical times, no signs of volcanic activity have, I believe, been manifested in any part of St. Jago. Even the form of a crater can but rarely be discovered on the summits of the many red cindery hills; yet the more recent streams can be distinguished on the coast, forming lines of cliffs of less height, but stretching out in advance of those belonging to an older series: the height of the cliffs thus affording a rude measure of the age of the streams. During our stay, I observed the habits of some marine animals. A large Aplysia is very common. This sea-slug is about five inches long; and is of a dirty yellowish colour veined with purple. On each side of the lower surface, or foot, there is a broad membrane, which appears sometimes to act as a ventilator, in causing a current of water to flow over the dorsal branchiae or lungs. It feeds on the delicate sea-weeds which grow among the stones in muddy and shallow water; and I found in its stomach several small pebbles, as in the gizzard of a bird. This slug, when disturbed, emits a very fine purplish-red fluid, which stains the water for the space of a foot around. Besides this means of defence, an acrid secretion, which is spread over its body, causes a sharp, stinging sensation, similar to that produced by the Physalia, or Portuguese man-of-war. I was much interested, on several occasions, by watching the habits of an Octopus, or cuttle-fish. Although common in the pools of water left by the retiring tide, these animals were not easily caught. By means of their long arms and suckers, they could drag their bodies into very narrow crevices; and when thus fixed, it required great force to remove them. At other times they darted tail first, with the rapidity of an arrow, from one side of the pool to the other, at the same instant discolouring the water with a dark chestnut-brown ink. These animals also escape detection by a very extraordinary, chameleon-like power of changing their colour. They appear to vary their tints according to the nature of the ground over which they pass: when in deep water, their general shade was brownish purple, but when placed on the land, or in shallow water, this dark tint changed into one of a-yellowish green. The colour, examined more carefully, was a French grey, with numerous minute spots of bright yellow: the former of these varied in intensity; the latter entirely disappeared and appeared again by turns. These changes were effected in such a manner, that clouds, varying in tint between a hyacinth red and a chestnut-brown, were continually passing over the body. Any part, being subjected to a slight shock of galvanism, became almost black: a similar effect, but in a less degree, was produced by scratching the skin with a needle. These clouds, or blushes as they may be called, are said to be produced by the alternate expansion and contraction of minute vesicles containing variously coloured fluids. This cuttle-fish displayed its chameleon-like power both during the act of swimming and whilst remaining stationary at the bottom. I was much amused by the various arts to escape detection used by one individual, which seemed fully aware that I was watching it. Remaining for a time motionless, it would then stealthily advance an inch or two, like a cat after a mouse; sometimes changing its colour: it thus proceeded, till having gained a deeper part, it darted away, leaving a dusky train of ink to hide the hole into which it had crawled. While looking for marine animals, with my head about two feet above the rocky shore, I was more than once saluted by a jet of water, accompanied by a slight grating noise. At first I could not think what it was, but afterwards I found out that it was this cuttle-fish, which, though concealed in a hole, thus often led me to its discovery. That it possesses the power of ejecting water there is no doubt, and it appeared to me that it could certainly take good aim by directing the tube or siphon on the under side of its body. From the difficulty which these animals have in carrying their heads, they cannot crawl with ease when placed on the ground. I observed that one which I kept in the cabin was slightly phosphorescent in the dark. ST. PAUL'S ROCKS.—In crossing the Atlantic we hove-to during the morning of February 16th, close to the island of St. Paul's. This cluster of rocks is situated in 0 degs. 58' north latitude, and 29 degs. 15' west longitude. It is 540 miles distant from the coast of America, and 350 from the island of Fernando Noronha. The highest point is only fifty feet above the level of the sea, and the entire circumference is under three-quarters of a mile. This small point rises abruptly out of the depths of the ocean. Its mineralogical constitution is not simple; in some parts the rock is of a cherty, in others of a felspathic nature, including thin veins of serpentine. It is a remarkable fact, that all the many small islands, lying far from any continent, in the Pacific, Indian, and Atlantic Oceans, with the exception of the Seychelles and this little point of rock, are, I believe, composed either of coral or of erupted matter. The volcanic nature of these oceanic islands is evidently an extension of that law, and the effect of those same causes, whether chemical or mechanical, from which it results that a vast majority of the volcanoes now in action stand either near sea-coasts or as islands in the midst of the sea. The rocks of St. Paul appear from a distance of a brilliantly white colour. This is partly owing to the dung of a vast multitude of seafowl, and partly to a coating of a hard glossy substance with a pearly lustre, which is intimately united to the surface of the rocks. This, when examined with a lens, is found to consist of numerous exceedingly thin layers, its total thickness being about the tenth of an inch. It contains much animal matter, and its origin, no doubt, is due to the action of the rain or spray on the birds' dung. Below some small masses of guano at Ascension, and on the Abrolhos Islets, I found certain stalactitic branching bodies, formed apparently in the same manner as the thin white coating on these rocks. The branching bodies so closely resembled in general appearance certain nulliporae (a family of hard calcareous sea-plants), that in lately looking hastily over my collection I did not perceive the difference. The globular extremities of the branches are of a pearly texture, like the enamel of teeth, but so hard as just to scratch plate-glass. I may here mention, that on a part of the coast of Ascension, where there is a vast accumulation of shelly sand, an incrustation is deposited on the tidal rocks by the water of the sea, resembling, as represented in the woodcut, certain cryptogamic plants (Marchantiae) often seen on damp walls. The surface of the fronds is beautifully glossy; and those parts formed where fully exposed to the light are of a jet black colour, but those shaded under ledges are only grey. I have shown specimens of this incrustation to several geologists, and they all thought that they were of volcanic or igneous origin! In its hardness and translucency—in its polish, equal to that of the finest oliva-shell—in the bad smell given out, and loss of colour under the blowpipe—it shows a close similarity with living sea-shells. Moreover, in sea-shells, it is known that the parts habitually covered and shaded by the mantle of the animal, are of a paler colour than those fully exposed to the light, just as is the case with this incrustation. When we remember that lime, either as a phosphate or carbonate, enters into the composition of the hard parts, such as bones and shells, of all living animals, it is an interesting physiological fact to find substances harder than the enamel of teeth, and coloured surfaces as well polished as those of a fresh shell, reformed through inorganic means from dead organic matter—mocking, also, in shape, some of the lower vegetable productions. We found on St. Paul's only two kinds of birds—the booby and the noddy. The former is a species of gannet, and the latter a tern. Both are of a tame and stupid disposition, and are so unaccustomed to visitors, that I could have killed any number of them with my geological hammer. The booby lays her eggs on the bare rock; but the tern makes a very simple nest with sea-weed. By the side of many of these nests a small flying-fish was placed; which I suppose, had been brought by the male bird for its partner. It was amusing to watch how quickly a large and active crab (Graspus), which inhabits the crevices of the rock, stole the fish from the side of the nest, as soon as we had disturbed the parent birds. Sir W. Symonds, one of the few persons who have landed here, informs me that he saw the crabs dragging even the young birds out of their nests, and devouring them. Not a single plant, not even a lichen, grows on this islet; yet it is inhabited by several insects and spiders. The following list completes, I believe, the terrestrial fauna: a fly (Olfersia) living on the booby, and a tick which must have come here as a parasite on the birds; a small brown moth, belonging to a genus that feeds on feathers; a beetle (Quedius) and a woodlouse from beneath the dung; and lastly, numerous spiders, which I suppose prey on these small attendants and scavengers of the water-fowl. The often repeated description of the stately palm and other noble tropical plants, then birds, and lastly man, taking possession of the coral islets as soon as formed, in the Pacific, is probably not correct; I fear it destroys the poetry of this story, that feather and dirt-feeding and parasitic insects and spiders should be the first inhabitants of newly formed oceanic land. The smallest rock in the tropical seas, by giving a foundation for the growth of innumerable kinds of seaweed and compound animals, supports likewise a large number of fish. The sharks and the seamen in the boats maintained a constant struggle which should secure the greater share of the prey caught by the fishing-lines. I have heard that a rock near the Bermudas, lying many miles out at sea, and at a considerable depth, was first discovered by the circumstance of fish having been observed in the neighbourhood. FERNANDO NORONHA, Feb. 20th.—As far as I was enabled to observe, during the few hours we stayed at this place, the constitution of the island is volcanic, but probably not of a recent date. The most remarkable feature is a conical hill, about one thousand feet high, the upper part of which is exceedingly steep, and on one side overhangs its base. The rock is phonolite, and is divided into irregular columns. On viewing one of these isolated masses, at first one is inclined to believe that it has been suddenly pushed up in a semi-fluid state. At St. Helena, however, I ascertained that some pinnacles, of a nearly similar figure and constitution, had been formed by the injection of melted rock into yielding strata, which thus had formed the moulds for these gigantic obelisks. The whole island is covered with wood; but from the dryness of the climate there is no appearance of luxuriance. Half-way up the mountain, some great masses of the columnar rock, shaded by laurel-like trees, and ornamented by others covered with fine pink flowers but without a single leaf, gave a pleasing effect to the nearer parts of the scenery. BAHIA, OR SAN SALVADOR. BRAZIL, Feb. 29th.—The day has passed delightfully. Delight itself, however, is a weak term to express the feelings of a naturalist who, for the first time, has wandered by himself in a Brazilian forest. The elegance of the grasses, the novelty of the parasitical plants, the beauty of the flowers, the glossy green of the foliage, but above all the general luxuriance of the vegetation, filled me with admiration. A most paradoxical mixture of sound and silence pervades the shady parts of the wood. The noise from the insects is so loud, that it may be heard even in a vessel anchored several hundred yards from the shore; yet within the recesses of the forest a universal silence appears to reign. To a person fond of natural history, such a day as this brings with it a deeper pleasure than he can ever hope to experience again. After wandering about for some hours, I returned to the landing-place; but, before reaching it, I was overtaken by a tropical storm. I tried to find shelter under a tree, which was so thick that it would never have been penetrated by common English rain; but here, in a couple of minutes, a little torrent flowed down the trunk. It is to this violence of the rain that we must attribute the verdure at the bottom of the thickest woods: if the showers were like those of a colder climate, the greater part would be absorbed or evaporated before it reached the ground. I will not at present attempt to describe the gaudy scenery of this noble bay, because, in our homeward voyage, we called here a second time, and I shall then have occasion to remark on it. Along the whole coast of Brazil, for a length of at least 2000 miles, and certainly for a considerable space inland, wherever solid rock occurs, it belongs to a granitic formation. The circumstance of this enormous area being constituted of materials which most geologists believe to have been crystallized when heated under pressure, gives rise to many curious reflections. Was this effect produced beneath the depths of a profound ocean? or did a covering of strata formerly extend over it, which has since been removed? Can we believe that any power, acting for a time short of infinity, could have denuded the granite over so many thousand square leagues? On a point not far from the city, where a rivulet entered the sea, I observed a fact connected with a subject discussed by Humboldt. At the cataracts of the great rivers Orinoco, Nile, and Congo, the syenitic rocks are coated by a black substance, appearing as if they had been polished with plumbago. The layer is of extreme thinness; and on analysis by Berzelius it was found to consist of the oxides of manganese and iron. In the Orinoco it occurs on the rocks periodically washed by the floods, and in those parts alone where the stream is rapid; or, as the Indians say, "the rocks are black where the waters are white." Here the coating is of a rich brown instead of a black colour, and seems to be composed of ferruginous matter alone. Hand specimens fail to give a just idea of these brown burnished stones which glitter in the sun's rays. They occur only within the limits of the tidal waves; and as the rivulet slowly trickles down, the surf must supply the polishing power of the cataracts in the great rivers. In like manner, the rise and fall of the tide probably answer to the periodical inundations; and thus the same effects are produced under apparently different but really similar circumstances. The origin, however, of these coatings of metallic oxides, which seem as if cemented to the rocks, is not understood; and no reason, I believe, can be assigned for their thickness remaining the same. One day I was amused by watching the habits of the Diodon antennatus, which was caught swimming near the shore. This fish, with its flabby skin, is well known to possess the singular power of distending itself into a nearly spherical form. After having been taken out of water for a short time, and then again immersed in it, a considerable quantity both of water and air is absorbed by the mouth, and perhaps likewise by the branchial orifices. This process is effected by two methods: the air is swallowed, and is then forced into the cavity of the body, its return being prevented by a muscular contraction which is externally visible: but the water enters in a gentle stream through the mouth, which is kept wide open and motionless; this latter action must, therefore, depend on suction. The skin about the abdomen is much looser than that on the back; hence, during the inflation, the lower surface becomes far more distended than the upper; and the fish, in consequence, floats with its back downwards. Cuvier doubts whether the Diodon in this position is able to swim; but not only can it thus move forward in a straight line, but it can turn round to either side. This latter movement is effected solely by the aid of the pectoral fins; the tail being collapsed, and not used. From the body being buoyed up with so much air, the branchial openings are out of water, but a stream drawn in by the mouth constantly flows through them. The fish, having remained in this distended state for a short time, generally expelled the air and water with considerable force from the branchial apertures and mouth. It could emit, at will, a certain portion of the water, and it appears, therefore, probable that this fluid is taken in partly for the sake of regulating its specific gravity. This Diodon possessed several means of defence. It could give a severe bite, and could eject water from its mouth to some distance, at the same time making a curious noise by the movement of its jaws. By the inflation of its body, the papillae, with which the skin is covered, become erect and pointed. But the most curious circumstance is, that it secretes from the skin of its belly, when handled, a most beautiful carmine-red fibrous matter, which stains ivory and paper in so permanent a manner that the tint is retained with all its brightness to the present day: I am quite ignorant of the nature and use of this secretion. I have heard from Dr. Allan of Forres, that he has frequently found a Diodon, floating alive and distended, in the stomach of the shark, and that on several occasions he has known it to eat its way, not only through the coats of the stomach, but through the sides of the monster, which has thus been killed. Who would ever have imagined that a little soft fish could have destroyed the great and savage shark? March 18th.—We sailed from Bahia. A few days afterwards, when not far distant from the Abrolhos Islets, my attention was called to a reddish-brown appearance in the sea. The whole surface of the water, as it appeared under a weak lens, seemed as if covered by chopped bits of hay, with their ends jagged. These are minute cylindrical confervae, in bundles or rafts of from twenty to sixty in each. Mr. Berkeley informs me that they are the same species (Trichodesmium erythraeum) with that found over large spaces in the Red Sea, and whence its name of Red Sea is derived. Their numbers must be infinite: the ship passed through several bands of them, one of which was about ten yards wide, and, judging from the mud-like colour of the water, at least two and a half miles long. In almost every long voyage some account is given of these confervae. They appear especially common in the sea near Australia; and off Cape Leeuwin I found an allied but smaller and apparently different species. Captain Cook, in his third voyage, remarks, that the sailors gave to this appearance the name of sea-sawdust. Near Keeling Atoll, in the Indian Ocean, I observed many little masses of confervae a few inches square, consisting of long cylindrical threads of excessive thinness, so as to be barely visible to the naked eye, mingled with other rather larger bodies, finely conical at both ends. Two of these are shown in the woodcut united together. They vary in length from .04 to .06, and even to .08 of an inch in length; and in diameter from .006 to .008 of an inch. Near one extremity of the cylindrical part, a green septum, formed of granular matter, and thickest in the middle, may generally be seen. This, I believe, is the bottom of a most delicate, colourless sac, composed of a pulpy substance, which lines the exterior case, but does not extend within the extreme conical points. In some specimens, small but perfect spheres of brownish granular matter supplied the places of the septa; and I observed the curious process by which they were produced. The pulpy matter of the internal coating suddenly grouped itself into lines, some of which assumed a form radiating from a common centre; it then continued, with an irregular and rapid movement, to contract itself, so that in the course of a second the whole was united into a perfect little sphere, which occupied the position of the septum at one end of the now quite hollow case. The formation of the granular sphere was hastened by any accidental injury. I may add, that frequently a pair of these bodies were attached to each other, as represented above, cone beside cone, at that end where the septum occurs. I will add here a few other observations connected with the discoloration of the sea from organic causes. On the coast of Chile, a few leagues north of Concepcion, the Beagle one day passed through great bands of muddy water, exactly like that of a swollen river; and again, a degree south of Valparaiso, when fifty miles from the land, the same appearance was still more extensive. Some of the water placed in a glass was of a pale reddish tint; and, examined under a microscope, was seen to swarm with minute animalcula darting about, and often exploding. Their shape is oval, and contracted in the middle by a ring of vibrating curved ciliae. It was, however, very difficult to examine them with care, for almost the instant motion ceased, even while crossing the field of vision, their bodies burst. Sometimes both ends burst at once, sometimes only one, and a quantity of coarse, brownish, granular matter was ejected. The animal an instant before bursting expanded to half again its natural size; and the explosion took place about fifteen seconds after the rapid progressive motion had ceased: in a few cases it was preceded for a short interval by a rotatory movement on the longer axis. About two minutes after any number were isolated in a drop of water, they thus perished. The animals move with the narrow apex forwards, by the aid of their vibratory ciliae, and generally by rapid starts. They are exceedingly minute, and quite invisible to the naked eye, only covering a space equal to the square of the thousandth of an inch. Their numbers were infinite; for the smallest drop of water which I could remove contained very many. In one day we passed through two spaces of water thus stained, one of which alone must have extended over several square miles. What incalculable numbers of these microscopical animals! The colour of the water, as seen at some distance, was like that of a river which has flowed through a red clay district, but under the shade of the vessel's side it was quite as dark as chocolate. The line where the red and blue water joined was distinctly defined. The weather for some days previously had been calm, and the ocean abounded, to an unusual degree, with living creatures. In the sea around Tierra del Fuego, and at no great distance from the land, I have seen narrow lines of water of a bright red colour, from the number of crustacea, which somewhat resemble in form large prawns. The sealers call them whale-food. Whether whales feed on them I do not know; but terns, cormorants, and immense herds of great unwieldy seals derive, on some parts of the coast, their chief sustenance from these swimming crabs. Seamen invariably attribute the discoloration of the water to spawn; but I found this to be the case only on one occasion. At the distance of several leagues from the Archipelago of the Galapagos, the ship sailed through three strips of a dark yellowish, or mud-like water; these strips were some miles long, but only a few yards wide, and they were separated from the surrounding water by a sinuous yet distinct margin. The colour was caused by little gelatinous balls, about the fifth of an inch in diameter, in which numerous minute spherical ovules were imbedded: they were of two distinct kinds, one being of a reddish colour and of a different shape from the other. I cannot form a conjecture as to what two kinds of animals these belonged. Captain Colnett remarks, that this appearance is very common among the Galapagos Islands, and that the directions of the bands indicate that of the currents; in the described case, however, the line was caused by the wind. The only other appearance which I have to notice, is a thin oily coat on the water which displays iridescent colours. I saw a considerable tract of the ocean thus covered on the coast of

Brazil; the seamen attributed it to the putrefying carcase of some whale, which probably was floating at no great distance. I do not here mention the minute gelatinous particles, hereafter to be referred to, which are frequently dispersed throughout the water, for they are not sufficiently abundant to create any change of colour. There are two circumstances in the above accounts which appear remarkable: first, how do the various bodies which form the bands with defined edges keep together? In the case of the prawn-like crabs, their movements were as co-instantaneous as in a regiment of soldiers; but this cannot happen from anything like voluntary action with the ovules, or the confervae, nor is it probable among the infusoria. Secondly, what causes the length and narrowness of the bands? The appearance so much resembles that which may be seen in every torrent, where the stream uncoils into long streaks the froth collected in the eddies, that I must attribute the effect to a similar action either of the currents of the air or sea. Under this supposition we must believe that the various organized bodies are produced in certain favourable places, and are thence removed by the set of either wind or water. I confess, however, there is a very great difficulty in imagining any one spot to be the birthplace of the millions of millions of animalcula and confervae: for whence come the germs at such points?—the parent bodies having been distributed by the winds and waves over the immense ocean. But on no other hypothesis can I understand their linear grouping. I may add that Scoresby remarks that green water abounding with pelagic animals is invariably found in a certain part of the Arctic Sea. [...]

Our Voyage having come to an end, I will take a short retrospect of the advantages and disadvantages, the pains and pleasures, of our circumnavigation of the world. If a person asked my advice, before undertaking a long voyage, my answer would depend upon his possessing a decided taste for some branch of knowledge, which could by this means be advanced. No doubt it is a high satisfaction to behold various countries and the many races of mankind, but the pleasures gained at the time do not counterbalance the evils. It is necessary to look forward to a harvest, however distant that may be, when some fruit will be reaped, some good effected. Many of the losses which must be experienced are obvious; such as that of the society of every old friend, and of the sight of those places with which every dearest remembrance is so intimately connected. These losses, however, are at the time partly relieved by the exhaustless delight of anticipating the long wished-for day of return. If, as poets say, life is a dream, I am sure in a voyage these are the visions which best serve to pass away the long night. Other losses, although not at first felt, tell heavily after a period: these are the want of room, of seclusion, of rest; the jading feeling of constant hurry; the privation of small luxuries, the loss of domestic society and even of music and the other pleasures of imagination. When such trifles are mentioned, it is evident that the real grievances, excepting from accidents, of a sea-life are at an end. The short space of sixty years has made an astonishing difference in the facility of distant navigation. Even in the time of Cook, a man who left his fireside for such expeditions underwent severe privations. A yacht now, with every luxury of life, can circumnavigate the globe. Besides the vast improvements in ships and naval resources, the whole western shores of America are thrown open, and Australia has become the capital of a rising continent. How different are the circumstances to a man shipwrecked at the present day in the Pacific, to what they were in the time of Cook! Since his voyage a hemisphere has been added to the civilized world. If a person suffer much from sea-sickness, let him weigh it heavily in the balance. I speak from experience: it is no trifling evil, cured in a week. If, on the other hand, he take pleasure in naval tactics, he will assuredly have full scope for his taste. But it must be borne in mind, how large a proportion of the time, during a long voyage, is spent on the water, as compared with the days in harbour. And what are the boasted glories of the illimitable ocean. A tedious waste, a desert of water, as the Arabian calls it. No doubt there are some delightful scenes. A moonlight night, with the clear heavens and the dark glittering sea, and the white sails filled by the soft air of a gently blowing trade-wind, a dead calm, with the heaving surface polished like a mirror, and all still except the occasional flapping of the canvas. It is well once to behold a squall with its rising arch and coming fury, or the heavy gale of wind and mountainous waves. I confess, however, my imagination had painted something more grand, more terrific in the full-grown storm. It is an incomparably finer spectacle when beheld on shore, where the waving trees, the wild flight of the birds, the dark shadows and bright lights, the rushing of the torrents all proclaim the strife of the unloosed elements. At sea the albatross and little petrel fly as if the storm were their proper sphere, the water rises and sinks as if fulfilling its usual task, the ship alone and its inhabitants seem the objects of wrath. On a forlorn and weather-beaten coast, the scene is indeed different, but the feelings partake more of horror than of wild delight. Let us now look at the brighter side of the past time. The pleasure derived from beholding the scenery and the general aspect of the various countries we have visited, has decidedly been the most constant and highest source of enjoyment. It is probable that the picturesque beauty of many parts of Europe exceeds anything which we beheld. But there is a growing pleasure in comparing the character of the scenery in different countries, which to a certain degree is distinct from merely admiring its beauty. It depends chiefly on an acquaintance with the individual parts of each view. I am strongly induced to believe that as in music, the person who understands every note will, if he also possesses a proper taste, more thoroughly enjoy the whole, so he who examines each part of a fine view, may also thoroughly comprehend the full and combined effect. Hence, a traveller should be a botanist, for in all views plants form the chief embellishment. Group masses of naked rock, even in the wildest forms, and they may for a time afford a sublime spectacle, but they will soon grow monotonous. Paint them with bright and varied colours, as in Northern Chile, they will become fantastic; clothe them with vegetation, they must form a decent, if not a beautiful picture. When I say that the scenery of parts of Europe is probably superior to anything which we beheld, I except, as a class by itself, that of the intertropical zones. The two classes cannot be compared together; but I have already often enlarged on the grandeur of those regions. As the force of impressions generally depends on preconceived ideas, I may add, that mine were taken from the vivid descriptions in the Personal Narrative of Humboldt, which far exceed in merit anything else which I have read. Yet with these high-wrought ideas, my feelings were far from partaking of a tinge of disappointment on my first and final landing on the shores of Brazil. Among the scenes which are deeply impressed on my mind, none exceed in sublimity the primeval forests undefaced by the hand of man; whether those of Brazil, where the powers of Life are predominant, or those of Tierra del Fuego, where Death and decay prevail. Both are temples filled with the varied productions of the God of Nature:—no one can stand in these solitudes unmoved, and not feel that there is more in man than the mere breath of his body. In calling up images of the past, I find that the plains of Patagonia frequently cross before my eyes; yet these plains are pronounced by all wretched and useless. They can be described only by negative characters; without habitations, without water, without trees, without mountains, they support merely a few dwarf plants. Why, then, and the case is not peculiar to myself, have these arid wastes taken so firm a hold on my memory? Why have not the still more level, the greener and more fertile Pampas, which are serviceable to mankind, produced an equal impression? I can scarcely analyze these feelings: but it must be partly owing to the free scope given to the imagination. The plains of Patagonia are boundless, for they are scarcely passable, and hence unknown: they bear the stamp of having lasted, as they are now, for ages, and there appears no limit to their duration through future time. If, as the ancients supposed, the flat earth was surrounded by an impassable breadth of water, or by deserts heated to an intolerable excess, who would not look at these last boundaries to man's knowledge with deep but ill-defined sensations? Lastly, of natural scenery, the views from lofty mountains, through certainly in one sense not beautiful, are very memorable. When looking down from the highest crest of the Cordillera, the mind, undisturbed by minute details, was filled with the stupendous dimensions of the surrounding masses. Of individual objects, perhaps nothing is more certain to create astonishment than the first sight in his native haunt of a barbarian—of man in his lowest and most savage state. One's mind hurries back over past centuries, and then asks, could our progenitors have been men like these?—men, whose very signs and expressions are less intelligible to us than those of the domesticated animals; men, who do not possess the instinct of those animals, nor yet appear to boast of human reason, or at least of arts consequent on that reason. I do not believe it is possible to describe or paint the difference between savage and civilized man. It is the difference between a wild and tame animal: and part of the interest in beholding a savage, is the same which would lead every one to desire to see the lion in his desert, the tiger tearing his prey in the jungle, or the rhinoceros wandering over the wild plains of Africa. Among the other most remarkable spectacles which we have beheld, may be ranked, the Southern Cross, the cloud of Magellan, and the other constellations of the southern hemisphere—the water-spout—the glacier leading its blue stream of ice, overhanging the sea in a bold precipice—a lagoon-island raised by the reef-building corals—an active volcano—and the overwhelming effects of a violent earthquake. These latter phenomena, perhaps, possess for me a peculiar interest, from their intimate connection with the geological structure of the world. The earthquake, however, must be to every one a most impressive event: the earth, considered from our earliest childhood as the type of solidity, has oscillated like a thin crust beneath our feet; and in seeing the laboured works of man in a moment overthrown, we feel the insignificance of his boasted power. It has been said, that the love of the chase is an inherent delight in man—a relic of an instinctive passion. If so, I am sure the pleasure of living in the open air, with the sky for a roof and the ground for a table, is part of the same feeling, it is the savage returning to his wild and native habits. I always look back to our boat cruises, and my land journeys, when through unfrequented countries, with an extreme delight, which no scenes of civilization could have created. I do not doubt that every traveller must remember the glowing sense of happiness which he experienced, when he first breathed in a foreign clime, where the civilized man had seldom or never trod. There are several other sources of enjoyment in a long voyage, which are of a more reasonable nature. The map of the world ceases to be a blank; it becomes a picture full of the most varied and animated figures. Each part assumes its proper dimensions: continents are not looked at in the light of islands, or islands considered as mere specks, which are, in truth, larger than many kingdoms of Europe. Africa, or North and South America, are well-sounding names, and easily pronounced; but it is not until having sailed for weeks along small portions of their shores, that one is thoroughly convinced what vast spaces on our immense world these names imply. From seeing the present state, it is impossible not to look forward with high expectations to the future progress of nearly an entire hemisphere. The march of improvement, consequent on the introduction of Christianity throughout the South Sea, probably stands by itself in the records of history. It is the more striking when we remember that only sixty years since, Cook, whose excellent judgment none will dispute, could foresee no prospect of a change. Yet these changes have now been effected by the philanthropic spirit of the British nation. In the same quarter of the globe Australia is rising, or indeed may be said to have risen, into a grand centre of civilization, which, at some not very remote period, will rule as empress over the southern hemisphere. It is impossible for an Englishman to behold these distant colonies, without a high pride and satisfaction. To hoist the British flag, seems to draw with it as a certain consequence, wealth, prosperity, and civilization. In conclusion, it appears to me that nothing can be more improving to a young naturalist, than a journey in distant countries. It both sharpens, and partly allays that want and craving, which, as Sir J. Herschel remarks, a man experiences although every corporeal sense be fully satisfied. The excitement from the novelty of objects, and the chance of success, stimulate him to increased activity. Moreover, as a number of isolated facts soon become uninteresting, the habit of comparison leads to generalization. On the other hand, as the traveller stays but a short time in each place, his descriptions must generally consist of mere sketches, instead of detailed observations. Hence arises, as I have found to my cost, a constant tendency to fill up the wide gaps of knowledge, by inaccurate and superficial hypotheses. But I have too deeply enjoyed the voyage, not to recommend any naturalist, although he must not expect to be so fortunate in his companions as I have been, to take all chances, and to start, on travels by land if possible, if otherwise, on a long voyage. He may feel assured, he will meet with no difficulties or dangers, excepting in rare cases, nearly so bad as he beforehand anticipates. In a moral point of view, the effect ought to be, to teach him good-humoured patience, freedom from selfishness, the habit of acting for himself, and of making the best of every occurrence. In short, he ought to partake of the characteristic qualities of most sailors. Travelling ought also to teach him distrust; but at the same time he will discover, how many truly kind-hearted people there are, with whom he never before had, or ever again will have any further communication, who yet are ready to offer him the most disinterested assistance.

On the Origin of Species by Means of Natural Selection, or The Preservation of Favoured Races in the Struggle for Life

Introduction

When on board H.M.S. "Beagle," as naturalist, I was much struck with certain facts in the distribution of the inhabitants of South America, and in the geological relations of the present to the past inhabitants of that continent. These facts seemed to me to throw some light on the origin of species—that mystery of mysteries, as it has been called by one of our greatest philosophers. On my return home, it occurred to me, in 1837, that something might perhaps be made out on this question by patiently accumulating and reflecting on all sorts of facts which could possibly have any bearing on it. After five years' work I allowed myself to speculate on the subject, and drew up some short notes; these I enlarged in 1844 into a sketch of the conclusions, which then seemed to me probable: from that period to the present day I have steadily pursued the same object. I hope that I may be excused for entering on these personal details, as I give them to show that I have not been hasty in coming to a decision. My work is now nearly finished; but as it will take me two or three more years to complete it, and as my health is far from strong, I have been urged to publish this Abstract. I have more especially been induced to do this, as Mr. Wallace, who is now studying the natural history of the Malay archipelago, has arrived at almost exactly the same general conclusions that I have on the origin of species. Last year he sent to me a memoir on this subject, with a request that I would forward it to Sir Charles Lyell, who sent it to the Linnean Society, and it is published in the third volume of the Journal of that Society. Sir C. Lyell and Dr. Hooker, who both knew of my work—the latter having read my sketch of 1844—honoured me by thinking it advisable to publish, with Mr. Wallace's excellent memoir, some brief extracts from my manuscripts. This Abstract, which I now publish, must necessarily be imperfect. I cannot here give references and authorities for my several statements; and I must trust to the reader reposing some confidence in my accuracy. No doubt errors will have crept in, though I hope I have always been cautious in trusting to good authorities alone. I can here give only the general conclusions at which I have arrived, with a few facts in illustration, but which, I hope, in most cases will suffice. No one can feel more sensible than I do of the necessity of hereafter publishing in detail all the facts, with references, on which my conclusions have been grounded; and I hope in a future work to do this. For I am well aware that scarcely a single point is discussed in this volume on which facts cannot be adduced, often apparently leading to conclusions directly opposite to those at which I have arrived. A fair result can be obtained only by fully stating and balancing the facts and arguments on both sides of each question; and this cannot possibly be here done. I much regret that want of space prevents my having the satisfaction of acknowledging the generous assistance which I have received from very many naturalists, some of them personally unknown to me. I cannot, however, let this opportunity pass without expressing my deep obligations to Dr. Hooker, who for the last fifteen years has aided me in every possible way by his large stores of knowledge and his excellent judgment. In considering the Origin of Species, it is quite conceivable that a naturalist, reflecting on the mutual affinities of organic beings, on their embryological relations, their geographical distribution, geological succession, and other such facts, might come to the conclusion that each species had not been independently created, but had descended, like varieties, from other species. Nevertheless, such a conclusion, even if well founded, would be unsatisfactory, until it could be shown how the innumerable species inhabiting this world have been modified, so as to acquire that perfection of structure and coadaptation which most justly excites our admiration. Naturalists continually refer to external conditions, such as climate, food, etc., as the only possible cause of variation. In one very limited sense, as we shall hereafter see, this may be true; but it is preposterous to attribute to mere external conditions, the structure, for instance, of the woodpecker, with its feet, tail, beak, and tongue, so admirably adapted to catch insects under the bark of trees. In the case of the misseltoe, which draws its nourishment from certain trees, which has seeds that must be transported by certain birds, and which has flowers with separate sexes absolutely requiring the agency of certain insects to bring pollen from one flower to the other, it is equally preposterous to account for the structure of this parasite, with its relations to several distinct organic beings, by the effects of external conditions, or of habit, or of the volition of the plant itself. The author of the "Vestiges of Creation" would, I presume, say that, after a certain unknown number of generations, some bird had given birth to a woodpecker, and some plant to the misseltoe, and that these had been produced perfect as we now see them; but this assumption seems to me to be no explanation, for it leaves the case of the coadaptations of organic beings to each other and to their physical conditions of life, untouched and unexplained. It is, therefore, of the highest importance to gain a clear insight into the means of modification and coadaptation. At the commencement of my observations it seemed to me probable that a careful study of domesticated animals and of cultivated plants would offer the best chance of making out this obscure problem. Nor have I been disappointed; in this and in all other perplexing cases I have invariably found that our knowledge, imperfect though it be, of variation under domestication, afforded the best and safest clue. I may venture to express my conviction of the high value of such studies, although they have been very commonly neglected by naturalists. From these considerations, I shall devote the first chapter of this Abstract to Variation under Domestication. We shall thus see that a large amount of hereditary modification is at least possible, and, what is equally or more important, we shall see how great is the power of man in accumulating by his Selection successive slight variations. I will then pass on to the variability of species in a state of nature; but I shall, unfortunately, be compelled to treat this subject far too briefly, as it can be treated properly only by giving long catalogues of facts. We shall, however, be enabled to discuss what circumstances are most favourable to variation. In the next chapter the Struggle for Existence amongst all organic beings throughout the world, which inevitably follows from their high geometrical powers of increase, will be treated of. This is the doctrine of Malthus, applied to the whole animal and vegetable kingdoms. As many more individuals of each species are born than can possibly survive; and as, consequently, there is a frequently recurring struggle for existence, it follows that any being, if it vary however slightly in any manner profitable to itself, under the complex and sometimes varying conditions of life, will have a better chance of surviving, and thus be NATURALLY SELECTED. From the strong principle of inheritance, any selected variety will tend to propagate its new and modified form. This fundamental subject of Natural Selection will be treated at some length in the fourth chapter; and we shall then see how Natural Selection almost inevitably causes much Extinction of the less improved forms of life and induces what I have called Divergence of Character. In the next chapter I shall discuss the complex and little known laws of variation and of correlation of growth. In the four succeeding chapters, the most apparent and gravest difficulties on the theory will be given: namely, first, the difficulties of transitions, or in understanding how a simple being or a simple organ can be changed and perfected into a highly developed being or elaborately constructed organ; secondly the subject of Instinct, or the mental powers of animals; thirdly, Hybridism, or the infertility of species and the fertility of varieties when intercrossed; and fourthly, the imperfection of the Geological Record. In the next chapter I shall consider the geological succession of organic beings throughout time; in the eleventh and twelfth, their geographical distribution throughout space; in the thirteenth, their classification or mutual affinities, both when mature and in an embryonic condition. In the last chapter I shall give a brief recapitulation of the whole work, and a few concluding remarks. No one ought to feel surprise at much remaining as yet unexplained in regard to the origin of species and varieties, if he makes due allowance for our profound ignorance in regard to the mutual relations of all the beings which live around us. Who can explain why one species ranges widely and is very numerous, and why another allied species has a narrow range and is rare? Yet these relations are of the highest importance, for they determine the present welfare, and, as I believe, the future success and modification of every inhabitant of this world. Still less do we know of the mutual relations of the innumerable inhabitants of the world during the many past geological epochs in its history. Although much remains obscure, and will long remain obscure, I can entertain no doubt, after the most deliberate study and dispassionate judgment of which I am capable, that the view which most naturalists entertain, and which I formerly entertained—namely, that each species has been independently created—is erroneous. I am fully convinced that species are not immutable; but that those belonging to what are called the same genera are lineal descendants of some other and generally extinct species, in the same manner as the acknowledged varieties of any one species are the descendants of that species. Furthermore, I am convinced that Natural Selection has been the main but not exclusive means of modification. [...]

Chapter 14. Recapitulation and Conclusion

As this whole volume is one long argument, it may be convenient to the reader to have the leading facts and inferences briefly recapitulated. That many and grave objections may be advanced against the theory of descent with modification through natural selection, I do not deny. I have endeavoured to give to them their full force. Nothing at first can appear more difficult to believe than that the more complex organs and instincts should have been perfected, not by means superior to, though analogous with, human reason, but by the accumulation of innumerable slight variations, each good for the individual possessor. Nevertheless, this difficulty, though appearing to our imagination insuperably great, cannot be considered real if we admit the following propositions, namely,—that gradations in the perfection of any organ or instinct, which we may consider, either do now exist or could have existed, each good of its kind,—that all organs and instincts are, in ever so slight a degree, variable,—and, lastly, that there is a struggle for existence leading to the preservation of each profitable deviation of structure or instinct. The truth of these propositions cannot, I think, be disputed. It is, no doubt, extremely difficult even to conjecture by what gradations many structures have been perfected, more especially amongst broken and failing groups of organic beings; but we see so many strange gradations in nature, as is proclaimed by the canon, "Natura non facit saltum," that we ought to be extremely cautious in saying that any organ or instinct, or any whole being, could not have arrived at its present state by many graduated steps. There are, it must be admitted, cases of special difficulty on the theory of natural selection; and one of the most curious of these is the existence of two or three defined castes of workers or sterile females in the same community of ants; but I have attempted to show how this difficulty can be mastered. With respect to the almost universal sterility of species when first crossed, which forms so remarkable a contrast with the almost universal fertility of varieties when crossed, I must refer the reader to the recapitulation of the facts given at the end of the eighth chapter, which seem to me conclusively to show that this sterility is no more a special endowment than is the incapacity of two trees to be grafted together, but that it is incidental on constitutional differences in the reproductive systems of the intercrossed species. We see the truth of this conclusion in the vast difference in the result, when the same two species are crossed reciprocally; that is, when one species is first used as the father and then as the mother. The fertility of varieties when intercrossed and of their mongrel offspring cannot be considered as universal; nor is their very general fertility surprising when we remember that it is not likely that either their constitutions or their reproductive systems should have been profoundly modified. Moreover, most of the varieties which have been experimentised on have been produced under domestication; and as domestication apparently tends to eliminate sterility, we ought not to expect it also to produce sterility. The sterility of hybrids is a very different case from that of first crosses, for their reproductive organs are more or less functionally impotent; whereas in first crosses the organs on both sides are in a perfect condition. As we continually see that organisms of all kinds are rendered in some degree sterile from their constitutions having been disturbed by slightly different and new conditions of life, we need not feel surprise at hybrids being in some degree sterile, for their constitutions can hardly fail to have been disturbed from being compounded of two distinct organisations. This parallelism is supported by another parallel, but directly opposite, class of facts; namely, that the vigour and fertility of all organic beings are increased by slight changes in their conditions of life, and that the offspring of slightly modified forms or varieties acquire from being crossed increased vigour and fertility. So that, on the one hand, considerable changes in the conditions of life and crosses between greatly modified forms, lessen fertility; and on the other hand, lesser changes in the conditions of life and crosses between less modified forms, increase fertility. Turning to geographical distribution, the difficulties encountered on the theory of descent with modification are grave enough. All the individuals of the same species, and all the species of the same genus, or even higher group, must have descended from common parents; and therefore, in however distant and isolated parts of the world they are now found, they must in the course of successive generations have passed from some one part to the others. We are often wholly unable even to conjecture how this could have been effected. Yet, as we have reason to believe that some species have retained the same specific form for very long periods, enormously long as measured by years, too much stress ought not to be laid on the occasional wide diffusion of the same species; for during very long periods of time there will always be a good chance for wide migration by many means. A broken or interrupted range may often be accounted for by the extinction of the species in the intermediate regions. It cannot be denied that we are as yet very ignorant of the full extent of the various climatal and geographical changes which have affected the earth during modern periods; and such changes will obviously have greatly facilitated migration. As an example, I have attempted to show how potent has been the influence of the Glacial period on the distribution both of the same and of representative species throughout the world. We are as yet profoundly ignorant of the many occasional means of transport. With respect to distinct species of the same genus inhabiting very distant and isolated regions, as the process of modification has necessarily been slow, all the means of migration will have been possible during a very long period; and consequently the difficulty of the wide diffusion of species of the same genus is in some degree lessened. As on the theory of natural selection an interminable number of intermediate forms must have existed, linking together all the species in each group by gradations as fine as our present varieties, it may be asked, Why do we not see these linking forms all around us? Why are not all organic beings blended together in an inextricable chaos? With respect to existing forms, we should remember that we have no right to expect (excepting in rare cases) to discover DIRECTLY connecting links between them, but only between each and some extinct and supplanted form. Even on a wide area, which has during a long period remained continuous, and of which the climate and other conditions of life change insensibly in going from a district occupied by one species into another district occupied by a closely allied species, we have no just right to expect often to find intermediate varieties in the intermediate zone. For we have reason to believe that only a few species are undergoing change at any one period; and all changes are slowly effected. I have also shown that the intermediate varieties which will at first probably exist in the intermediate zones, will be liable to be supplanted by the allied forms on either hand; and the latter, from existing in greater numbers, will generally be modified and improved at a quicker rate than the intermediate varieties, which exist in lesser numbers; so that the intermediate varieties will, in the long run, be supplanted and exterminated. On this doctrine of the extermination of an infinitude of connecting links, between the living and extinct inhabitants of the world, and at each successive period between the extinct and still older species, why is not every geological formation charged with such links? Why does not every collection of fossil remains afford plain evidence of the gradation and mutation of the forms of life? We meet with no such evidence, and this is the most obvious and forcible of the many objections which may be urged against my theory. Why, again, do whole groups of allied species appear, though certainly they often falsely appear, to have come in suddenly on the several geological stages? Why do we not find great piles of strata beneath the Silurian system, stored with the remains of the progenitors of the Silurian groups of fossils? For certainly on my theory such strata must somewhere have been deposited at these ancient and utterly unknown epochs in the world's history. I can answer these questions and grave objections only on the supposition that the geological record is far more imperfect than most geologists believe. It cannot be objected that there has not been time sufficient for any amount of organic change; for the lapse of time has been so great as to be utterly inappreciable by the human intellect. The number of specimens in all our museums is absolutely as nothing compared with the countless generations of countless species which certainly have existed. We should not be able to recognise a species as the parent of any one or more species if we were to examine them ever so closely, unless we likewise possessed many of the intermediate links between their past or parent and present states; and these many links we could hardly ever expect to discover, owing to the imperfection of the geological record. Numerous existing doubtful forms could be named which are probably varieties; but who will pretend that in future ages so many fossil links will be discovered, that naturalists will be able to decide, on the common view, whether or not these doubtful forms are varieties? As long as most of the links between any two species are unknown, if any one link or intermediate variety be discovered, it will simply be classed as another and distinct species. Only a small portion of the world has been geologically explored. Only organic beings of certain classes can be preserved in a fossil condition, at least in any great number. Widely ranging species vary most, and varieties are often at first local,—both causes rendering the discovery of intermediate links less likely. Local varieties will not spread into other and distant regions until they are considerably modified and improved; and when they do spread, if discovered in a geological formation, they will appear as if suddenly created there, and will be simply classed as new species. Most formations have been intermittent in their accumulation; and their duration, I am inclined to believe, has been shorter than the average duration of specific forms. Successive formations are separated from each other by enormous blank intervals of time; for fossiliferous formations, thick enough to resist future degradation, can be accumulated only where much sediment is deposited on the subsiding bed of the sea. During the alternate periods of elevation and of stationary level the record will be blank. During these latter periods there will probably be more variability in the forms of life; during periods of subsidence, more extinction. With respect to the absence of fossiliferous formations beneath the lowest Silurian strata, I can only recur to the hypothesis given in the ninth chapter. That the geological record is imperfect all will admit; but that it is imperfect to the degree which I require, few will be inclined to admit. If we look to long enough intervals of time, geology plainly declares that all species have changed; and they have changed in the manner which my theory requires, for they have changed slowly and in a graduated manner. We clearly see this in the fossil remains from consecutive formations invariably being much more closely related to each other, than are the fossils from formations distant from each other in time. Such is the sum of the several chief objections and difficulties which may justly be urged against my theory; and I have now briefly recapitulated the answers and explanations which can be given to them. I have felt these difficulties far too heavily during many years to doubt their weight. But it deserves especial notice that the more important objections relate to questions on which we are confessedly ignorant; nor do we know how ignorant we are. We do not know all the possible transitional gradations between the simplest and the most perfect organs; it cannot be pretended that we know all the varied means of Distribution during the long lapse of years, or that we know how imperfect the Geological Record is. Grave as these several difficulties are, in my judgment they do not overthrow the theory of descent with modification. Now let us turn to the other side of the argument. Under domestication we see much variability. This seems to be mainly due to the reproductive system being eminently susceptible to changes in the conditions of life; so that this system, when not rendered impotent, fails to reproduce offspring exactly like the parent-form. Variability is governed by many complex laws,—by correlation of growth, by use and disuse, and by the direct action of the physical conditions of life. There is much difficulty in ascertaining how much modification our domestic productions have undergone; but we may safely infer that the amount has been large, and that modifications can be inherited for long periods. As long as the conditions of life remain the same, we have reason to believe that a modification, which has already been inherited for many generations, may continue to be inherited for an almost infinite number of generations. On the other hand we have evidence that variability, when it has once come into play, does not wholly cease; for new varieties are still occasionally produced by our most anciently domesticated productions. Man does not actually produce variability; he only unintentionally exposes organic beings to new conditions of life, and then nature acts on the organisation, and causes variability. But man can and does select the variations given to him by nature, and thus accumulate them in any desired manner. He thus adapts animals and plants for his own benefit or pleasure. He may do this methodically, or he may do it unconsciously by preserving the individuals most useful to him at the time, without any thought of altering the breed. It is certain that he can largely influence the character of a breed by selecting, in each successive generation, individual differences so slight as to be quite inappreciable by an uneducated eye. This process of selection has been the great agency in the production of the most distinct and useful domestic breeds. That many of the breeds produced by man have to a large extent the character of natural species, is shown by the inextricable doubts whether very many of them are varieties or aboriginal species. There is no obvious reason why the principles which have acted so efficiently under domestication should not have acted under nature. In the preservation of favoured individuals and races, during the constantly-recurrent Struggle for Existence, we see the most powerful and ever-acting means of selection. The struggle for existence inevitably follows from the high geometrical ratio of increase which is common to all organic beings. This high rate of increase is proved by calculation, by the effects of a succession of peculiar seasons, and by the results of naturalisation, as explained in the third chapter. More individuals are born than can possibly survive. A grain in the balance will determine which individual shall live and which shall die,—which variety or species shall increase in number, and which shall decrease, or finally become extinct. As the individuals of the same species come in all respects into the closest competition with each other, the struggle will generally be most severe between them; it will be almost equally severe between the varieties of the same species, and next in severity between the species of the same genus. But the struggle will often be very severe between beings most remote in the scale of nature. The slightest advantage in one being, at any age or during any season, over those with which it comes into competition, or better adaptation in however slight a degree to the surrounding physical conditions, will turn the balance. With animals having separated sexes there will in most cases be a struggle between the males for possession of the females. The most vigorous individuals, or those which have most successfully struggled with their conditions of life, will generally leave most progeny. But success will often depend on having special weapons or means of defence, or on the charms of the males; and the slightest advantage will lead to victory. As geology plainly proclaims that each land has undergone great physical changes, we might have expected that organic beings would have varied under nature, in the same way as they generally have varied under the changed conditions of domestication. And if there be any variability under nature, it would be an unaccountable fact if natural selection had not come into play. It has often been asserted, but the assertion is quite incapable of proof, that the amount of variation under nature is a strictly limited quantity. Man, though acting on external characters alone and often capriciously, can produce within a short period a great result by adding up mere individual differences in his domestic productions; and every one admits that there are at least individual differences in species under nature. But, besides such differences, all naturalists have admitted the existence of varieties, which they think sufficiently distinct to be worthy of record in systematic works. No one can draw any clear distinction between individual differences and slight varieties; or between more plainly marked varieties and sub-species, and species. Let it be observed how naturalists differ in the rank which they assign to the many representative forms in Europe and North America. If then we have under nature variability and a powerful agent always ready to act and select, why should we doubt that variations in any way useful to beings, under their excessively complex relations of life, would be preserved, accumulated, and inherited? Why, if man can by patience select variations most useful to himself, should nature fail in selecting variations useful, under changing conditions of life, to her living products? What limit can be put to this power, acting during long ages and rigidly scrutinising the whole constitution, structure, and habits of each creature,—favouring the good and rejecting the bad? I can see no limit to this power, in slowly and beautifully adapting each form to the most complex relations of life. The theory of natural selection, even if we looked no further than this, seems to me to be in itself probable. I have already recapitulated, as fairly as I could, the opposed difficulties and objections: now let us turn to the special facts and arguments in favour of the theory. On the view that species are only strongly marked and permanent varieties, and that each species first existed as a variety, we can see why it is that no line of demarcation can be drawn between species, commonly supposed to have been produced by special acts of creation, and varieties which are acknowledged to have been produced by secondary laws. On this same view we can understand how it is that in each region where many species of a genus have been produced, and where they now flourish, these same species should present many varieties; for where the manufactory of species has been active, we might expect, as a general rule, to find it still in action; and this is the case if varieties be incipient species. Moreover, the species of the larger genera, which afford the greater number of varieties or incipient species, retain to a certain degree the character of varieties; for they differ from each other by a less amount of difference than do the species of smaller genera. The closely allied species also of the larger genera apparently have restricted ranges, and they are clustered in little groups round other species—in which respects they resemble varieties. These are strange relations on the view of each species having been independently created, but are intelligible if all species first existed as varieties. As each species tends by its geometrical ratio of reproduction to increase inordinately in number; and as the modified descendants of each species will be enabled to increase by so much the more as they become more diversified in habits and structure, so as to be enabled to seize on many and widely different places in the economy of nature, there will be a constant tendency in natural selection to preserve the most divergent offspring of any one species. Hence during a long-continued course of modification, the slight differences, characteristic of varieties of the same species, tend to be augmented into the greater differences characteristic of species of the same genus. New and improved varieties will inevitably supplant and exterminate the older, less improved and intermediate varieties; and thus species are rendered to a large extent defined and distinct objects. Dominant species belonging to the larger groups tend to give birth to new and dominant forms; so that each large group tends to become still larger, and at the same time more divergent in character. But as all groups cannot thus succeed in increasing in size, for the world would not hold them, the more dominant groups beat the less dominant. This tendency in the large groups to go on increasing in size and diverging in character, together with the almost inevitable contingency of much extinction, explains the arrangement of all the forms of life, in groups subordinate to groups, all within a few great classes, which we now see everywhere around us, and which has prevailed throughout all time. This grand fact of the grouping of all organic beings seems to me utterly inexplicable on the theory of creation. As natural selection acts solely by accumulating slight, successive, favourable variations, it can produce no great or sudden modification; it can act only by very short and slow steps. Hence the canon of "Natura non facit saltum," which every fresh addition to our knowledge tends to make more strictly correct, is on this theory simply intelligible. We can plainly see why nature is prodigal in variety, though niggard in innovation. But why this should be a law of nature if each species has been independently created, no man can explain. Many other facts are, as it seems to me, explicable on this theory. How strange it is that a bird, under the form of woodpecker, should have been created to prey on insects on the ground; that upland geese, which never or rarely swim, should have been created with webbed feet; that a thrush should have been created to dive and feed on sub-aquatic insects; and that a petrel should have been created with habits and structure fitting it for the life of an auk or grebe! and so on in endless other cases. But on the view of each species constantly trying to increase in number, with natural selection always ready to adapt the slowly varying descendants of each to any unoccupied or ill-occupied place in nature, these facts cease to be strange, or perhaps might even have been anticipated. As natural selection acts by competition, it adapts the inhabitants of each country only in relation to the degree of perfection of their associates; so that we need feel no surprise at the inhabitants of any one country, although on the ordinary view supposed to have been specially created and adapted for that country, being beaten and supplanted by the naturalised productions from another land. Nor ought we to marvel if all the contrivances in nature be not, as far as we can judge, absolutely perfect; and if some of them be abhorrent to our ideas of fitness. We need not marvel at the sting of the bee causing the bee's own death; at drones being produced in such vast numbers for one single act, and being then slaughtered by their sterile sisters; at the astonishing waste of pollen by our fir-trees; at the instinctive hatred of the queen bee for her own fertile daughters; at ichneumonidae feeding within the live bodies of caterpillars; and at other such cases. The wonder indeed is, on the theory of natural selection, that more cases of the want of absolute perfection have not been observed. The complex and little known laws governing variation are the same, as far as we can see, with the laws which have governed the production of so-called specific forms. In both cases physical conditions seem to have produced but little direct effect; yet when varieties enter any zone, they occasionally assume some of the characters of the species proper to that zone. In both varieties and species, use and disuse seem to have produced some effect; for it is difficult to resist this conclusion when we look, for instance, at the logger-headed duck, which has wings incapable of flight, in nearly the same condition as in the domestic duck; or when we look at the burrowing tucutucu, which is occasionally blind, and then at certain moles, which are habitually blind and have their eyes covered with skin; or when we look at the blind animals inhabiting the dark caves of America and Europe. In both varieties and species correlation of growth seems to have played a most important part, so that when one part has been modified other parts are necessarily modified. In both varieties and species reversions to long-lost characters occur. How inexplicable on the theory of creation is the occasional appearance of stripes on the shoulder and legs of the several species of the horse-genus and in their hybrids! How simply is this fact explained if we believe that these species have descended from a striped progenitor, in the same manner as the several domestic breeds of pigeon have descended from the blue and barred rock-pigeon! On the ordinary view of each species having been independently created, why should the specific characters, or those by which the species of the same genus differ from each other, be more variable than the generic characters in which they all agree? Why, for instance, should the colour of a flower be more likely to vary in any one species of a genus, if the other species, supposed to have been created independently, have differently coloured flowers, than if all the species of the genus have the same coloured flowers? If species are only well-marked varieties, of which the characters have become in a high degree permanent, we can understand this fact; for they have already varied since they branched off from a common progenitor in certain characters, by which they have come to be specifically distinct from each other; and therefore these same characters would be more likely still to be variable than the generic characters which have been inherited without change for an enormous period. It is inexplicable on the theory of creation why a part developed in a very unusual manner in any one species of a genus, and therefore, as we may naturally infer, of great importance to the species, should be eminently liable to variation; but, on my view, this part has undergone, since the several species branched off from a common progenitor, an unusual amount of variability and modification, and therefore we might expect this part generally to be still variable. But a part may be developed in the most unusual manner, like the wing of a bat, and yet not be more variable than any other structure, if the part be common to many subordinate forms, that is, if it has been inherited for a very long period; for in this case it will have been rendered constant by long-continued natural selection. Glancing at instincts, marvellous as some are, they offer no greater difficulty than does corporeal structure on the theory of the natural selection of successive, slight, but profitable modifications. We can thus understand why nature moves by graduated steps in endowing different animals of the same class with their several instincts. I have attempted to show how much light the principle of gradation throws on the admirable architectural powers of the hive-bee. Habit no doubt sometimes comes into play in modifying instincts; but it certainly is not indispensable, as we see, in the case of neuter insects, which leave no progeny to inherit the effects of long-continued habit. On the view of all the species of the same genus having descended from a common parent, and having inherited much in common, we can understand how it is that allied species, when placed under considerably different conditions of life, yet should follow nearly the same instincts; why the thrush of South America, for instance, lines her nest with mud like our British species. On the view of instincts having been slowly acquired through natural selection we need not marvel at some instincts being apparently not perfect and liable to mistakes, and at many instincts causing other animals to suffer. If species be only well-marked and permanent varieties, we can at once see why their crossed offspring should follow the same complex laws in their degrees and kinds of resemblance to their parents,—in being absorbed into each other by successive crosses, and in other such points,—as do the crossed offspring of acknowledged varieties. On the other hand, these would be strange facts if species have been independently created, and varieties have been produced by secondary laws. If we admit that the geological record is imperfect in an extreme degree, then such facts as the record gives, support the theory of descent with modification. New species have come on the stage slowly and at successive intervals; and the amount of change, after equal intervals of time, is widely different in different groups. The extinction of species and of whole groups of species, which has played so conspicuous a part in the history of the organic world, almost inevitably follows on the principle of natural selection; for old forms will be supplanted by new and improved forms. Neither single species nor groups of species reappear when the chain of ordinary generation has once been broken. The gradual diffusion of dominant forms, with the slow modification of their descendants, causes the forms of life, after long intervals of time, to appear as if they had changed simultaneously throughout the world. The fact of the fossil remains of each formation being in some degree intermediate in character between the fossils in the formations above and below, is simply explained by their intermediate position in the chain of descent. The grand fact that all extinct organic beings belong to the same system with recent beings, falling either into the same or into intermediate groups, follows from the living and the extinct being the offspring of common parents. As the groups which have descended from an ancient progenitor have generally diverged in character, the progenitor with its early descendants will often be intermediate in character in comparison with its later descendants; and thus we can see why the more ancient a fossil is, the oftener it stands in some degree intermediate between existing and allied groups. Recent forms are generally looked at as being, in some vague sense, higher than ancient and extinct forms; and they are in so far higher as the later and more improved forms have conquered the older and less improved organic beings in the struggle for life. Lastly, the law of the long endurance of allied forms on the same continent,—of marsupials in Australia, of edentata in America, and other such cases,—is intelligible, for within a confined country, the recent and the extinct will naturally be allied by descent. Looking to geographical distribution, if we admit that there has been during the long course of ages much migration from one part of the world to another, owing to former climatal and geographical changes and to the many occasional and unknown means of dispersal, then we can understand, on the theory of descent with modification, most of the great leading facts in Distribution. We can see why there should be so striking a parallelism in the distribution of organic beings throughout space, and in their geological succession throughout time; for in both cases the beings have been connected by the bond of ordinary generation, and the means of modification have been the same. We see the full meaning of the wonderful fact, which must have struck every traveller, namely, that on the same continent, under the most diverse conditions, under heat and cold, on mountain and lowland, on deserts and marshes, most of the inhabitants within each great class are plainly related; for they will generally be descendants of the same progenitors and early colonists. On this same principle of former migration, combined in most cases with modification, we can understand, by the aid of the Glacial period, the identity of some few plants, and the close alliance of many others, on the most distant mountains, under the most different climates; and likewise the close alliance of some of the inhabitants of the sea in the northern and southern temperate zones, though separated by the whole intertropical ocean. Although two areas may present the same physical conditions of life, we need feel no surprise at their inhabitants being widely different, if they have been for a long period completely separated from each other; for as the relation of organism to organism is the most important of all relations, and as the two areas will have received colonists from some third source or from each other, at various periods and in different proportions, the course of modification in the two areas will inevitably be different. On this view of migration, with subsequent modification, we can see why oceanic islands should be inhabited by few species, but of these, that many should be peculiar. We can clearly see why those animals which cannot cross wide spaces of ocean, as frogs and terrestrial mammals, should not inhabit oceanic islands; and why, on the other hand, new and peculiar species of bats, which can traverse the ocean, should so often be found on islands far distant from any continent. Such facts as the presence of peculiar species of bats, and the absence of all other mammals, on oceanic islands, are utterly inexplicable on the theory of independent acts of creation. The existence of closely allied or representative species in any two areas, implies, on the theory of descent with modification, that the same parents formerly inhabited both areas; and we almost invariably find that wherever many closely allied species inhabit two areas, some identical species common to both still exist. Wherever many closely allied yet distinct species occur, many doubtful forms and varieties of the same species likewise occur. It is a rule of high generality that the inhabitants of each area are related to the inhabitants of the nearest source whence immigrants might have been derived. We see this in nearly all the plants and animals of the Galapagos archipelago, of Juan Fernandez, and of the other American islands being related in the most striking manner to the plants and animals of the neighbouring American mainland; and those of the Cape de Verde archipelago and other African islands to the African mainland. It must be admitted that these facts receive no explanation on the theory of creation. The fact, as we have seen, that all past and present organic beings constitute one grand natural system, with group subordinate to group, and with extinct groups often falling in between recent groups, is intelligible on the theory of natural selection with its contingencies of extinction and divergence of character. On these same principles we see how it is, that the mutual affinities of the species and genera within each class are so complex and circuitous. We see why certain characters are far more serviceable than others for classification;—why adaptive characters, though of paramount importance to the being, are of hardly any importance in classification; why characters derived from rudimentary parts, though of no service to the being, are often of high classificatory value; and why embryological characters are the most valuable of all. The real affinities of all organic beings are due to inheritance or community of descent. The natural system is a genealogical arrangement, in which we have to discover the lines of descent by the most permanent characters, however slight their vital importance may be. The framework of bones being the same in the hand of a man, wing of a bat, fin of the porpoise, and leg of the horse,—the same number of vertebrae forming the neck of the giraffe and of the elephant,—and innumerable other such facts, at once explain themselves on the theory of descent with slow and slight successive modifications. The similarity of pattern in the wing and leg of a bat, though used for such different purpose,—in the jaws and legs of a crab,—in the petals, stamens, and pistils of a flower, is likewise intelligible on the view of the gradual modification of parts or organs, which were alike in the early progenitor of each class. On the principle of successive variations not always supervening at an early age, and being inherited at a corresponding not early period of life, we can clearly see why the embryos of mammals, birds, reptiles, and fishes should be so closely alike, and should be so unlike the adult forms. We may cease marvelling at the embryo of an air-breathing mammal or bird having branchial slits and arteries running in loops, like those in a fish which has to breathe the air dissolved in water, by the aid of well-developed branchiae. Disuse, aided sometimes by natural selection, will often tend to reduce an organ, when it has become useless by changed habits or under changed conditions of life; and we can clearly understand on this view the meaning of rudimentary organs. But disuse and selection will generally act on each creature, when it has come to maturity and has to play its full part in the struggle for existence, and will thus have little power of acting on an organ during early life; hence the organ will not be much reduced or rendered rudimentary at this early age. The calf, for instance, has inherited teeth, which never cut through the gums of the upper jaw, from an early progenitor having well-developed teeth; and we may believe, that the teeth in the mature animal were reduced, during successive generations, by disuse or by the tongue and palate having been fitted by natural selection to browse without their aid; whereas in the calf, the teeth have been left untouched by selection or disuse, and on the principle of inheritance at corresponding ages have been inherited from a remote period to the present day. On the view of each organic being and each separate organ having been specially created, how utterly inexplicable it is that parts, like the teeth in the embryonic calf or like the shrivelled wings under the soldered wing-covers of some beetles, should thus so frequently bear the plain stamp of inutility! Nature may be said to have taken pains to reveal, by rudimentary organs and by homologous structures, her scheme of modification, which it seems that we wilfully will not understand. I have now recapitulated the chief facts and considerations which have thoroughly convinced me that species have changed, and are still slowly changing by the preservation and accumulation of successive slight favourable variations. Why, it may be asked, have all the most eminent living naturalists and geologists rejected this view of the mutability of species? It cannot be asserted that organic beings in a state of nature are subject to no variation; it cannot be proved that the amount of variation in the course of long ages is a limited quantity; no clear distinction has been, or can be, drawn between species and well-marked varieties. It cannot be maintained that species when intercrossed are invariably sterile, and varieties invariably fertile; or that sterility is a special endowment and sign of creation. The belief that species were immutable productions was almost unavoidable as long as the history of the world was thought to be of short duration; and now that we have acquired some idea of the lapse of time, we are too apt to assume, without proof, that the geological record is so perfect that it would have afforded us plain evidence of the mutation of species, if they had undergone mutation. But the chief cause of our natural unwillingness to admit that one species has given birth to other and distinct species, is that we are always slow in admitting any great change of which we do not see the intermediate steps. The difficulty is the same as that felt by so many geologists, when Lyell first insisted that long lines of inland cliffs had been formed, and great valleys excavated, by the slow action of the coast-waves. The mind cannot possibly grasp the full meaning of the term of a hundred million years; it cannot add up and perceive the full effects of many slight variations, accumulated during an almost infinite number of generations. Although I am fully convinced of the truth of the views given in this volume under the form of an abstract, I by no means expect to convince experienced naturalists whose minds are stocked with a multitude of facts all viewed, during a long course of years, from a point of view directly opposite to mine. It is so easy to hide our ignorance under such expressions as the "plan of creation," "unity of design," etc., and to think that we give an explanation when we only restate a fact. Any one whose disposition leads him to attach more weight to unexplained difficulties than to the explanation of a certain number of facts will certainly reject my theory. A few naturalists, endowed with much flexibility of mind, and who have already begun to doubt on the immutability of species, may be influenced by this volume; but I look with confidence to the future, to young and rising naturalists, who will be able to view both sides of the question with impartiality. Whoever is led to believe that species are mutable will do good service by conscientiously expressing his conviction; for only thus can the load of prejudice by which this subject is overwhelmed be removed. Several eminent naturalists have of late published their belief that a multitude of reputed species in each genus are not real species; but that other species are real, that is, have been independently created. This seems to me a strange conclusion to arrive at. They admit that a multitude of forms, which till lately they themselves thought were special creations, and which are still thus looked at by the majority of naturalists, and which consequently have every external characteristic feature of true species,—they admit that these have been produced by variation, but they refuse to extend the same view to other and very slightly different forms. Nevertheless they do not pretend that they can define, or even conjecture, which are the created forms of life, and which are those produced by secondary laws. They admit variation as a vera causa in one case, they arbitrarily reject it in another, without assigning any distinction in the two cases. The day will come when this will be given as a curious illustration of the blindness of preconceived opinion. These authors seem no more startled at a miraculous act of creation than at an ordinary birth. But do they really believe that at innumerable periods in the earth's history certain elemental atoms have been commanded suddenly to flash into living tissues? Do they believe that at each supposed act of creation one individual or many were produced? Were all the infinitely numerous kinds of animals and plants created as eggs or seed, or as full grown? and in the case of mammals, were they created bearing the false marks of nourishment from the mother's womb? Although naturalists very properly demand a full explanation of every difficulty from those who believe in the mutability of species, on their own side they ignore the whole subject of the first appearance of species in what they consider reverent silence. It may be asked how far I extend the doctrine of the modification of species. The question is difficult to answer, because the more distinct the forms are which we may consider, by so much the arguments fall away in force. But some arguments of the greatest weight extend very far. All the members of whole classes can be connected together by chains of affinities, and all can be classified on the same principle, in groups subordinate to groups. Fossil remains sometimes tend to fill up very wide intervals between existing orders. Organs in a rudimentary condition plainly show that an early progenitor had the organ in a fully developed state; and this in some instances necessarily implies an enormous amount of modification in the descendants. Throughout whole classes various structures are formed on the same pattern, and at an embryonic age the species closely resemble each other. Therefore I cannot doubt that the theory of descent with modification embraces all the members of the same class. I believe that animals have descended from at most only four or five progenitors, and plants from an equal or lesser number. Analogy would lead me one step further, namely, to the belief that all animals and plants have descended from some one prototype. But analogy may be a deceitful guide. Nevertheless all living things have much in common, in their chemical composition, their germinal vesicles, their cellular structure, and their laws of growth and reproduction. We see this even in so trifling a circumstance as that the same poison often similarly affects plants and animals; or that the poison secreted by the gall-fly produces monstrous growths on the wild rose or oak-tree. Therefore I should infer from analogy that probably all the organic beings which have ever lived on this earth have descended from some one primordial form, into which life was first breathed. When the views entertained in this volume on the origin of species, or when analogous views are generally admitted, we can dimly foresee that there will be a considerable revolution in natural history. Systematists will be able to pursue their labours as at present; but they will not be incessantly haunted by the shadowy doubt whether this or that form be in essence a species. This I feel sure, and I speak after experience, will be no slight relief. The endless disputes whether or not some fifty species of British brambles are true species will cease. Systematists will have only to decide (not that this will be easy) whether any form be sufficiently constant and distinct from other forms, to be capable of definition; and if definable, whether the differences be sufficiently important to deserve a specific name. This latter point will become a far more essential consideration than it is at present; for differences, however slight, between any two forms, if not blended by intermediate gradations, are looked at by most naturalists as sufficient to raise both forms to the rank of species. Hereafter we shall be compelled to acknowledge that the only distinction between species and well-marked varieties is, that the latter are known, or believed, to be connected at the present day by intermediate gradations, whereas species were formerly thus connected. Hence, without quite rejecting the consideration of the present existence of intermediate gradations between any two forms, we shall be led to weigh more carefully and to value higher the actual amount of difference between them. It is quite possible that forms now generally acknowledged to be merely varieties may hereafter be thought worthy of specific names, as with the primrose and cowslip; and in this case scientific and common language will come into accordance. In short, we shall have to treat species in the same manner as those naturalists treat genera, who admit that genera are merely artificial combinations made for convenience. This may not be a cheering prospect; but we shall at least be freed from the vain search for the undiscovered and undiscoverable essence of the term species. The other and more general departments of natural history will rise greatly in interest. The terms used by naturalists of affinity, relationship, community of type, paternity, morphology, adaptive characters, rudimentary and aborted organs, etc., will cease to be metaphorical, and will have a plain signification. When we no longer look at an organic being as a savage looks at a ship, as at something wholly beyond his comprehension; when we regard every production of nature as one which has had a history; when we contemplate every complex structure and instinct as the summing up of many contrivances, each useful to the possessor, nearly in the same way as when we look at any great mechanical invention as the summing up of the labour, the experience, the reason, and even the blunders of numerous workmen; when we thus view each organic being, how far more interesting, I speak from experience, will the study of natural history become! A grand and almost untrodden field of inquiry will be opened, on the causes and laws of variation, on correlation of growth, on the effects of use and disuse, on the direct action of external conditions, and so forth. The study of domestic productions will rise immensely in value. A new variety raised by man will be a far more important and interesting subject for study than one more species added to the infinitude of already recorded species. Our classifications will come to be, as far as they can be so made, genealogies; and will then truly give what may be called the plan of creation. The rules for classifying will no doubt become simpler when we have a definite object in view. We possess no pedigrees or armorial bearings; and we have to discover and trace the many diverging lines of descent in our natural genealogies, by characters of any kind which have long been inherited. Rudimentary organs will speak infallibly with respect to the nature of long-lost structures. Species and groups of species, which are called aberrant, and which may fancifully be called living fossils, will aid us in forming a picture of the ancient forms of life. Embryology will reveal to us the structure, in some degree obscured, of the prototypes of each great class. When we can feel assured that all the individuals of the same species, and all the closely allied species of most genera, have within a not very remote period descended from one parent, and have migrated from some one birthplace; and when we better know the many means of migration, then, by the light which geology now throws, and will continue to throw, on former changes of climate and of the level of the land, we shall surely be enabled to trace in an admirable manner the former migrations of the inhabitants of the whole world. Even at present, by comparing the differences of the inhabitants of the sea on the opposite sides of a continent, and the nature of the various inhabitants of that continent in relation to their apparent means of immigration, some light can be thrown on ancient geography. The noble science of Geology loses glory from the extreme imperfection of the record. The crust of the earth with its embedded remains must not be looked at as a well-filled museum, but as a poor collection made at hazard and at rare intervals. The accumulation of each great fossiliferous formation will be recognised as having depended on an unusual concurrence of circumstances, and the blank intervals between the successive stages as having been of vast duration. But we shall be able to gauge with some security the duration of these intervals by a comparison of the preceding and succeeding organic forms. We must be cautious in attempting to correlate as strictly contemporaneous two formations, which include few identical species, by the general succession of their forms of life. As species are produced and exterminated by slowly acting and still existing causes, and not by miraculous acts of creation and by catastrophes; and as the most important of all causes of organic change is one which is almost independent of altered and perhaps suddenly altered physical conditions, namely, the mutual relation of organism to organism,—the improvement of one being entailing the improvement or the extermination of others; it follows, that the amount of organic change in the fossils of consecutive formations probably serves as a fair measure of the lapse of actual time. A number of species, however, keeping in a body might remain for a long period unchanged, whilst within this same period, several of these species, by migrating into new countries and coming into competition with foreign associates, might become modified; so that we must not overrate the accuracy of organic change as a measure of time. During early periods of the earth's history, when the forms of life were probably fewer and simpler, the rate of change was probably slower; and at the first dawn of life, when very few forms of the simplest structure existed, the rate of change may have been slow in an extreme degree. The whole history of the world, as at present known, although of a length quite incomprehensible by us, will hereafter be recognised as a mere fragment of time, compared with the ages which have elapsed since the first creature, the progenitor of innumerable extinct and living descendants, was created. In the distant future I see open fields for far more important researches. Psychology will be based on a new foundation, that of the necessary acquirement of each mental power and capacity by gradation. Light will be thrown on the origin of man and his history. Authors of the highest eminence seem to be fully satisfied with the view that each species has been independently created. To my mind it accords better with what we know of the laws impressed on matter by the Creator, that the production and extinction of the past and present inhabitants of the world should have been due to secondary causes, like those determining the birth and death of the individual. When I view all beings not as special creations, but as the lineal descendants of some few beings which lived long before the first bed of the Silurian system was deposited, they seem to me to become ennobled. Judging from the past, we may safely infer that not one living species will transmit its unaltered likeness to a distant futurity. And of the species now living very few will transmit progeny of any kind to a far distant futurity; for the manner in which all organic beings are grouped, shows that the greater number of species of each genus, and all the species of many genera, have left no descendants, but have become utterly extinct. We can so far take a prophetic glance into futurity as to foretell that it will be the common and widely-spread species, belonging to the larger and dominant groups, which will ultimately prevail and procreate new and dominant species. As all the living forms of life are the lineal descendants of those which lived long before the Silurian epoch, we may feel certain that the ordinary succession by generation has never once been broken, and that no cataclysm has desolated the whole world. Hence we may look with some confidence to a secure future of equally inappreciable length. And as natural selection works solely by and for the good of each being, all corporeal and mental endowments will tend to progress towards perfection. It is interesting to contemplate an entangled bank, clothed with many plants of many kinds, with birds singing on the bushes, with various insects flitting about, and with worms crawling through the damp earth, and to reflect that these elaborately constructed forms, so different from each other, and dependent on each other in so complex a manner, have all been produced by laws acting around us. These laws, taken in the largest sense, being Growth with Reproduction; Inheritance which is almost implied by reproduction; Variability from the indirect and direct action of the external conditions of life, and from use and disuse; a Ratio of Increase so high as to lead to a Struggle for Life, and as a consequence to Natural Selection, entailing Divergence of Character and the Extinction of less-improved forms. Thus, from the war of nature, from famine and death, the most exalted object which we are capable of conceiving, namely, the production of the higher animals, directly follows. There is grandeur in this view of life, with its several powers, having been originally breathed into a few forms or into one; and that, whilst this planet has gone cycling on according to the fixed law of gravity, from so simple a beginning endless forms most beautiful and most wonderful have been, and are being, evolved.

DESCENT OF MAN: AND SELECTION IN RELATION TO SEX

Introduction

The nature of the following work will be best understood by a brief account of how it came to be written. During many years I collected notes on the origin or descent of man, without any intention of publishing on the subject, but rather with the determination not to publish, as I thought that I should thus only add to the prejudices against my views. It seemed to me sufficient to indicate, in the first edition of my "Origin of Species," that by this work "light would be thrown on the origin of man and his history;" and this implies that man must be included with other organic beings in any general conclusion respecting his manner of appearance on this earth. Now the case wears a wholly different aspect. When a naturalist like

Carl Vogt ventures to say in his address as President of the National Institution of Geneva (1869), "personne, en Europe au moins, n'ose plus soutenir la creation independante et de toutes pieces, des especes," it is manifest that at least a large number of naturalists must admit that species are the modified descendants of other species; and this especially holds good with the younger and rising naturalists. The greater number accept the agency of natural selection; though some urge, whether with justice the future must decide, that I have greatly overrated its importance. Of the older and honoured chiefs in natural science, many unfortunately are still opposed to evolution in every form. In consequence of the views now adopted by most naturalists, and which will ultimately, as in every other case, be followed by others who are not scientific, I have been led to put together my notes, so as to see how far the general conclusions arrived at in my former works were applicable to man. This seemed all the more desirable, as I had never deliberately applied these views to a species taken singly. When we confine our attention to any one form, we are deprived of the weighty arguments derived from the nature of the affinities which connect together whole groups of organisms—their geographical distribution in past and present times, and their geological succession. The homological structure, embryological development, and rudimentary organs of a species remain to be considered, whether it be man or any other animal, to which our attention may be directed; but these great classes of facts afford, as it appears to me, ample and conclusive evidence in favour of the principle of gradual evolution. The strong support derived from the other arguments should, however, always be kept before the mind. The sole object of this work is to consider, firstly, whether man, like every other species, is descended from some pre-existing form; secondly, the manner of his development; and thirdly, the value of the differences between the so-called races of man. As I shall confine myself to these points, it will not be necessary to describe in detail the differences between the several races—an enormous subject which has been fully described in many valuable works. The high antiquity of man has recently been demonstrated by the labours of a host of eminent men, beginning with M. Boucher de Perthes; and this is the indispensable basis for understanding his origin. I shall, therefore, take this conclusion for granted, and may refer my readers to the admirable treatises of Sir Charles Lyell, Sir John Lubbock, and others. Nor shall I have occasion to do more than to allude to the amount of difference between man and the anthropomorphous apes; for Prof. Huxley, in the opinion of most competent judges, has conclusively shewn that in every visible character man differs less from the higher apes, than these do from the lower members of the same order of Primates. This work contains hardly any original facts in regard to man; but as the conclusions at which I arrived, after drawing up a rough draft, appeared to me interesting, I thought that they might interest others. It has often and confidently been asserted, that man's origin can never be known: but ignorance more frequently begets confidence than does knowledge: it is those who know little, and not those who know much, who so positively assert that this or that problem will never be solved by science. The conclusion that man is the co-descendant with other species of some ancient, lower, and extinct form, is not in any degree new. Lamarck long ago came to this conclusion, which has lately been maintained by several eminent naturalists and philosophers; for instance, by Wallace, Huxley, Lyell, Vogt, Lubbock, Buchner, Rolle, etc. I will not attempt to give references to all the authors who have taken the same side of the question. Thus G. Canestrini has published [...] a very curious paper on rudimentary characters, as bearing on the origin of man. Another work has (1869) been published by Dr. Francesco Barrago, bearing in Italian the title of "Man, made in the image of God, was also made in the image of the ape"), and especially by Haeckel. This last naturalist, besides his great work, "Generelle Morphologie" (1866), has recently (1868, with a second edition in 1870), published his "Naturliche Schopfungsgeschichte," in which he fully discusses the genealogy of man. If this work had appeared before my essay had been written, I should probably never have completed it. Almost all the conclusions at which I have arrived I find confirmed by this naturalist, whose knowledge on many points is much fuller than mine. Wherever I have added any fact or view from Prof. Haeckel's writings, I give his authority in the text; other statements I leave as they originally stood in my manuscript, occasionally giving in the foot-notes references to his works, as a confirmation of the more doubtful or interesting points. During many years it has seemed to me highly probable that sexual selection has played an important part in differentiating the races of man; but in my "Origin of Species" (first edition, page 199) I contented myself by merely alluding to this belief. When I came to apply this view to man, I found it indispensable to treat the whole subject in full detail. [...] Consequently the second part of the present work, treating of sexual selection, has extended to an inordinate length, compared with the first part; but this could not be avoided. I had intended adding to the present volumes an essay on the expression of the various emotions by man and the lower animals. My attention was called to this subject many years ago by Sir Charles Bell's admirable work. This illustrious anatomist maintains that man is endowed with certain muscles solely for the sake of expressing his emotions. As this view is obviously opposed to the belief that man is descended from some other and lower form, it was necessary for me to consider it. I likewise wished to ascertain how far the emotions are expressed in the same manner by the different races of man. But owing to the length of the present work, I have thought it better to reserve my essay for separate publication.

Part I. The Descent or Origin of Man

Chapter I. The Evidence of the Descent of Man from Some Lower Form

Nature of the evidence bearing on the origin of man—Homologous structures in man and the lower animals—Miscellaneous points of correspondence—Development—Rudimentary structures, muscles, sense-organs, hair, bones, reproductive organs, etc.—The bearing of these three great classes of facts on the origin of man. He who wishes to decide whether man is the modified descendant of some pre-existing form, would probably first enquire whether man varies, however slightly, in bodily structure and in mental faculties; and if so, whether the variations are transmitted to his offspring in accordance with the laws which prevail with the lower animals. Again, are the variations the result, as far as our ignorance permits us to judge, of the same general causes, and are they governed by the same general laws, as in the case of other organisms; for instance, by correlation, the inherited effects of use and disuse, etc.? Is man subject to similar malconformations, the result of arrested development, of reduplication of parts, etc., and does he display in any of his anomalies reversion to some former and ancient type of structure? It might also naturally be enquired whether man, like so many other animals, has given rise to varieties and sub-races, differing but slightly from each other, or to races differing so much that they must be classed as doubtful species? How are such races distributed over the world; and how, when crossed, do they react on each other in the first and succeeding generations? And so with many other points. The enquirer would next come to the important point, whether man tends to increase at so rapid a rate, as to lead to occasional severe struggles for existence; and consequently to beneficial variations, whether in body or mind, being preserved, and injurious ones eliminated. Do the races or species of men, whichever term may be applied, encroach on and replace one another, so that some finally become extinct? We shall see that all these questions, as indeed is obvious in respect to most of them, must be answered in the affirmative, in the same manner as with the lower animals. But the several considerations just referred to may be conveniently deferred for a time: and we will first see how far the bodily structure of man shews traces, more or less plain, of his descent from some lower form. In succeeding chapters the mental powers of man, in comparison with those of the lower animals, will be considered.

The Bodily Structure of Man

It is notorious that man is constructed on the same general type or model as other mammals. All the bones in his skeleton can be compared with corresponding bones in a monkey, bat, or seal. So it is with his muscles, nerves, blood-vessels and internal viscera. The brain, the most important of all the organs, follows the same law, as shewn by Huxley and other anatomists. Bischoff, who is a hostile witness, admits that every chief fissure and fold in the brain of man has its analogy in that of the orang; but he adds that at no period of development do their brains perfectly agree; nor could perfect agreement be expected, for otherwise their mental powers would have been the same. Vulpian remarks: "Les differences reelles qui existent entre l'encephale de l'homme et celui des singes superieurs, sont bien minimes. Il ne faut pas se faire d'illusions a cet egard. L'homme est bien plus pres des singes anthropomorphes par les caracteres anatomiques de son cerveau que ceux-ci ne le sont non seulement des autres mammiferes, mais meme de certains quadrumanes, des guenons et des macaques." But it would be superfluous here to give further details on the correspondence between man and the higher mammals in the structure of the brain and all other parts of the body. It may, however, be worth while to specify a few points, not directly or obviously connected with structure, by which this correspondence or relationship is well shewn. Man is liable to receive from the lower animals, and to communicate to them, certain diseases, as hydrophobia, variola, the glanders, syphilis, cholera, herpes, etc.; and this fact proves the close similarity of their tissues and blood, both in minute structure and composition, far more plainly than does their comparison under the best microscope, or by the aid of the best chemical analysis. Monkeys are liable to many of the same non-contagious diseases as we are; thus Rengger, who carefully observed for a long time the Cebus Azarae in its native land, found it liable to catarrh, with the usual symptoms, and which, when often recurrent, led to consumption. These monkeys suffered also from apoplexy, inflammation of the bowels, and cataract in the eye. The younger ones when shedding their milk-teeth often died from fever. Medicines produced the same effect on them as on us. Many kinds of monkeys have a strong taste for tea, coffee, and spiritous liquors: they will also, as I have myself seen, smoke tobacco with pleasure. Brehm asserts that the natives of north-eastern Africa catch the wild baboons by exposing vessels with strong beer, by which they are made drunk. He has seen some of these animals, which he kept in confinement, in this state; and he gives a laughable account of their behaviour and strange grimaces. On the following morning they were very cross and dismal; they held their aching heads with both hands, and wore a most pitiable expression: when beer or wine was offered them, they turned away with disgust, but relished the juice of lemons. An American monkey, an Ateles, after getting drunk on brandy, would never touch it again, and thus was wiser than many men. These trifling facts prove how similar the nerves of taste must be in monkeys and man, and how similarly their whole nervous system is affected. Man is infested with internal parasites, sometimes causing fatal effects; and is plagued by external parasites, all of which belong to the same genera or families as those infesting other mammals, and in the case of scabies to the same species. Man is subject, like other mammals, birds, and even insects, to that mysterious law, which causes certain normal processes, such as gestation, as well as the maturation and duration of various diseases, to follow lunar periods. His wounds are repaired by the same process of healing; and the stumps left after the amputation of his limbs, especially during an early embryonic period, occasionally possess some power of regeneration, as in the lowest animals. The whole process of that most important function, the reproduction of the species, is strikingly the same in all mammals, from the first act of courtship by the male, to the birth and nurturing of the young. Monkeys are born in almost as helpless a condition as our own infants; and in certain genera the young differ fully as much in appearance from the adults, as do our children from their full-grown parents. It has been urged by some writers, as an important distinction, that with man the young arrive at maturity at a much later age than with any other animal: but if we look to the races of mankind which inhabit tropical countries the difference is not great, for the orang is believed not to be adult till the age of from ten to fifteen years. Man differs from woman in size, bodily strength, hairiness, etc., as well as in mind, in the same manner as do the two sexes of many mammals. So that the correspondence in general structure, in the minute structure of the tissues, in chemical composition and in constitution, between man and the higher animals, especially the anthropomorphous apes, is extremely close.

Embryonic Development

Man is developed from an ovule, about the 125th of an inch in diameter, which differs in no respect from the ovules of other animals. The embryo itself at a very early period can hardly be distinguished from that of other members of the verte-brate kingdom. At this period the arteries run in arch-like branches, as if to carry the blood to branchiae which are not present in the higher Vertebrata, though the slits on the sides of the neck still remain..., marking their former position. At a somewhat later period, when the extremities are developed, "the feet of lizards and mammals," as the illustrious Von Baer remarks, "the wings and feet of birds, no less than the hands and feet of man, all arise from the same fundamental form." It is, says Prof. Huxley "quite in the later stages of development that the young human being presents marked differences from the young ape, while the latter departs as much from the dog in its developments, as the man does. Startling as this last as-sertion may appear to be, it is demonstrably true." [...]

After the foregoing statements made by such high authorities, it would be su-perfluous on my part to give a number of borrowed details, shewing that the embryo of man closely resembles that of other mammals. It may, however, be added, that the human embryo likewise resembles certain low forms when adult in various points of structure. For instance, the heart at first exists as a simple pul-sating vessel; the excreta are voided through a cloacal passage; and the os coccyx projects like a true tail, "extending considerably beyond the rudimentary legs." In the embryos of all air-breathing vertebrates, certain glands, called the corpora Wolffiana, correspond with, and act like the kidneys of mature fishes. Even at a later embryonic period, some striking resemblances between man and the lower animals may be observed. Bischoff says that "the convolutions of the brain in a human foetus at the end of the seventh month reach about the same stage of de-velopment as in a baboon when adult." The great toe, as Professor Owen remarks, "which forms the fulcrum when standing or walking, is perhaps the most charac-teristic peculiarity in the human structure;" but in an embryo, about an inch in length, Prof. Wyman found "that the great toe was shorter than the others; and, instead of being parallel to them, projected at an angle from the side of the foot, thus corresponding with the permanent condition of this part in the quadru-mana." I will conclude with a quotation from Huxley who after asking, does man originate in a different way from a dog, bird, frog or fish? says, "the reply is not doubtful for a moment; without question, the mode of origin, and the early stages of the development of man, are identical with those of the animals immediately below him in the scale: without a doubt in these respects, he is far nearer to apes than the apes are to the dog."

Rudiments

This subject, though not intrinsically more important than the two last, will for several reasons be treated here more fully. Not one of the higher animals can be named which does not bear some part in a rudimentary condition; and man forms no exception to the rule. Rudimentary organs must be distinguished from those that are nascent; though in some cases the distinction is not easy. The former are either absolutely useless, such as the mammae of male quadrupeds, or the incisor teeth of ruminants which never cut through the gums; or they are of such slight service to their present possessors, that we can hardly suppose that they were developed under the conditions which now exist. Organs in this latter state are not strictly rudimentary, but they are tending in this direction. Nascent organs, on the other hand, though not fully developed, are of high service to their possessors, and are capable of further development. Rudimentary organs are eminently variable; and this is partly intelligible, as they are useless, or nearly useless, and consequently are no longer subjected to natural selection. They often become wholly suppressed. When this occurs, they are nevertheless liable to occasional reappearance through reversion—a circumstance well worthy of attention. The chief agents in causing organs to become rudimentary seem to have been disuse at that period of life when the organ is chiefly used (and this is generally during maturity), and also inheritance at a corresponding period of life. The term "disuse" does not relate merely to the lessened action of muscles, but includes a diminished flow of blood to a part or organ, from being subjected to fewer alternations of pressure, or from becoming in any way less habitually active. Rudiments, however, may occur in one sex of those parts which are normally present in the other sex; and such rudiments, as we shall hereafter see, have often originated in a way distinct from those here referred to. In some cases, organs have been reduced by means of natural selection, from having become injurious to the species under changed habits of life. The process of reduction is probably often aided through the two principles of compensation and economy of growth; but the later stages of reduction, after disuse has done all that can fairly be attributed to it, and when the saving to be effected by the economy of growth would be very small, are difficult to understand. The final and complete suppression of a part, already useless and much reduced in size, in which case neither compensation nor economy can come into play, is perhaps intelligible by the aid of the hypothesis of pangenesis. But as the whole subject of rudimentary organs has been discussed and illustrated in my former works, I need here say no more on this head. Rudiments of various muscles have been observed in many parts of the human body; and not a few muscles, which are regularly present in some of the lower animals can occasionally be detected in man in a greatly reduced condition. Every one must have noticed the power which many animals, especially horses, possess of moving or twitching their skin; and this is effected by the panniculus carnosus. Remnants of this muscle in an efficient state are found in various parts of our bodies; for instance, the muscle on the forehead, by which the eyebrows are raised. The platysma myoides, which is well developed on the neck, belongs to this system. Prof. Turner, of Edinburgh, has occasionally detected, as he informs me, muscular fasciculi in five different situations, namely in the axillae, near the scapulae, etc., all of which must be referred to the system of the panniculus. He has also shewn that the musculus sternalis or sternalis brutorum, which is not an extension of the rectus abdominalis, but is closely allied to the panniculus, occurred in the proportion of about three per cent. in upwards of 600 bodies: he adds, that this muscle affords "an excellent illustration of the statement that occasional and rudimentary structures are especially liable to variation in arrangement." Some few persons have the power of contracting the superficial muscles on their scalps; and these muscles are in a variable and partially rudimentary condition. M. A. de Candolle has communicated to me a curious instance of the long-continued persistence or inheritance of this power, as well as of its unusual development. He knows a family, in which one member, the present head of the family, could, when a youth, pitch several heavy books from his head by the movement of the scalp alone; and he won wagers by performing this feat. His father, uncle, grandfather, and his three children possess the same power to the same unusual degree. This family became divided eight generations ago into two branches; so that the head of the above-mentioned branch is cousin in the seventh degree to the head of the other branch. This distant cousin resides in another part of France; and on being asked whether he possessed the same faculty, immediately exhibited his power. This case offers a good illustration how persistent may be the transmission of an absolutely useless faculty, probably derived from our remote semi-human progenitors; since many monkeys have, and frequently use the power, of largely moving their scalps up and down. The extrinsic muscles which serve to move the external ear, and the intrinsic muscles which move the different parts, are in a rudimentary condition in man, and they all belong to the system of the panniculus; they are also variable in development, or at least in function. I have seen one man who could draw the whole ear forwards; other men can draw it upwards; another who could draw it backwards to the same effect; and from what one of these persons told me, it is probable that most of us, by often touching our ears, and thus directing our attention towards them, could recover some power of movement by repeated trials. The power of erecting and directing the shell of the ears to the various points of the compass, is no doubt of the highest service to many animals, as they thus perceive the direction of danger; but I have never heard, on sufficient evidence, of a man who possessed this power, the one which might be of use to him. The whole external shell may be considered a rudiment, together with the various folds and prominences (helix and anti-helix, tragus and anti-tragus, etc.) which in the lower animals strengthen and support the ear when erect, without adding much to its weight. Some authors, however, suppose that the cartilage of the shell serves to transmit vibrations to the acoustic nerve; but Mr. Toynbee, after collecting all the known evidence on this head, concludes that the external shell is of no distinct use. The ears of the chimpanzee and orang are curiously like those of man, and the proper muscles are likewise but very slightly developed. I am also assured by the keepers in the Zoological Gardens that these animals never move or erect their ears; so that they are in an equally rudimentary condition with those of man, as far as function is concerned. Why these animals, as well as the progenitors of man, should have lost the power of erecting their ears, we cannot say. It may be, though I am not satisfied with this view, that owing to their arboreal habits and great strength they were but little exposed to danger, and so during a lengthened period moved their ears but little, and thus gradually lost the power of moving them. This would be a parallel case with that of those large and heavy birds, which, from inhabiting oceanic islands, have not been exposed to the attacks of beasts of prey, and have consequently lost the power of using their wings for flight. The inability to move the ears in man and several apes is, however, partly compensated by the freedom with which they can move the head in a horizontal plane, so as to catch sounds from all directions. It has been asserted that the ear of man alone possesses a lobule; but "a rudiment of it is found in the gorilla." [...]

The celebrated sculptor, Mr. Woolner, informs me of one little peculiarity in the external ear, which he has often observed both in men and women, and of which he perceived the full significance. His attention was first called to the subject whilst at work on his figure of Puck, to which he had given pointed ears. He was thus led to examine the ears of various monkeys, and subsequently more carefully those of man. The peculiarity consists in a little blunt point, projecting from the inwardly folded margin, or helix. When present, it is developed at birth, and, according to Prof. Ludwig Meyer, more frequently in man than in woman. [...] These points not only project inwards towards the centre of the ear, but often a little outwards from its plane, so as to be visible when the head is viewed from directly in front or behind. They are variable in size, and somewhat in position, standing either a little higher or lower; and they sometimes occur on one ear and not on the other. They are not confined to mankind, for I observed a case in one of the spider-monkeys (Ateles beelzebuth) in our Zoological Gardens; and Mr. E. Ray Lankester informs me of another case in a chimpanzee in the gardens at Hamburg. The helix obviously consists of the extreme margin of the ear folded inwards; and this folding appears to be in some manner connected with the whole external ear being permanently pressed backwards. In many monkeys, which do not stand high in the order, as baboons and some species of macacus, the upper portion of the ear is slightly pointed, and the margin is not at all folded inwards; but if the margin were to be thus folded, a slight point would necessarily project inwards towards the centre, and probably a little outwards from the plane of the ear; and this I believe to be their origin in many cases. On the other hand, Prof. L. Meyer, in an able paper recently published, maintains that the whole case is one of mere variability; and that the projections are not real ones, but are due to the internal cartilage on each side of the points not having been fully developed. I am quite ready to admit that this is the correct explanation in many instances, as in those figured by Prof. Meyer, in which there are several minute points, or the whole margin is sinuous. I have myself seen, through the kindness of Dr. L. Down, the ear of a microcephalous idiot, on which there is a projection on the outside of the helix, and not on the inward folded edge, so that this point can have no relation to a former apex of the ear. Nevertheless in some cases, my original view, that the points are vestiges of the tips of formerly erect and pointed ears, still seems to me probable. I think so from the frequency of their occurrence, and from the general correspondence in position with that of the tip of a pointed ear. In one case, of which a photograph has been sent me, the projection is so large, that supposing, in accordance with Prof. Meyer's view, the ear to be made perfect by the equal development of the cartilage throughout the whole extent of the margin, it would have covered fully one-third of the whole ear. Two cases have been communicated to me, one in North America, and the other in England, in which the upper margin is not at all folded inwards, but is pointed, so that it closely resembles the pointed ear of an ordinary quadruped in outline.

In one of these cases, which was that of a young child, the father compared the ear with the drawing which I have given of the ear of a monkey, the Cynopithecus niger, and says that their outlines are closely similar. If, in these two cases, the margin had been folded inwards in the normal manner, an inward projection must have been formed. I may add that in two other cases the outline still remains somewhat pointed, although the margin of the upper part of the ear is normally folded inwards—in one of them, however, very narrowly. [...] On the whole, it still seems to me probable that the points in question are in some cases, both in man and apes, vestiges of a former condition. The nictitating membrane, or third eyelid, with its accessory muscles and other structures, is especially well developed in birds, and is of much functional importance to them, as it can be rapidly drawn across the whole eye-ball. It is found in some reptiles and amphibians, and in certain fishes, as in sharks. It is fairly well developed in the two lower divisions of the mammalian series, namely, in the monotremata and marsupials, and in some few of the higher mammals, as in the walrus. But in man, the quadrumana, and most other mammals, it exists, as is admitted by all anatomists, as a mere rudiment, called the semilunar fold. The sense of smell is of the highest importance to the greater number of mammals—to some, as the ruminants, in warning them of danger; to others, as the Carnivora, in finding their prey; to others, again, as the wild boar, for both purposes combined. But the sense of smell is of extremely slight service, if any, even to the dark coloured races of men, in whom it is much more highly developed than in the white and civilised races. Nevertheless it does not warn them of danger, nor guide them to their food; nor does it prevent the Esquimaux from sleeping in the most fetid atmosphere, nor many savages from eating half-putrid meat. In Europeans the power differs greatly in different individuals, as I am assured by an eminent naturalist who possesses this sense highly developed, and who has attended to the subject. Those who believe in the principle of gradual evolution, will not readily admit that the sense of smell in its present state was originally acquired by man, as he now exists. He inherits the power in an enfeebled and so far rudimentary condition, from some early progenitor, to whom it was highly serviceable, and by whom it was continually used. In those animals which have this sense highly developed, such as dogs and horses, the recollection of persons and of places is strongly associated with their odour; and we can thus perhaps understand how it is, as Dr. Maudsley has truly remarked, that the sense of smell in man "is singularly effective in recalling vividly the ideas and images of forgotten scenes and places." Man differs conspicuously from all the other primates in being almost naked. But a few short straggling hairs are found over the greater part of the body in the man, and fine down on that of the woman. The different races differ much in hairiness; and in the individuals of the same race the hairs are highly variable, not only in abundance, but likewise in position: thus in some Europeans the shoulders are quite naked, whilst in others they bear thick tufts of hair. There can be little doubt that the hairs thus scattered over the body are the rudiments of the uniform hairy coat of the lower animals. This view is rendered all the more probable, as it is known that fine, short, and pale-coloured hairs on the limbs and other parts of the body, occasionally become developed into "thickset, long, and rather coarse dark hairs," when abnormally nourished near old-standing inflamed surfaces. I am informed by Sir James Paget that often several members of a family have a few hairs in their eyebrows much longer than the others; so that even this slight peculiarity seems to be inherited. These hairs, too, seem to have their representatives; for in the chimpanzee, and in certain species of Macacus, there are scattered hairs of considerable length rising from the naked skin above the eyes, and corresponding to our eyebrows; similar long hairs project from the hairy covering of the superciliary ridges in some baboons. The fine wool-like hair, or so-called lanugo, with which the human foetus during the sixth month is thickly covered, offers a more curious case. It is first developed, during the fifth month, on the eyebrows and face, and especially round the mouth, where it is much longer than that on the head. A moustache of this kind was observed by Eschricht on a female foetus; but this is not so surprising a circumstance as it may at first appear, for the two sexes generally resemble each other in all external characters during an early period of growth. The direction and arrangement of the hairs on all parts of the foetal body are the same as in the adult, but are subject to much variability. The whole surface, including even the forehead and ears, is thus thickly clothed; but it is a significant fact that the palms of the hands and the soles of the feet are quite naked, like the inferior surfaces of all four extremities in most of the lower animals. As this can hardly be an accidental coincidence, the woolly covering of the foetus probably represents the first permanent coat of hair in those mammals which are born hairy. Three or four cases have been recorded of persons born with their whole bodies and faces thickly covered with fine long hairs; and this strange condition is strongly inherited, and is correlated with an abnormal condition of the teeth. Prof. Alex. Brandt informs me that he has compared the hair from the face of a man thus characterised, aged thirty-five, with the lanugo of a foetus, and finds it quite similar in texture; therefore, as he remarks, the case may be attributed to an arrest of development in the hair, together with its continued growth. Many delicate children, as I have been assured by a surgeon to a hospital for children, have their backs covered by rather long silky hairs; and such cases probably come under the same head. It appears as if the posterior molar or wisdom-teeth were tending to become rudimentary in the more civilised races of man. These teeth are rather smaller than the other molars, as is likewise the case with the corresponding teeth in the chimpanzee and orang; and they have only two separate fangs. They do not cut through the gums till about the seventeenth year, and I have been assured that they are much more liable to decay, and are earlier lost than the other teeth; but this is denied by some eminent dentists. They are also much more liable to vary, both in structure and in the period of their development, than the other teeth. In the Melanian races, on the other hand, the wisdom-teeth are usually furnished with three separate fangs, and are generally sound; they also differ from the other molars in size, less than in the Caucasian races. Prof. Schaaffhausen accounts for this difference between the races by "the posterior dental portion of the jaw being always shortened" in those that are civilised, and this shortening may, I presume, be attributed to civilised men habitually feeding on soft, cooked food, and thus using their jaws less. I am informed by Mr. Brace that it is becoming quite a common practice in the United States to remove some of the molar teeth of children, as the jaw does not grow large enough for the perfect development of the normal number. With respect to the alimentary canal, I have met with an account of only a single rudiment, namely the vermiform appendage of the caecum. The caecum is a branch or diverticulum of the intestine, ending in a cul-de-sac, and is extremely long in many of the lower vegetable-feeding mammals. In the marsupial koala it is actually more than thrice as long as the whole body. It is sometimes produced into a long gradually-tapering point, and is sometimes constricted in parts. It appears as if, in consequence of changed diet or habits, the caecum had become much shortened in various animals, the vermiform appendage being left as a rudiment of the shortened part. That this appendage is a rudiment, we may infer from its small size, and from the evidence which Prof. Canestrini has collected of its variability in man. It is occasionally quite absent, or again is largely developed. The passage is sometimes completely closed for half or two-thirds of its length, with the terminal part consisting of a flattened solid expansion. In the orang this appendage is long and convoluted: in man it arises from the end of the short caecum, and is commonly from four to five inches in length, being only about the third of an inch in diameter. Not only is it useless, but it is sometimes the cause of death, of which fact I have lately heard two instances: this is due to small hard bodies, such as seeds, entering the passage, and causing inflammation. In some of the lower Quadrumana, in the Lemuridae and Carnivora, as well as in many marsupials, there is a passage near the lower end of the humerus, called the supra-condyloid foramen, through which the great nerve of the fore limb and often the great artery pass. Now in the humerus of man, there is generally a trace of this passage, which is sometimes fairly well developed, being formed by a depending hook-like process of bone, completed by a band of ligament. Dr. Struthers, who has closely attended to the subject, has now shewn that this peculiarity is sometimes inherited, as it has occurred in a father, and in no less than four out of his seven children. When present, the great nerve invariably passes through it; and this clearly indicates that it is the homologue and rudiment of the supra-condyloid foramen of the lower animals. Prof. Turner estimates, as he informs me, that it occurs in about one per cent. of recent skeletons. But if the occasional development of this structure in man is, as seems probable, due to reversion, it is a return to a very ancient state of things, because in the higher Quadrumana it is absent. There is another foramen or perforation in the humerus, occasionally present in man, which may be called the inter-condyloid. This occurs, but not constantly, in various anthropoid and other apes, and likewise in many of the lower animals. It is remarkable that this perforation seems to have been present in man much more frequently during ancient times than recently. Mr. Busk has collected the following evidence on this head: Prof. Broca "noticed the perforation in four and a half per cent. of the arm-bones collected in the 'Cimetiere du Sud,' at Paris; and in the Grotto of Orrony, the contents of which are referred to the Bronze period, as many as eight humeri out of thirty-two were perforated; but this extraordinary proportion, he thinks, might be due to the cavern having been a sort of 'family vault.' Again, M. Dupont found thirty per cent. of perforated bones in the caves of the Valley of the Lesse, belonging to the Reindeer period; whilst M. Leguay, in a sort of dolmen at Argenteuil, observed twenty-five per cent. to be perforated; and M. Pruner-Bey found twenty-six per cent. in the same condition in bones from Vaureal. Nor should it be left unnoticed that M. Pruner-Bey states that this condition is common in Guanche skeletons." It is an interesting fact that ancient races, in this and several other cases, more frequently present structures which resemble those of the lower animals than do the modern. One chief cause seems to be that the ancient races stand somewhat nearer in the long line of descent to their remote animal-like progenitors. In man, the os coccyx, together with certain other vertebrae hereafter to be described, though functionless as a tail, plainly represent this part in other vertebrate animals. At an early embryonic period it is free, and projects beyond the lower extremities; ... Even after birth it has been known, in certain rare and anomalous cases, to form a small external rudiment of a tail. The os coccyx is short, usually including only four vertebrae, all anchylosed together: and these are in a rudimentary condition, for they consist, with the exception of the basal one, of the centrum alone. They are furnished with some small muscles; one of which, as I am informed by Prof. Turner, has been expressly described by Theile as a rudimentary repetition of the extensor of the tail, a muscle which is so largely developed in many mammals. The spinal cord in man extends only as far downwards as the last dorsal or first lumbar vertebra; but a thread-like structure (the filum terminale) runs down the axis of the sacral part of the spinal canal, and even along the back of the coccygeal bones. The upper part of this filament, as Prof. Turner informs me, is undoubtedly homologous with the spinal cord; but the lower part apparently consists merely of the pia mater, or vascular investing membrane. Even in this case the os coccyx may be said to possess a vestige of so important a structure as the spinal cord, though no longer enclosed within a bony canal. The following fact, for which I am also indebted to Prof. Turner, shews how closely the os coccyx corresponds with the true tail in the lower animals: Luschka has recently discovered at the extremity of the coccygeal bones a very peculiar convoluted body, which is continuous with the middle sacral artery; and this discovery led Krause and Meyer to examine the tail of a monkey (Macacus), and of a cat, in both of which they found a similarly convoluted body, though not at the extremity. The reproductive system offers various rudimentary structures; but these differ in one important respect from the foregoing cases. Here we are not concerned with the vestige of a part which does not belong to the species in an efficient state, but with a part efficient in the one sex, and represented in the other by a mere rudiment. Nevertheless, the occurrence of such rudiments is as difficult to explain, on the belief of the separate creation of each species, as in the foregoing cases. Hereafter I shall have to recur to these rudiments, and shall shew that their presence generally depends merely on inheritance, that is, on parts acquired by one sex having been partially transmitted to the other. I will in this place only give some instances of such rudiments. It is well known that in the males of all mammals, including man, rudimentary mammae exist. These in several instances have become well developed, and have yielded a copious supply of milk. Their essential identity in the two sexes is likewise shewn by their occasional sympathetic enlargement in both during an attack of the measles. The vesicula prostatica, which has been observed in many male mammals, is now universally acknowledged to be the homologue of the female uterus, together with the connected passage. It is impossible to read Leuckart's able description of this organ, and his reasoning, without admitting the justness of his conclusion. This is especially clear in the case of those mammals in which the true female uterus bifurcates, for in the males of these the vesicula likewise bifurcates. Some other rudimentary structures belonging to the reproductive system might have been here adduced. The bearing of the three great classes of facts now given is unmistakeable. But it would be superfluous fully to recapitulate the line of argument given in detail in my "Origin of Species." The homological construction of the whole frame in the members of the same class is intelligible, if we admit their descent from a common progenitor, together with their subsequent adaptation to diversified conditions. On any other view, the similarity of pattern between the hand of a man or monkey, the foot of a horse, the flipper of a seal, the wing of a bat, etc., is utterly inexplicable. It is no scientific explanation to assert that they have all been formed on the same ideal plan. With respect to development, we can clearly understand, on the principle of variations supervening at a rather late embryonic period, and being inherited at a corresponding period, how it is that the embryos of wonderfully different forms should still retain, more or less perfectly, the structure of their common progenitor. No other explanation has ever been given of the marvellous fact that the embryos of a man, dog, seal, bat, reptile, etc., can at first hardly be distinguished from each other. In order to understand the existence of rudimentary organs, we have only to suppose that a former progenitor possessed the parts in question in a perfect state, and that under changed habits of life they became greatly reduced, either from simple disuse, or through the natural selection of those individuals which were least encumbered with a superfluous part, aided by the other means previously indicated. Thus we can understand how it has come to pass that man and all other vertebrate animals have been constructed on the same general model, why they pass through the same early stages of development, and why they retain certain rudiments in common. Consequently we ought frankly to admit their community of descent: to take any other view, is to admit that our own structure, and that of all the animals around us, is a mere snare laid to entrap our judgment. This conclusion is greatly strengthened, if we look to the members of the whole animal series, and consider the evidence derived from their affinities or classification, their geographical distribution and geological succession. It is only our natural prejudice, and that arrogance which made our forefathers declare that they were descended from demi-gods, which leads us to demur to this conclusion. But the time will before long come, when it will be thought wonderful that naturalists, who were well acquainted with the comparative structure and development of man, and other mammals, should have believed that each was the work of a separate act of creation.

THE AUTOBIOGRAPHY OF CHARLES DARWIN

From *The Life and Letters of Charles Darwin*
Edited by his Son
Francis Darwin

[My father's autobiographical recollections, given in the present chapter, were written for his children,—and written without any thought that they would ever be published. To many this may seem an impossibility; but those who knew my father will understand how it was not only possible, but natural. The autobiography bears the heading, "Recollections of the Development of my Mind and Character," and end with the following note:—"Aug. 3, 1876. This sketch of my life was begun about May 28th at Hopedene (Mr. Hensleigh Wedgwood's house in Surrey), and since then I have written for nearly an hour on most afternoons." It will easily be understood that, in a narrative of a personal and intimate kind written for his wife and children, passages should occur which must here be omitted; and I have not thought it necessary to indicate where such omissions are made. It has been found necessary to make a few corrections of obvious verbal slips, but the number of such alterations has been kept down to the minimum.—F.D.] [. . .]

When I left the school I was for my age neither high nor low in it; and I believe that I was considered by all my masters and by my father as a very ordinary boy, rather below the common standard in intellect. To my deep mortification my father once said to me, "You care for nothing but shooting, dogs, and rat-catching, and you will be a disgrace to yourself and all your family." But my father, who was the kindest man I ever knew and whose memory I love with all my heart, must have been angry and somewhat unjust when he used such words.

Looking back as well as I can at my character during my school life, the only qualities which at this period promised well for the future, were, that I had strong and diversified tastes, much zeal for whatever interested me, and a keen pleasure in understanding any complex subject or thing. I was taught Euclid by a private tutor, and I distinctly remember the intense satisfaction which the clear geometrical proofs gave me. I remember, with equal distinctness, the delight which my uncle gave me (the father of Francis Galton) by explaining the principle of the vernier of a barometer. With respect to diversified tastes, independently of science, I was fond of reading various books, and I used to sit for hours reading the historical plays of Shakespeare, generally in an old window in the thick walls of the school. I read also other poetry, such as Thomson's "Seasons," and the recently published poems of Byron and Scott. I mention this because later in life I wholly lost, to my great regret, all pleasure from poetry of any kind, including Shakespeare. In connection with pleasure from poetry, I may add that in 1822 a vivid delight in scenery was first awakened in my mind, during a riding tour on the borders of Wales, and this has lasted longer than any other aesthetic pleasure. [. . .]

Cambridge 1828–1831

After having spent two sessions in Edinburgh, my father perceived, or he heard from my sisters, that I did not like the thought of being a physician, so he proposed that I should become a clergyman. He was very properly vehement against my turning into an idle sporting man, which then seemed my probable destination. I asked for some time to consider, as from what little I had heard or thought on the subject I had scruples about declaring my belief in all the dogmas of the Church of England; though otherwise I liked the thought of being a country clergyman. Accordingly I read with care "Pearson on the Creed," and a few other books on divinity; and as I did not then in the least doubt the strict and literal truth of every word in the Bible, I soon persuaded myself that our Creed must be fully accepted.

Considering how fiercely I have been attacked by the orthodox, it seems ludicrous that I once intended to be a clergyman. Nor was this intention and my father's wish ever formerly given up, but died a natural death when, on leaving Cambridge, I joined the "Beagle" as naturalist. [...]

During the three years which I spent at Cambridge my time was wasted, as far as the academical studies were concerned, as completely as at Edinburgh and at school. I attempted mathematics, and even went during the summer of 1828 with a private tutor (a very dull man) to Barmouth, but I got on very slowly. The work was repugnant to me, chiefly from my not being able to see any meaning in the early steps in algebra. This impatience was very foolish, and in after years I have deeply regretted that I did not proceed far enough at least to understand something of the great leading principles of mathematics, for men thus endowed seem to have an extra sense. But I do not believe that I should ever have succeeded beyond a very low grade. With respect to Classics I did nothing except attend a few compulsory college lectures, and the attendance was almost nominal. In my second year I had to work for a month or two to pass the Little-Go, which I did easily. Again, in my last year I worked with some earnestness for my final degree of B.A., and brushed up my Classics, together with a little Algebra and Euclid, which latter gave me much pleasure, as it did at school. In order to pass the B.A. examination, it was also necessary to get up Paley's "Evidences of Christianity," and his "Moral Philosophy." This was done in a thorough manner, and I am convinced that I could have written out the whole of the "Evidences" with perfect correctness, but not of course in the clear language of Paley. The logic of this book and, as I may add, of his "Natural Theology," gave me as much delight as did Euclid. The careful study of these works, without attempting to learn any part by rote, was the only part of the academical course which, as I then felt and as I still believe, was of the least use to me in the education of my mind. I did not at that time trouble myself about Paley's premises; and taking these on trust, I was charmed and convinced by the long line of argumentation. By answering well the examination questions in Paley, by doing Euclid well, and by not failing miserably in Classics, I gained a good place among the oi polloi or crowd of men who do not go in for honours. Oddly enough, I cannot remember how high I stood, and my memory fluctuates between the fifth, tenth, or twelfth, name on the list. (Tenth in the list of January 1831.) [...]

I have not as yet mentioned a circumstance which influenced my whole career more than any other. This was my friendship with Professor Henslow. Before coming up to Cambridge, I had heard of him from my brother as a man who knew every branch of science, and I was accordingly prepared to reverence him. He kept open house once every week when all undergraduates, and some older members of the University, who were attached to science, used to meet in the evening. I soon got, through Fox, an invitation, and went there regularly. Before long I became well acquainted with Henslow, and during the latter half of my time at Cambridge took long walks with him on most days; so that I was called by some of the dons "the man who walks with Henslow;" and in the evening I was very often asked to join his family dinner. His knowledge was great in botany, entomology, chemistry, mineralogy, and geology. His strongest taste was to draw conclusions from long-continued minute observations. His judgment was excellent, and his whole mind well balanced; but I do not suppose that any one would say that he possessed much original genius. He was deeply religious, and so orthodox that he told me one day he should be grieved if a single word of the Thirty-nine Articles were altered. His moral qualities were in every way admirable. He was free from every tinge of vanity or other petty feeling; and I never saw a man who thought so little about himself or his own concerns. His temper was imperturbably good, with the most winning and courteous manners; yet, as I have seen, he could be roused by any bad action to the warmest indignation and prompt action. [...]

Voyage of the "Beagle" from December 27, 1831, to October 2, 1836

On returning home from my short geological tour in North Wales, I found a letter from Henslow, informing me that Captain Fitz-Roy was willing to give up part of his own cabin to any young man who would volunteer to go with him without pay as naturalist to the Voyage of the "Beagle". I have given, as I believe, in my MS. Journal an account of all the circumstances which then occurred; I will here only say that I was instantly eager to accept the offer, but my father strongly objected, adding the words, fortunate for me, "If you can find any man of common sense who advises you to go I will give my consent." So I wrote that evening and refused the offer. On the next morning I went to Maer to be ready for September 1st, and, whilst out shooting, my uncle (Josiah Wedgwood.) sent for me, offering to drive me over to Shrewsbury and talk with my father, as my uncle thought it would be wise in me to accept the offer. My father always maintained that he was one of the most sensible men in the world, and he at once consented in the kindest manner. I had been rather extravagant at Cambridge, and to console my father, said, "that I should be deuced clever to spend more than my allowance whilst on board the 'Beagle';" but he answered with a smile, "But they tell me you are very clever."

Next day I started for Cambridge to see Henslow, and thence to London to see Fitz-Roy, and all was soon arranged. Afterwards, on becoming very intimate with Fitz-Roy, I heard that I had run a very narrow risk of being rejected, on account of the shape of my nose! He was an ardent disciple of Lavater, and was convinced that he could judge of a man's character by the outline of his features; and he doubted whether any one with my nose could possess sufficient energy and determination for the voyage. But I think he was afterwards well satisfied that my nose had spoken falsely.

Fitz-Roy's character was a singular one, with very many noble features: he was devoted to his duty, generous to a fault, bold, determined, and indomitably energetic, and an ardent friend to all under his sway. He would undertake any sort of trouble to assist those whom he thought deserved assistance. He was a handsome man, strikingly like a gentleman, with highly courteous manners, which resembled those of his maternal uncle, the famous Lord Castlereagh, as I was told by the Minister at Rio. Nevertheless he must have inherited much in his appearance from Charles II, for Dr. Wallich gave me a collection of photographs which he had made, and I was struck with the resemblance of one to Fitz-Roy; and on looking at the name, I found it Ch. E. Sobieski Stuart, Count d'Albanie, a descendant of the same monarch.

Fitz-Roy's temper was a most unfortunate one. It was usually worst in the early morning, and with his eagle eye he could generally detect something amiss about the ship, and was then unsparing in his blame. He was very kind to me, but was a man very difficult to live with on the intimate terms which necessarily followed from our messing by ourselves in the same cabin. We had several quarrels; for instance, early in the voyage at Bahia, in Brazil, he defended and praised slavery, which I abominated, and told me that he had just visited a great slave-owner, who had called up many of his slaves and asked them whether they were happy, and whether they wished to be free, and all answered "No." I then asked him, perhaps with a sneer, whether he thought that the answer of slaves in the presence of their master was worth anything? This made him excessively angry, and he said that as I doubted his word we could not live any longer together. I thought that I should have been compelled to leave the ship; but as soon as the news spread, which it did quickly, as the captain sent for the first lieutenant to assuage his anger by abusing me, I was deeply gratified by receiving an invitation from all the gun-room officers to mess with them. But after a few hours Fitz-Roy showed his usual magnanimity by sending an officer to me with an apology and a request that I would continue to live with him.

The voyage of the "Beagle" has been by far the most important event in my life, and has determined my whole career; yet it depended on so small a circumstance as my uncle offering to drive me thirty miles to Shrewsbury, which few uncles would have done, and on such a trifle as the shape of my nose. I have always felt that I owe to the voyage the first real training or education of my mind; I was led to attend closely to several branches of natural history, and thus my powers of observation were improved, though they were always fairly developed. [...]

My Several Publications

[...] From September 1854 I devoted my whole time to arranging my huge pile of notes, to observing, and to experimenting in relation to the transmutation of species. During the voyage of the "Beagle" I had been deeply impressed by discovering in the Pampean formation great fossil animals covered with armour like that on the existing armadillos; secondly, by the manner in which closely allied animals replace one another in proceeding southwards over the Continent; and thirdly, by the South American character of most of the productions of the Galapagos archipelago, and more especially by the manner in which they differ slightly on each island of the group; none of the islands appearing to be very ancient in a geological sense.

It was evident that such facts as these, as well as many others, could only be explained on the supposition that species gradually become modified; and the subject haunted me. But it was equally evident that neither the action of the surrounding conditions, nor the will of the organisms (especially in the case of plants) could account for the innumerable cases in which organisms of every kind are beautifully adapted to their habits of life—for instance, a woodpecker or a tree-frog to climb trees, or a seed for dispersal by hooks or plumes. I had always been much struck by such adaptations, and until these could be explained it seemed to me almost useless to endeavour to prove by indirect evidence that species have been modified.

After my return to England it appeared to me that by following the example of Lyell in Geology, and by collecting all facts which bore in any way on the variation of animals and plants under domestication and nature, some light might perhaps be thrown on the whole subject. My first note-book was opened in July 1837. I worked on true Baconian principles, and without any theory collected facts on a wholesale scale, more especially with respect to domesticated productions, by printed enquiries, by conversation with skilful breeders and gardeners, and by extensive reading. When I see the list of books of all kinds which I read and abstracted, including whole series of Journals and Transactions, I am surprised at my industry. I soon perceived that selection was the keystone of man's success in making useful races of animals and plants. But how selection could be applied to organisms living in a state of nature remained for some time a mystery to me.

In October 1838, that is, fifteen months after I had begun my systematic enquiry, I happened to read for amusement "Malthus on Population," and being well prepared to appreciate the struggle for existence which everywhere goes on from long-continued observation of the habits of animals and plants, it at once struck me that under these circumstances favourable variations would tend to be preserved, and unfavourable ones to be destroyed. The result of this would be the formation of new species. Here then I had at last got a theory by which to work; but I was so anxious to avoid prejudice, that I determined not for some time to write even the briefest sketch of it. In June 1842 I first allowed myself the satisfaction of writing a very brief abstract of my theory in pencil in 35 pages; and this was enlarged during the summer of 1844 into one of 230 pages, which I had fairly copied out and still possess.

But at that time I overlooked one problem of great importance; and it is astonishing to me, except on the principle of Columbus and his egg, how I could have overlooked it and its solution. This problem is the tendency in organic beings descended from the same stock to diverge in character as they become modified. That they have diverged greatly is obvious from the manner in which species of all kinds can be classed under genera, genera under families, families under sub-orders and so forth; and I can remember the very spot in the road, whilst in my carriage, when to my joy the solution occurred to me; and this was long after I had come to Down. The solution, as I believe, is that the modified offspring of all dominant and increasing forms tend to become adapted to many and highly diversified places in the economy of nature.

Early in 1856 Lyell advised me to write out my views pretty fully, and I began at once to do so on a scale three or four times as extensive as that which was afterwards followed in my "Origin of Species;" yet it was only an abstract of the materials which I had collected, and I got through about half the work on this scale. But my plans were overthrown, for early in the summer of 1858 Mr. Wallace, who was then in the Malay archipelago, sent me an essay "On the Tendency of Varieties to depart indefinitely from the Original Type;" and this essay contained exactly the same theory as mine. Mr. Wallace expressed the wish that if I thought well of his essay, I should send it to Lyell for perusal.

The circumstances under which I consented at the request of Lyell and Hooker to allow of an abstract from my MS., together with a letter to Asa Gray, dated September 5, 1857, to be published at the same time with Wallace's Essay, are given in the "Journal of the Proceedings of the Linnean Society," 1858, page 45. I was at first very unwilling to consent, as I thought Mr. Wallace might consider my doing so unjustifiable, for I did not then know how generous and noble was his disposition. The extract from my MS. and the letter to Asa Gray had neither been intended for publication, and were badly written. Mr. Wallace's essay, on the other hand, was admirably expressed and quite clear. Nevertheless, our joint productions excited very little attention, and the only published notice of them which I can remember was by Professor Haughton of Dublin, whose verdict was that all that was new in them was false, and what was true was old. This shows how necessary it is that any new view should be explained at considerable length in order to arouse public attention.

In September 1858 I set to work by the strong advice of Lyell and Hooker to prepare a volume on the transmutation of species, but was often interrupted by ill-health, and short visits to Dr. Lane's delightful hydropathic establishment at Moor Park. I abstracted the MS. begun on a much larger scale in 1856, and completed the volume on the same reduced scale. It cost me thirteen months and ten days' hard labour. It was published under the title of the "Origin of Species," in November 1859. Though considerably added to and corrected in the later editions, it has remained substantially the same book.

It is no doubt the chief work of my life. It was from the first highly successful. The first small edition of 1250 copies was sold on the day of publication, and a second edition of 3000 copies soon afterwards. Sixteen thousand copies have now (1876) been sold in England; and considering how stiff a book it is, this is a large sale. It has been translated into almost every European tongue, even into such languages as Spanish, Bohemian, Polish, and Russian. It has also, according to Miss Bird, been translated into Japanese (Miss Bird is mistaken, as I learn from Prof. Mitsukuri.—F.D.), and is there much studied. Even an essay in Hebrew has appeared on it, showing that the theory is contained in the Old Testament! The reviews were very numerous; for some time I collected all that appeared on the "Origin" and on my related books, and these amount (excluding newspaper reviews) to 265; but after a time I gave up the attempt in despair. Many separate essays and books on the subject have appeared; and in Germany a catalogue or bibliography on "Darwinismus" has appeared every year or two.

The success of the "Origin" may, I think, be attributed in large part to my having long before written two condensed sketches, and to my having finally abstracted a much larger manuscript, which was itself an abstract. By this means I was enabled to select the more striking facts and conclusions. I had, also, during many years followed a golden rule, namely, that whenever a published fact, a new observation or thought came across me, which was opposed to my general results, to make a memorandum of it without fail and at once; for I had found by experience that such facts and thoughts were far more apt to escape from the memory than favourable ones. Owing to this habit, very few objections were raised against my views which I had not at least noticed and attempted to answer.

It has sometimes been said that the success of the "Origin" proved "that the subject was in the air," or "that men's minds were prepared for it." I do not think that this is strictly true, for I occasionally sounded not a few naturalists, and never happened to come across a single one who seemed to doubt about the permanence of species. Even Lyell and Hooker, though they would listen with interest to me, never seemed to agree. I tried once or twice to explain to able men what I meant by Natural Selection, but signally failed. What I believe was strictly true is that innumerable well-observed facts were stored in the minds of naturalists ready to take their proper places as soon as any theory which would receive them was sufficiently explained. Another element in the success of the book was its moderate size; and this I owe to the appearance of Mr. Wallace's essay; had I published on the scale in which I began to write in 1856, the book would have been four or five times as large as the "Origin," and very few would have had the patience to read it.

I gained much by my delay in publishing from about 1839, when the theory was clearly conceived, to 1859; and I lost nothing by it, for I cared very little whether men attributed most originality to me or Wallace; and his essay no doubt aided in the reception of the theory. I was forestalled in only one important point, which my vanity has always made me regret, namely, the explanation by means of the Glacial period of the presence of the same species of plants and of some few animals on distant mountain summits and in the arctic regions. This view pleased me so much that I wrote it out in extenso, and I believe that it was read by Hooker some years before E. Forbes published his celebrated memoir ("Geolog. Survey Mem.," 1846.) on the subject. In the very few points in which we differed, I still think that I was in the right. I have never, of course, alluded in print to my having independently worked out this view. [...]

This leads me to remark that I have almost always been treated honestly by my reviewers, passing over those without scientific knowledge as not worthy of notice. My views have often been grossly misrepresented, bitterly opposed and ridiculed, but this has been generally done, as I believe, in good faith. On the whole I do not doubt that my works have been over and over again greatly overpraised. I rejoice that I have avoided controversies, and this I owe to Lyell, who many years ago, in reference to my geological works, strongly advised me never to get entangled in a controversy, as it rarely did any good and caused a miserable loss of time and temper.

Whenever I have found out that I have blundered, or that my work has been imperfect, and when I have been contemptuously criticised, and even when I have been overpraised, so that I have felt mortified, it has been my greatest comfort to say hundreds of times to myself that "I have worked as hard and as well as I could, and no man can do more than this." I remember when in Good Success Bay, in Tierra del Fuego, thinking (and, I believe, that I wrote home to the effect) that I could not employ my life better than in adding a little to Natural Science. This I have done to the best of my abilities, and critics may say what they like, but they cannot destroy this conviction. [. . .]

My "Descent of Man" was published in February, 1871. As soon as I had become, in the year 1837 or 1838, convinced that species were mutable productions, I could not avoid the belief that man must come under the same law. Accordingly I collected notes on the subject for my own satisfaction, and not for a long time with any intention of publishing. Although in the "Origin of Species" the derivation of any particular species is never discussed, yet I thought it best, in order that no honourable man should accuse me of concealing my views, to add that by the work "light would be thrown on the origin of man and his history." It would have been useless and injurious to the success of the book to have paraded, without giving any evidence, my conviction with respect to his origin.

But when I found that many naturalists fully accepted the doctrine of the evolution of species, it seemed to me advisable to work up such notes as I possessed, and to publish a special treatise on the origin of man. I was the more glad to do so, as it gave me an opportunity of fully discussing sexual selection—a subject which had always greatly interested me. This subject, and that of the variation of our domestic productions, together with the causes and laws of variation, inheritance, and the intercrossing of plants, are the sole subjects which I have been able to write about in full, so as to use all the materials which I have collected. The "Descent of Man" took me three years to write, but then as usual some of this time was lost by ill health, and some was consumed by preparing new editions and other minor works. A second and largely corrected edition of the "Descent" appeared in 1874. [. . .]

I have now mentioned all the books which I have published, and these have been the milestones in my life, so that little remains to be said. I am not conscious of any change in my mind during the last thirty years, excepting in one point presently to be mentioned; nor, indeed, could any change have been expected unless one of general deterioration. But my father lived to his eighty-third year with his mind as lively as ever it was, and all his faculties undimmed; and I hope that I may die before my mind fails to a sensible extent. I think that I have become a little more skilful in guessing right explanations and in devising experimental tests; but this may probably be the result of mere practice, and of a larger store of knowledge. I have as much difficulty as ever in expressing myself clearly and concisely; and this difficulty has caused me a very great loss of time; but it has had the compensating advantage of forcing me to think long and intently about every sentence, and thus I have been led to see errors in reasoning and in my own observations or those of others.

There seems to be a sort of fatality in my mind leading me to put at first my statement or proposition in a wrong or awkward form. Formerly I used to think about my sentences before writing them down; but for several years I have found that it saves time to scribble in a vile hand whole pages as quickly as I possibly can, contracting half the words; and then correct deliberately. Sentences thus scribbled down are often better ones than I could have written deliberately.

Having said thus much about my manner of writing, I will add that with my large books I spend a good deal of time over the general arrangement of the matter. I first make the rudest outline in two or three pages, and then a larger one in several pages, a few words or one word standing for a whole discussion or series of facts. Each one of these headings is again enlarged and often transferred before I begin to write in extenso. As in several of my books facts observed by others have been very extensively used, and as I have always had several quite distinct subjects in hand at the same time, I may mention that I keep from thirty to forty large portfolios, in cabinets with labelled shelves, into which I can at once put a detached reference or memorandum. I have bought many books, and at their ends I make an index of all the facts that concern my work; or, if the book is not my own, write out a separate abstract, and of such abstracts I have a large drawer full. Before beginning on any subject I look to all the short indexes and make a general and classified index, and by taking the one or more proper portfolios I have all the information collected during my life ready for use. [...]

I have no great quickness of apprehension or wit which is so remarkable in some clever men, for instance, Huxley. I am therefore a poor critic: a paper or book, when first read, generally excites my admiration, and it is only after considerable reflection that I perceive the weak points. My power to follow a long and purely abstract train of thought is very limited; and therefore I could never have succeeded with metaphysics or mathematics. My memory is extensive, yet hazy: it suffices to make me cautious by vaguely telling me that I have observed or read something opposed to the conclusion which I am drawing, or on the other hand in favour of it; and after a time I can generally recollect where to search for my authority. So poor in one sense is my memory, that I have never been able to remember for more than a few days a single date or a line of poetry.

Some of my critics have said, "Oh, he is a good observer, but he has no power of reasoning!" I do not think that this can be true, for the "Origin of Species" is one long argument from the beginning to the end, and it has convinced not a few able men. No one could have written it without having some power of reasoning. I have a fair share of invention, and of common sense or judgment, such as every fairly successful lawyer or doctor must have, but not, I believe, in any higher degree.

On the favourable side of the balance, I think that I am superior to the common run of men in noticing things which easily escape attention, and in observing them carefully. My industry has been nearly as great as it could have been in the observation and collection of facts. What is far more important, my love of natural science has been steady and ardent.

This pure love has, however, been much aided by the ambition to be esteemed by my fellow naturalists. From my early youth I have had the strongest desire to understand or explain whatever I observed,—that is, to group all facts under some general laws. These causes combined have given me the patience to reflect or ponder for any number of years over any unexplained problem. As far as I can judge, I am not apt to follow blindly the lead of other men. I have steadily endeavoured to keep my mind free so as to give up any hypothesis, however much beloved (and I cannot resist forming one on every subject), as soon as facts are shown to be opposed to it. Indeed, I have had no choice but to act in this manner, for with the exception of the Coral Reefs, I cannot remember a single first-formed hypothesis which had not after a time to be given up or greatly modified. This has naturally led me to distrust greatly deductive reasoning in the mixed sciences. On the other hand, I am not very sceptical,—a frame of mind which I believe to be injurious to the progress of science. A good deal of scepticism in a scientific man is advisable to avoid much loss of time, but I have met with not a few men, who, I feel sure, have often thus been deterred from experiment or observations, which would have proved directly or indirectly serviceable. [...]

My habits are methodical, and this has been of not a little use for my particular line of work. Lastly, I have had ample leisure from not having to earn my own bread. Even ill-health, though it has annihilated several years of my life, has saved me from the distractions of society and amusement.

Therefore my success as a man of science, whatever this may have amounted to, has been determined, as far as I can judge, by complex and diversified mental qualities and conditions. Of these, the most important have been—the love of science—unbounded patience in long reflecting over any subject—industry in observing and collecting facts—and a fair share of invention as well as of common sense. With such moderate abilities as I possess, it is truly surprising that I should have influenced to a considerable extent the belief of scientific men on some important points.

General Bibliography

Biographies of Charles Robert Darwin

Bowlby, John. 1990. *Charles Darwin: A New Biography*. London: Hutchinson.
Brown, Janet. 1995. *Charles Darwin. Vol. 1: Voyaging*. London: Jonathon Cape.
Brown, Janet. 2002. *Charles Darwin. Vol. 2: The Power of Place*. London: Jonathon Cape.
Desmond, Adrian and James Moore. 1991. *Darwin*. London: Michael Joseph.
George, Wilma. 1982. *Darwin* (Modern Masters Series). London: Fontana Paperbacks.

Darwin's Final Illness and Death

Moore, James. 1994. *The Darwin Legend*. Grand Rapids, MI: Baker Books.

The *Beagle* Voyage: General Accounts

Keynes, Richard. 2002. *Fossils, Finches and Fuegians: Charles Darwin's Adventures and Discoveries on the Beagle, 1832–1836*. London: HarperCollins.
Moorehead, Alan. 1969. *Darwin and the Beagle*. London: Hamish Hamilton.

Emma Darwin

Healey, Edna. 2001. *Emma Darwin: The Inspirational Wife of a Genius*. London: Headline.

Charles Darwin's Family and Descendants

Keynes, Randal. 2001. *Annie's Box: Charles Darwin, His Daughter and Human Evolution*. London: Fourth Estate.
Raverat, Gwen. 1952. *Period Piece: A Cambridge Childhood*. London: Faber and Faber.
Spalding, Frances. 2004. *Gwen Raverat: Family, Friends, Affections*. London: Pimlico.

Captain Robert FitzRoy

Mellersh, H.E.L. 1968. *FitzRoy of the Beagle*. London: Rupert Hart-Davis.

Nichols, Peter. 2003. *Evolution's Captain: The Dark Fate of the Man Who Sailed Charles Darwin around the World*. London: HarperCollins.

Darwin's Ideas and Their Influence

Bowler, Peter J. 1990. *Charles Darwin: The Man and His Influence*. Oxford, England: Blackwell Publishers. Reissued by Cambridge University Press in 1996.

Eldredge, Niles. 1995. *Reinventing Darwin: The Great Evolutionary Debate*. New York: John Wiley and Sons.

Glick, Thomas F., ed. 1988. *The Comparative Reception of Darwinism*. Chicago: University of Chicago Press.

Livingstone, David N. 1987. *Darwin's Forgotten Defenders*. Grand Rapids, MI: William B. Eerdmans Publishing Company.

Lustig, Abigail, Robert J. Richards, and Miachael Ruse, eds. 2004. *Darwinian Heresies*. Cambridge, England: Cambridge University Press.

MacLeod, Roy and Philip E. Rehbock. 1994. *Darwin's Laboratory: Evolutionary Theory and Natural History in the Pacific*. Honolulu: University of Hawaii Press.

Manier, Edward. 1978. *The Young Darwin and His Cultural Circle*. Dordrech, The Netherlands: D. Reidel Publishing Company.

Oldroyd, D. R. 1980. *Darwinian Impacts: An Introduction to the Darwinian Revolution*. Milton Keynes, Australia: Open University Press.

Darwin's Associates

Allan, M. 1967. *The Hookers of Kew, 1785–1911*. London: Michael Joseph.

Russell-Gebbert, Jean. 1977. *Henslow of Hitcham*. Lavenham, England: Terence Dalton Ltd.

Wallace, Ian, ed. 2005. *Leonard Jenyns: Darwin's Lifelong Friend*. Bath, England: Bath Royal Literary and Scientific Institution.

Walters, S. M. and E. A Stow. 2001. *Darwin's Mentor: John Stevens Henslow, 1796–1861*. Cambridge, England: Cambridge University Press.

Index

Page numbers in **bold** indicate main entries.

About the Author

PATRICK H. ARMSTRONG taught Geography and Ecology at the University of Western Australia. He has written extensively on the life and work of Charles Darwin. Brought up in the university city of Cambridge, among Armstrong's earliest recollections was seeing Darwin's granddaughter painting pictures of the River Cam.